D1070302

Tree Whispering:

A Nature Lover's Guide to Touching, Healing, and Communicating with Trees, Plants, and All of Nature

Jim Conroy, PhD, *The Tree Whisperer*®

and

Basia Alexander, *The Chief Listener*

Plant Kingdom Communications™
www.PlantKingdomCommunications.com

First published in 2011 by Plant Kingdom Communications, Publisher.
P.O. Box 90, Morris Plains, NJ 07950 www.PlantKingdomCommunications.com

The mission of Plant Kingdom Communications is Peace and Balance Among the Beings of Earth.

Copyright ©2011 Jim Conroy, Basia Alexander, and Plant Health Alternatives, LLC.
ISBN-13: 978-0-9834114-0-6
Library of Congress Control Number: 2011929138

Plant Kingdom Communications books may be purchased for educational, business, or sales promotional use. For information, please write: Special Markets Department, Plant Kingdom Communications, LLC, P.O. Box 90, Morris Plains, NJ 07950 USA.

The Plant Kingdom Communications Speaker's Bureau can bring authors to your live event. For more information, please go to *www.PlantKingdomCommunications.com*

Printed by BookMasters®, Inc., Ashland, Ohio, www.BookMasters.com
Printed in the United States of America on recycled paper.

Cover's HeartHands and Author Photos: ©Jane B. Kellner, Kelley/Kellner Associates, Salisbury, CT, kel.kel@sbcglobal.net. Background Cover Photo: Shutterstock.com.

Cover by Basia Alexander and Jim Conroy. Interior design by Basia Alexander.
Copyeditor: Melissa Atkin. Proofreader: Erika Nein.

The following trademarks are the properties of their respective owners:

Tree Whispering®	*Tree Ambassador*®	*BioDynamics*™
The Tree Whisperer®	*Plant Ambassador*®	*Permaculture*®
Plant Whisper®	*Tree Protectors*™	*BodyTalk System*™
Healing Whispers™	*Have You Thanked*™*a Tree or*	*HeartMath*®
Holistic Chores™	*Plant Today?*	*Touch for Health*™
Strengthen Forests™	*Leave Leaves*™	*Therapeutic Touch*™
Cooperative BioBalance™	*Botany in Balance*™	*Matrix Energetics*®
Green Centrics™	*Apple*®	*Feldenkrais Method*®
Co-Existence Technologies™	*BioMimicry*™	*BookMasters*®

For Nature Lovers

For the Plant Kingdom

For All of Nature

For the Future

Personal Acknowledgments

Dr. Jim Conroy: I thank my dad, who understood my sensitivity and love for plants even when I didn't, for building a greenhouse out the cellar window when I was in high school, and for helping me get into Delaware Valley College to build my love for plants into a profession. To my mom, who always wanted to educate people, for her encouragement to complete my education and to go for a doctorate.

I thank Mr. R. Many for helping me learn some values in life over and above what a parent could teach. I thank Dr. Joshua Feldstein, Delaware Valley College, for taking me under his wing and giving me a great education in horticulture. You gave me a strong foundation for my future. I thank Dr. Ralph Green, Purdue University, for his help, guidance, and understanding through the Masters and PhD process. This valuable degree and your guidance has always remained a part of me throughout my career. To the agricultural chemical companies, for helping me see one side of caring for trees and plants. In contrast, I saw the more holistic side. I thank my sister Jan, other relatives, and friends–whom I call "like family"–including Tom and Barbara Grady for support and Ed and Linda Schoeps for including me.

I thank the trees, plants, bees, and other organisms for helping me develop the work. I thank the Angels, Guardian Angels, Higher Realms, Guides, Devas, Spirits, Plant and Tree Spirits, AMDLW, and Elementals. A special thanks to the teams that are always working with me, the "Lady in White," and my Life's Force and path. Special thanks to my business partner, Basia, for initial encouragement to develop the work, for creative vision to express the work, and to bring it forward so it could be a valuable contribution to humanity.

Ms. Basia Alexander: I thank my father for the music and for telling me about the extinction of the Passenger Pigeon. I thank my mother for love of beauty and for making sure that I wouldn't be afraid of thunderstorms. I know it was all "because you loved me." I thank Ron Praught for his loving patience. I thank my blood relations and "like family" for their support. I thank Susanna Opper for a lifetime of friendship, Day Merrill for a pivotal friendship, Carol Ohmart-Behan for kindred friendship, Doreen DiGiacomo for new friendship, and Norma Feldman for freedom in Spirit.

I thank my teachers: Julia Cameron for Morning Pages, Sibylle Preuschat and MSW for the path, Werner Erhard for distinguishing distinction, Stewart Emery for his gentle heart, Robert Fritz for his model of creativity, Michael Melia for the leap, Gerry Nierenberg for "everybody wins," Judy Beach (may she write in peace) for popcorn and candles, Nina Reimer for dolls that heal, and Jan Phillips for saying "Go first!" I also thank Hannelore Hahn and Elizabeth Julia for the International Women's Writer's Guild, Fritjof Capra for his good advice, the Beloit College Plan with Track II for opening my mind, Gene Roddenberry for his vision of the future, and Walt Disney for inspiring imagination. I thank "RED" in Muir Woods and the baby Maples for their lives. I thank Alyce, Aetero, the AMDLW, and all of the Rest for the rest of it All. And, not least, I thank Jim for good partnership.

Professional Acknowledgments ❧

Both Dr. Jim and Basia thank the following:

For believing in us and giving us a chance in the early days, we deeply thank Jeff Frank, Mike Nadeau, Jamie Laidlaw, and Joseph Heckman.

All of our students. For their long-time and enthusiastic support, we especially thank Linda Farmer, Adalea McLaughlin, Cheryl Smith, Leo Kelly, Paul O'Kula, Dwight Brooks, David Slade, Robin Rose Bennett, Maria Petrova, Madeline Thompson, Ann St. Germaine, Debbra Gill, Joan Lenart, Leslie Ashman, Linda Ludwig, Mary Cypress, Carrie Gilberti, and Dorrie Rosen.

Early adopter clients, especially Sheila, Melinda, Michael and Diane, Rita and Goeff, Bill and Henry and Clarence, Sabine Schoenberg, Pat Kenschaft, Mark Savage, "ArborMan" Dan, Mark, "Farmer" Bill, Sarna Strom, Alison Iati, Andy Boszhardt, and many others.

Sister Miriam MacGillis of Genesis Farm for her confidence in us. Mike Baki, Smadar English, and Judy VonHandorf of the Community Supported Garden at Genesis Farm for open-mindedness, cooperation, and welcoming us.

Strong supporters, especially Chris Donnelly, Bill Duesing, Cie Lael, Jason Hart, Marie Hedrick, Bill Dewey, James Urbanowski, Joan, Mary Anne Mitchell, Jon Estrin, Angie Buchanan, Ben Gosscup, David Yarrow, Rose Getch, Tom Sotoridy, "TallMan" McMahon, Scott, Jodie Bross, and many others.

The Omega Institute for bringing us back year after year.

Sally and Kevin Malanga for walking the talk with their hearts and pocketbook. Bobby Gianos for attentive caring for his trees.

Melissa Atkin for the amazing kind of editing and gentle listening that resulted in breakthroughs in expressing the work.

Eleanor Berger, author of *Stepping Out*, for her valuable guidance through the whole process. Maria Petrova and Jane Kellner for creativity with photos. Erika Nein for proofreading and fast turnaround.

Dorothy Maclean, 1960s co-founder of Findhorn Garden, Scotland, and spiritual ground-breaker, and Lorian Press, for their generosity.

Colorado test-site homeowners, especially Marie Hedrick, Leslie McCallum, Marie Koepke, Jill Suffin, and Graham and Louise Powers.

John Veltheim for inspiration. Werner Erhard for going forward from the future. Steve Jobs for great technology. David Austin for his roses.

Bethany Birkett for her insightful advice all these years. David Bursik for legal advice. Chuck Lota for taxes. Tim and all at BookMasters.

All people who have come out of hiding about already communicating with trees and plants, and who want to learn more.

All tree lovers and tree protectors, all visionaries and evolutionaries, all young and young-at-heart who will carry on this work.

Who Will Enjoy this Book?

- ❏ Tree people. Plant lovers.
- ❏ People who enjoy walking in the woods, or anyone who has a favorite tree or plant.
- ❏ People with a deep respect for Nature.
- ❏ Open-minded and innovative individuals.
- ❏ People who garden or interact with plants often.
- ❏ Those with a childhood connection to trees.
- ❏ Spiritually oriented people, or anyone who feels that Nature has Divinity within it.
- ❏ People who already talk to their plants or trees, or anyone who says "please," "thank you," or "sorry" to the greenery.
- ❏ Outdoor enthusiasts, hikers, campers, athletes.
- ❏ Fun-loving adventurists.
- ❏ Environmentalists or anyone who wants to honor, respect, and live lightly on Mother Earth.
- ❏ People aspiring to healthy or sustainable lifestyles.
- ❏ Healers. Therapists.
- ❏ Artists, designers, and creative people who feel inspiration.
- ❏ Anyone who wants a deeper connection with trees or plants.
- ❏ Compassionate, helpful people who are willing to try something new that will help another living Being.
- ❏ Tree and plant professionals, farmers, growers, or orchardists who are willing to consider a better way.
- ❏ Visionaries.
- ❏ People who feel a sense of belonging with other people who love trees, plants, and all of Nature.
- ❏ Dog, cat, bird, fish, crystal, rock, bug, insect, or horse people—anyone who already whispers with other Beings.
- ❏ People who feel sad when they see a tree cut down.

Contents

Acknowledgments   *vi*

Who will enjoy this book?   *viii*

Preface and How to Read this Book   *xi*

Chapter 1   A Quiet Walk in the Woods   *1*

Chapter 2   Your Trail Guides   *9*

Chapter 3   Messages from Trees and Plants   *21*

Chapter 4   Be a Better Receiver of Trees' and
             Plants' Communications   *51*

Chapter 5   Advice for Expanding Perceptions and
             Developing Intuitive Skills   *75*

Chapter 6   How Trees and Plants Really Operate   *97*

Chapter 7   The Five Heralds: Healing the
             Tree Whisperer's Way   *119*

Chapter 8   What You Can Do   *137*

Chapter 9   The Tree Whisperer's Insights   *183*

Chapter 10 An Idea Whose Time Has Come   *219*

Chapter 11 Futuristic Vision in Practice Now:
             Cooperative BioBalance   *231*

Afterword: Change and Celebrate   *259*

Appendix: The Philosophy and Relevant Sciences   *263*

Glossary: What Is Meant by Bold Words   *274*

Citations and More to Learn   *277*

Participate   *287*

Contact and About the Authors   *288*

Preface and How to Read This Book

Ms. Basia Alexander, The Chief Listener, tells the story: We were about three-quarters finished with what we thought would be our first book when we suddenly realized that it was being written in a technical way. We wanted to write a book from our hearts instead. We set aside much of what we wrote and started again. As an inspiration, I put collages of graduates' photos and class pictures all around my desk. When we teach our Tree Whispering® classes, we learn from our students and they touch our hearts. We hope that the feeling comes through and that this book will touch your heart.

Dr. Jim Conroy, The Tree Whisperer,® reveals: Basia and I are looking for you. Yes, personally, you. We want to find you because you are the one who loves trees, loves plants, and has a deep appreciation for **Nature**. Whether or not you know anything about botany doesn't matter at all. You know that trees and plants are living Beings. More than that, you realize that they have a lot to teach us. The idea of touching the Spirit within yourself and the Spirit of Nature is appealing to you and might be comfortable for you. You are the kind of person who gets distressed if you see a sick tree or if you see trees being cut down. If you can do some good for a tree or plant, you feel better about yourself and happy for the plant. Trees and plants seem like a part of your family! They are my family, too.

You'll soon learn more about how Basia and I got started with our touching, healing, and **communicating** work with trees and plants. We want you to know that we consider it to be a sacred mission.

What We Hope You Get from Reading this Book

Basia proposes: Read the whole book. However, don't read from your head, read with your heart open. Don't get caught up in trying to figure out why or how healing or communicating with trees and plants works. We will tell you how it works, rest assured. Engage with what we say while you remember how much you love trees, plants, and all of Nature.

Basia continues: We hope that you will try the "Try This" exercises in this book. They make reading into an experience. After all, the best way to learn is not by following another's words, but by doing something yourself.

Read, experience, and learn as if lives depended on it. The lives of your own trees and plants may, in fact, be involved. And, since everything is connected on this small planet, your own quality of life may also weigh in the balance.

If you read this book and become better informed, well, that is fine with me, but that is not why I do this. I am writing it so that your relationship with trees, plants, and all of Nature may become improved and transformed. Your opportunity is to shift to **holistic** and even spiritual partnership with trees, plants, and all of Nature.

I believe that each of us is facing a point of making important choices in our personal lives and within the context of global changes in consciousness, environment, and economy. Will each of us continue to live the same old way? Continue to have the same old assumptions? I believe the old ways are no longer sustainable. I hope that you will have a new resolve to open your heart, open your mind, and consider something new and different. I hope you try something that could make a difference in your life and in the lives of the living Beings of the Plant Kingdom.

Dr. Jim shares his suggestions: You've heard of having a bird's eye view of a situation. How about having a plant's eye view? How would your own life improve if your heart and inner self got in touch with the life form–the consciousness–that is a tree or a plant?

In the mid 2000s, Basia and I had a display booth at a garden show, and we remember how stunned a man was when we explained the idea of Tree Whispering. He said, "This idea could change everything about the way we grow plants and the way we feel about them!" He saw the opportunities and challenges that this approach offers.

We suggest that there is an opening for you to feel more inner peace in your own life by experiencing another life form's **Life Force**. You may also feel the goodness and benevolence of helping that other life form become healthier. How might your life improve? You'll know when you have the experience. This book will help you have the experience.

Then, you will probably want to do your garden chores differently. For instance, transplanting. You might take more time to correctly handle all the practical factors like soil amendment, planting depth, and adding water. You might be sensitive and ask the plant or tree exactly where it wants to go, which way it wants to be turned, and how far it wants to be from another. Chores done in a more cooperative manner yield greater success for you. Even if you don't understand why yet–doing chores with an attitude of partnership would make all the difference in the plant's or tree's world.

We hope that your whole perspective will change. When you look at plants or trees, you will see living Beings–**Green Beings**–worthy of attention. You will be even more appreciative than you already are of their gifts and generosity to humanity.

Most importantly, this book is a journey. It's a journey inside the Plant Kingdom. Trust the path.

The trees are waiting for you to communicate with them.

With deep gratitude to you, to the Plant Kingdom, and to all of Nature

Dr. Jim Conroy

Ms. Basia Alexander

TREE WHISPERING'S SIX MISSIONS

(1) Inspire people everywhere to have personal experiences with the **bioenergy** *and wisdom of trees and plants in ways that are healthy and healing for people in body, mind, and Spirit, and healthy for all trees and plants. It's a two-way* **dynamically balanced** *flow of health.*

(2) Bring about changes in people, organizations, and even governments. Beliefs, attitudes, and practices are transformed to be consistent with the principles of balance, the design of harmony, and the experience of coming from the plant's point of view. This is a **paradigm shift** *to cooperation, partnership, and equality between people and Nature and within Nature itself. This is not a matter of shuffling the chairs in people's attitudes and practices toward the Plant Kingdom. This shift to a new paradigm is a game-changer.*

(3) Lead the way with holistic, hands-on bioenergy healing techniques to strengthen and heal trees, plants, gardens, crops, forests, and ecosystems that have **compromised internal functionality***. The purpose of the inner healing is to establish and enhance sustainable balance within their parts, systems, and functions. This represents the new paradigm's new game.*

(4) Re-establish dynamic equilibrium between plants, insects, disease organisms, and other life forms so that they can all co-exist. This is Cooperative BioBalance™ *in action.*

(5) Reverse negative effects of climate change, pollution, and other destructive occurrences on individual trees or plants, as well as in larger areas and all the way up to bioregions of the planet.

(6) Found and ground a new category of knowledge and field of inquiry through the Institute for Cooperative BioBalance. The new discipline will include both the study and the conscious **co-creative** *practice of cooperative and dynamically balanced relationships among all living Beings.*

NOTES ON HOW TO READ THIS BOOK

Basia explains the formats: When either Dr. Jim or I are speaking, our words will be shown in standard typeface as you are reading now.

Sometimes our graduates are quoted. Graduates' words will also appear in standard typeface. Detailed information about each graduate can be found in the Citations.

Prior to anyone's words, you will see a **bold label** to indicate who is speaking.

To emphasize a point, you will see words in *italic text*.

If a word appears in the Glossary, it will be **bolded**.

Sometimes, words or phrases are in CAPITAL LETTERS. You will see this when we want to show you a repeating theme.

In a few chapters, trees speak. See trees' communications in a handwritten typeface like this: *Trees Speak*

As you read, there will be opportunities to do short exercises that will look like this:

TRY THIS: IMAGINE BELONGING
Read this exercise through first and decide whether you want to do it. Always take care of yourself and make sure that you feel comfortable. Don't do anything that would feel bad for you. If you have any concerns, do not do it.
Step 1: Sit down in a comfortable and private place where you won't be interrupted for ten to fifteen minutes.

Basia continues her explanation: Entire paragraphs or lists using italic typeface are used to indicate information or explanations that have no speaker. The Six Missions on the previous page are an example of information shown in italics with no speaker.

There are lots of photos, illustrations, and diagrams, which will support your understanding. We put detailed information in the Appendix and comments in the Citations, so we hope you find the book interesting right to the last page.

Contact information for Dr. Jim and me as well as ideas for continued activities for you are on the last page.

Chapter 1: A Quiet Walk in the Woods

YOUR FAVORITE TREE

Ms. Basia Alexander, The Chief Listener, suggests: Imagine your favorite tree. Or, think about your favorite plant. How do you feel when you see it? When you touch it? When you stand near it? It is probably your favorite because you feel peaceful, content, caring, or even inspired when you visit it. There is something about it that attracts you. Is it the beauty of the leaves? The strength of the trunk? The uniqueness of its form? The majesty of its size? Does the courage of the tree or plant that has survived or thrived in its environment draw you close?

FEELING GOOD—BODY AND SOUL

Dr. Jim Conroy, The Tree Whisperer,® asks: Don't you feel good—body and soul—when you feel connected with **Nature**? You leave behind your cares when you immerse yourself in the pleasures of the fragrance of pine needles or the rustle of a deep green canopy of leaves in the breeze. Perhaps on a quiet walk in the woods, you feel or believe that—for a moment—you leave your world and step into the trees' world.

Decades or perhaps hundreds of years old, the wise elders stand as witnesses to your quiet walk. They are patient Beings, masters of adaptation, skilled chemists with more sensory capacities than you may realize. They are transmitters of **bioenergy** frequencies. While walking, you feel the power and Spirit of the trees. In their world, you feel invigorated, enlivened, revitalized. You may even feel closer to the Divine. In your gratitude, perhaps you nod a thank-you to a special tree and feel appreciation for the whole forest as you depart.

You have a deep regard for Nature and go about your daily life doing the most respectful things you can do toward Nature.

KNOWING YOU'RE NOT ALONE

Dr. Jim encourages: Do you know that you are not alone in your appreciation of trees? Perhaps you think that there might be just a few other people who feel the way you do. But could you actually realize that millions and millions of people around the world are just like you in their enjoyment, caring, respect, warmheartedness, and, yes, love for trees? Take a moment to consider that you have something in common with a tremendous group of fellow human Beings.

LISTENING TO TREES

Dr. Jim continues: If you love trees and plants, then you know that they are living Beings–just different from us. They have a unique kind of **cognition** or **intelligence**: the genius of Nature's 4 billion years of development on this planet. Living Beings with a kind of intelligence are able to **communicate**. When you hike or stroll through the woods, you hear an orchestra of sounds because your ears are tuned to auditory frequencies. At the same time, the forest is also alive with the exchange of resonance waves among the trees, among the insects, and among other organisms going about the moment-by-moment business of sharing information about their lives.

As a tree and plant lover, you already know that they have a great deal to teach us. All you have to do is learn to listen.

Being receptive to a different kind of communication is the key. Nonverbal information comes to human senses all the time, and people are skilled at interpreting it. Perceiving in the old ways—ways long forgotten to modern culture—is how to listen to trees, plants, and all of Nature. It involves using all the senses. The customs of shamans, medicine men or women, aboriginal peoples, mundunugu, and natives of any land are no longer secrets; they are now open to all.

What if you are one of those people who already talk with the trees and hear, see, feel, or sense an intelligence, a presence, or a message? You are not alone. You are not crazy. The trees are expressing themselves, and you are already a good receiver, a good listener.

HELPING THE TREES AND PLANTS YOU LOVE

Basia asks: On that quiet walk in the woods, did you allow yourself to touch or hold a tree? Maybe you sat with your back leaning on it? Perhaps you stopped in a glade and beheld the wonder of life there.

When you felt this healthy renewal, did you notice whether the trees were healthy? Did you give anything back to them? How did the trees fare after your visit?

Feeling connected with Nature does not have to be a one-way street. Nature connects with you, too. Communication and sharing rejuvenating energies can go both ways. When the human's world and the plant's world merge, a **dynamically balanced** cycle of vitality and even an exchange of Spirit becomes possible. Each helps the other. Just as a tree makes you feel good, you can make a tree healthier. You can give back to trees, plants, and all of Nature's Beings. Giving back to Nature can be done through the ways of touching, healing, and communicating. Dr. Jim and I discuss that in this book and teach it in our classes. You can help sick trees and plants. You will feel good by doing good.

WHAT IS TREE WHISPERING®?

Basia reminds: The word "whisper" defined in the dictionary means to speak softly and privately with another. "Whispering" with horses, dogs, babies, one's own body, and even microbes became popular in the 1990s. The concept has come to signify an intuitive and deeply felt understanding of–or emotional kinship with–the "other" in ways that conventional science does not advocate or even approach.

Dr. Jim chimes in: With the name—Tree Whispering—you might think that it means leaning close to a tree and saying things very softly. You may do that, as I do. However, the focus of Tree Whispering is not about talking to trees and plants. Tree Whispering is, first and foremost, a deeply personal and profound experience of mutual connection with the **Life Force** and energy **biofield** of a living Being that happens to be green and has leaves and roots. It's about getting to know humanity's partners on the planet as fellow living Beings.

Lastly, Tree Whispering is not a set of tips or another product to use on trees and plants. It is not about doing things that you think should be done to a tree or plant. Tree Whispering opens the door to cooperating with these living Beings and forming partnerships with them.

ABOUT THIS BOOK: TOUCHING, HEALING, AND COMMUNICATING

Dr. Jim continues: Communication between people and the Plant Kingdom is possible. You may already feel that you are a tree's or plant's caregiver, protector, or even ambassador. That probably feels good. At the same time, you can do good. You can return the favors of life and well-being that trees and plants provide: you can become a friend, a helper, and a healer.

Become a friend. A new, even more satisfying relationship among you and members of the Plant Kingdom is possible. As you read this book, you will reawaken to their amazing qualities while your personal experience of their complexity and majesty deepens.

In any friendship or partnership, both beings share a common bond and show appreciation to each other. Soon, you will feel safe to admit that you not only love trees and plants but also have a special feeling of happiness when you are around them. If you already talk to trees and plants, you can come out of hiding. You know that you are not alone. Your friendship can mean a new lease on life for individual **Green Beings**.

Be a helper. Respect is at the heart of a good relationship. You will find practical ways to show your respect to trees and plants. By recognizing and using broad communication skills, you can feel good about yourself while you are helping your friends, the trees and plants. Your caring **intentions** and personal interactions will help them to survive and thrive.

Become a healer. There is both ignorance and misinformation about how trees and plants live and maintain their health. But, it doesn't have to be a mystery. Their parts, inner systems, and functions operate much like those of humans. There are many parallels.

Is it possible to heal a tree's inner health? Yes, their inner functionality can be restored to balance and harmony. Can you really heal plants that are sick or in **decline**? Yes, you can. Anyone can learn. Everyone has the ability. How? Read on...

TRY THIS: FEEL GOOD VISITING A TREE OR PLANT

Read through the steps. Decide whether you feel comfortable doing this exercise. If you do not feel comfortable or have any concern whatsoever, do not do it.

Step 1: Get a notebook or get the *Tree Whispering:Trust the Path* notebook. You may wish to make notes about this and other "Try This" exercises.

Step 2: If it is practical, go to your favorite tree or plant. Or, go to any tree or plant you like or you think is beautiful.

Step 3: Allow yourself the pleasure of feeling good in its presence. Don't try to think, analyze, or understand anything. Just feel good. Enjoy yourself.

Step 4: Slow and deliberate breathing can help. Stay with it for 5 to 10 minutes.

Step 5: In your *Tree Whispering:Trust the Path* notebook, jot down some notes to yourself. Focus on your impressions and on how good you feel.

TRY THIS: FEEL CONNECTED TO PEOPLE WHO ARE TREE, PLANT, AND NATURE LOVERS

Read through the steps. Decide whether you feel comfortable doing this exercise. If you do not feel comfortable or have any concern whatsoever, do not do it.

Step 1: Sit down in a comfortable and private place where you won't be interrupted for five to ten minutes. This exercise is best done with eyes closed, if you are comfortable closing your eyes.

Step 2: Millions and millions of people around the world are just like you in their enjoyment, caring, respect, warmheartedness, and love for trees, plants, and all of Nature. Take some time to feel or think about having something in common with a tremendous group of fellow human Beings.

Step 3: Imagine feeling a sense of belonging. We are all connected.

Step 4: Jot down a few notes in your *Tree Whispering:Trust the Path* notebook about that experience.

<u>Try This: Find out why you are Reading this Book</u>
Read through the steps. Decide whether you feel comfortable doing this exercise.
If you do not feel comfortable or have any concern whatsoever, do not do it.

Step 1: Sit down in a comfortable and private place where you won't be interrupted for about ten minutes.

Step 2: If you love trees, plants, forests, and the planet—and have a vision for a positive future—then check off ALL the reasons why you were attracted to this book and to the idea of communicating with trees, plants, and all of Nature.

❑ I love trees and plants. I am a "plant person."

❑ I already talk to trees and plants.

❑ Maybe, they talk to me, too.

❑ I want to know that I'm not alone; there are others like me.

❑ I want to be inspired.

❑ I'm curious.

❑ I want to get closer to Nature.

❑ I want to awaken perceptions I had as a child.

❑ I enjoy feeling good (healed in body and soul) when I am with plants or trees.

❑ I think this might be rejuvenating for me.

❑ I am concerned about the health of a certain tree in my yard or want to save an historic tree.

❑ I believe I can help sick trees; I want to do good for another living Being.

❑ I want to care for my trees or plants without chemicals.

❑ I want to preserve my investment in my home's landscape.

❑ I am a tree professional and want to explore something new.

❑ It sounded interesting, and I enjoy learning new things.

❑ I want to grow a better garden or do better farming.

❑ I am grateful for all that trees and plants give me.

❑ Trees have taught me about life.

❑ I have good memories of trees.

❑ I am concerned about the environment and the planet and want to help the trees, plants, crops, and forests in some way.

❑ I suspect that this fits into my expanding view of life and the global **paradigm shift** in consciousness that is going on now.

Step 3: Are there any other reasons you are reading? Please write them in your *Tree Whispering:Trust the Path* notebook.

Step 4: Jot down any other notes, impressions, or intentions.

Step 5: Congratulate yourself for finishing the exercise!

<u>TRY THIS: A QUIET WALK IN THE WOODS</u>

*Read through the steps. Decide whether you feel comfortable doing this exercise.
If you do not feel comfortable or have any concern whatsoever, do not do it.*

Step 1: Take your *Tree Whispering:Trust the Path* notebook with you to your favorite park, woods, forest, or path through trees.

Step 2: Begin your walk in the quiet as you normally would.

Step 3: In your heart or speaking in a whisper, express gratitude or thankfulness to the trees as you move among them. Notice how you feel.

Step 4: Stop for a moment. Say to the trees: "**I open my heart to you.**"

Step 5: Resume walking. Be receptive to feelings of their gratitude coming to you.

Step 6: As you walk or afterward, jot down notes in your *Tree Whispering: Trust the Path* notebook about how you feel, what you think, and what it was like for you to take this walk.

Dr. Jim Conroy,
The Tree Whisperer®

Ms. Basia Alexander,
The Chief Listener

BECOMING THE TREE WHISPERER

Dr. Jim Conroy, The Tree Whisperer, says: I love trees and plants. You probably love them, too. Trees and plants are alive like you and me. We are all living Beings. We are just different. By listening to them, I have come to know hundreds and hundreds of trees and plants as individuals. When they are sick, I help them heal themselves. I love each of them as if they were my children.

When you put your hands on a tree, you feel the bark. When I touch a tree, sure, I feel the bark, but I also feel the tree's **Life Force** flowing through it. I feel a rush of power or current moving from the roots to the branches. This power or current tells me details about the tree's inner health in ways that conventional science and technology cannot.

I tell people, "Do the right things from the beginning to keep your trees and plants healthy." Despite their best efforts, trees and plants still can get stressed. With today's weather extremes, most trees are stressed to some degree.

Dr. Jim continues: People started calling me "the tree whisperer" when I went to their properties, touched, and saved their precious but sick trees. Some people had already tried conventional approaches that were unsuccessful. I **holistically** heal the life processes of trees and plants when they are stressed or in **decline**, using **bioenergy**-based, hands-on healing methods. My interaction with the trees' **biofields** promotes healthy **dynamic balance** within their inner functionality and helps them heal themselves. I apply no products whatsoever.

With my gift and skills for "getting in touch with the Life Force" of trees and plants and by using my Green Centrics™ System, I discover malfunctions within trees' and plants' inner physiology. Then, I holistically restore their health through the use of commonly accepted bioenergy healing methods.

In 2002, I created the Green Centrics System as an organized, professional methodology. In early days of developing my system, trees and plants taught me why stress factors are additive for them and that three or more stresses can lead to their decline. After three years of research and development, I started doing this methodology professionally.

Not long afterward, I realized that people want a simple and easy way to help their own trees and to feel a deeper appreciation for all of **Nature**. So, my business partner, Basia Alexander, and I created Tree Whispering® and started teaching. Tree Whispering begins as a personal experience of the **Growth Energy** and Life Force of trees or plants. Tree Whispering is also a set of techniques for healing **internal functionality** that's been **compromised** by stress factors. Anyone can experience a tree's or plant's Life Force and learn the techniques!

Dr. Jim elaborates: To fully understand Tree Whispering, a shift in thinking is needed. People are accustomed to assuming that they know what is best for trees, but, in truth, they should ask trees about their inner health and about what they need.

You might be thinking: "Is he crazy? He's talking about asking a tree!" No. I am not crazy. Both wilderness trackers as well as indigenous peoples have always known how to pay close attention to Nature. They pay attention to physical signs like changes in foliage or animal footprints, but–more importantly– they pay attention to their gut feelings and intuitions. We

Westerners—who believe we are so advanced—need to cure our own insanity. It is crazy *not* to listen closely to Nature. Our enjoyment of a walk in the woods–if not our lives and our future on the planet–may depend on cultivating such skills.

When I "whisper," I am getting to know a tree or plant as an individual. I am coming from its point of view. Mostly, I am asking it about what conditions must be corrected in its internal functionality in order to improve its health. Yes, trees and plants contain that information since they are living systems, but they can't always accomplish the change in internal functionality for themselves. It's just like us–we might know about our own illnesses, but we can't always heal ourselves.

I don't use products or invasive techniques. I heal in these ways: by establishing a personal rapport–like being "in the zone"–with the tree's Life Force, by focusing my conscious **intentionality**, and by moving bioenergy flows within and around the tree. Since the turn of the century, many forward-looking hospitals have been offering **energy medicine** systems like Yoga, Reiki, Touch for Health and Therapeutic Touch™ in their programs for cancer, heart, and other patients. Trees may have a different physiology, but since they are alive, they respond to similar energy medicine healing techniques.

Dr. Jim emphasizes: I believe that we, as the human guardians of Earth, can cooperate to bring botany back into balance. Trees, plants, insects, diseases–even entire ecosystems–can again work in harmony and dynamic balance. I believe that balance can be reestablished in Nature but *not* because we are so smart, *not* because our science has all the answers, *not* because we can control or manipulate Nature. We can't control Nature. Attempts to dominate Nature have not worked out well. Instead, reestablishment of harmony and balance can result from our conscious and **co-creative** partnership with Nature. I call this new kind of relationship with Nature "Cooperative BioBalance.™" Through the practice of Tree Whispering, you can establish a personal partnership with your own trees and plants. You can help them thrive and grow with a holistic, respectful, bioenergy-based healing approach.

Dr. Jim Conroy followed a childhood love of plants all the way through a bachelor of science in horticulture from Delaware Valley College in

*Pennsylvania to a masters and doctorate in botany and plant pathology
from Purdue University in Indiana. In his corporate career, he started
by working directly with customers about improving the health of their
crops and other plants. During his more than 25 years in upper
management of Top 50 ag-chemical corporations, he promoted plant
health through research and development, customer contact, marketing
of products, and business development.*

Dr. Jim talks about his background: When I was a child, my
father built a greenhouse for me that stuck out of our raised
basement window. I had to climb up on a chair to get into it. My
high-school biology class bean-growing project took place in
that little greenhouse. I started with one little round bean that I
put in the soil. That bean actually grew to produce three new
beans in a pod. That was amazing to me and set my path for life.

Fast forward a few decades to my years working for various
agricultural chemical companies. While walking through fields
of crops or orchards, I knew that we–in science and
marketing–were missing something. We knew that plants
stopped growing when they were stressed. But, with the mindset
of the day and its existing tools and conventional products, we
couldn't do anything to repair the inner processes of plants and
trees. We could only *externally* apply products on the
symptoms. All we could do was kill the pests or throw around
fertilizer. We could not heal these plants that were so important
to growers, gardeners, consumers, and homeowners alike.
Ultimately, all we—the scientists, marketers, and growers—
could do was watch and hope that the trees and plants would
"grow through" their weaknesses.

I remember learning something important in my early days
working for one ag-chem company. During a visit to an Iowa
farmer's fields, I was told that he planted his soybean seeds into
the field in a timely way. They sprouted and started growing
well. Then, the weather turned cold and wet. I saw those two-
week-old plants. They turned yellow and stopped growing. He
knew—and I learned—that the soybeans had "locked-up." In
other words, something inside the plant became compromised
because of the stretch of cold, wet weather. No product could
help this condition. In the meantime, the grower would have to
wait patiently–perhaps for a couple weeks. The soybean plants

would have to survive until they could "grow through it" and could compensate inside themselves. It turned out that many growers in the area had the same problem that season. Since the growers lost this valuable growing time early in the season, the growers could only hope to get a long, warm autumn so they might harvest decently sized soybean pods for sale.

During his entire corporate career, Dr. Conroy remembered the lesson of the yellow soybean plants. He knew that a solution for healing plants and trees from the inside-out existed somewhere outside of the conventional mindset. He was determined to find a creative approach that did not involve applying products to the outside of plants or using invasive techniques on them.

In early 2002, he attended an introductory talk by Dr. John Veltheim, the founder of the BodyTalk System,™ a complementary energy medicine healing system for humans. Within the first hour, Dr. Conroy realized that he discovered his creative solution to healing plants and trees on the inside.

Dr. Jim recalls: I knew that tree and plants are living Beings. I asked myself: "Could the same ideas and techniques that are proven to work in human healing systems work with plants?" I set out to discover the answer.

I studied the BodyTalk System and found that it was an excellent protocol for achieving improvements in human health and well-being. Humans and plants, although both alive, are different physiologically. Therefore, plants needed their own system.

In the process of my studies, I realized and finally admitted that I have strong intuitive capabilities and sensory perceptive skills. When I am with trees and plants, I experience knowings, sounds, images, colors, and fragrances as **communications** from them.

With his combination of perceptive skills, strong scientific background, and willingness to be open-minded, Dr. Conroy started to develop his holistic system for healing trees and plants: the Green Centrics System. Three years of initial research and testing yielded results on plants, crops, and trees that were promising and sometimes stunning.

Dr. Jim talks about early development: My very first clients were rose bushes in my backyard. There were always a few weak bushes, so I started using my new biofield-based healing techniques on them. They revealed to me that their internal functionality was compromised when they were stressed. In other words, **feedback loops** of functionality between parts and systems that should have been interacting were broken. I realized that I could make an internal repair by touching and tapping on them while–in my consciousness–I focused on certain combinations of internal relationships. This process of repair yielded a spurt of new growth in a modest amount of time. It pleased me that weak bushes got stronger and bloomed.

I graduated to crop clients and tree clients. The master-growers at Community Supported Garden at Genesis Farm[1] in Blairstown, New Jersey, generously opened their fields and trees to my trials. Annual crops are especially fun to work on. When I tested my healing techniques on them, they responded positively within three to four days. When I worked on their trees, the response time was longer. Trees are just on a longer time scale than annuals. But, improve and grow, they did!

Among my first customers were people who had previous personal experience with the efficacy of biofield-based healing systems like the BodyTalk System, Rieki and Touch for Health. Those people immediately understood that the same kind of approach would work on their trees and plants.

By 2005, Dr. Conroy was satisfied with the Green Centrics System's state of development. He also increased his own proficiency. In 2006, he concentrated on raising his level of consistency. His tree and plant clients were recovering from stress. Declining trees were beginning to grow again. He did all this work without the application of any products or invasive techniques whatsoever.

Dr. Jim tells the story: I call the trees my "clients" because they receive the healing treatments. When I started offering the service to people, I decided to call them my "customers" because they pay for my services.

Many of my customers started calling me "the tree whisperer." When I lean close and put my hands on the trunk of a tree in order to feel its Life Force, I suppose it looks like I am whispering with it. Basia suggested that we go to public appearances and trade shows with a sign that said "The Tree Whisperer." Initially, I went with some hesitation using that label. But, people's reactions showed that they understood that this was something very different. I embraced the moniker: The

Tree Whisperer. The name expresses what I do in a way that most people can grasp quickly and with a smile.

BECOMING THE CHIEF LISTENER

Ms. Basia Alexander, The Chief Listener, created her own Track II bachelor of arts degree in communications at Beloit College in Beloit, Wisconsin. As training director for an Apple® Computer dealership and as an adjunct professor, Basia wrote and delivered all computer basics as well as desktop publishing trainings. In the late 1990s, she followed an inner calling to write on spiritual, self-help, health, and personal development topics. ReVitalizations™–her coaching and training company–produced local and regional workshops about expanding personal creativity and regaining radiant health. After becoming certified as a BodyTalk System practitioner, her love of trees and plants led her to co-found Plant Health Alternatives, LLC, with Dr. Conroy. Always a green-thumbed outdoor, indoor, and container gardener, Basia is proud of her two-story tall Norfolk Island Pine and thirty-five-year-old cactus. Basia writes all Tree Whispering manuals and teaches side-by-side with Dr. Conroy. She is also an innovator and author in the new discipline of Conscious Co-Creativity.

Ms. Basia Alexander, The Chief Listener, explains her title:
In the early days of Dr. Jim's test trials at the Community Supported Garden at Genesis Farm, he would return to the office with more questions than answers. He would describe what he felt and saw. I would listen. It was in the quiet of my listening that Dr. Jim could re-create his experience with the plant or tree in order to have insights into what was happening inside of it.

Together, we would arrive at an understanding of how effectively the trees and plants were able to interact with Dr. Jim's new treatments. By listening, I helped to facilitate a translation process. From his right-brained and heartfelt experiences evolved a left-brained, usable interpretation. This partnership led to the development of the Green Centrics System. I asked questions, too, as I believe that asking questions is an important part of listening. I helped him tease out the techniques and build the processes by which he was approaching trees and plants. So, Dr. Jim started calling me "the chief listener" and the name stuck.

Ms. Alexander, The Chief Listener, has a knack for hearing messages in-between the words. She speaks only American English, has a smattering of high-school French, and listened to her mother's family speak Polish when her father wasn't in the room. But, she is a translator of different kinds of languages–those of the heart and those of Nature.

Basia continues: I don't want to make this sound like something unusual, but I hear and see Nature communicate. But, then, most people hear Nature speak in the way the birds sing or frogs chirp and in seeing the rhythms of the seasons. Nature communicates all around us. Just look and listen!

In the Western culture, nearly 400 years of **Cartesian**-based reductionist and mechanistic thinking have discouraged people from developing senses and inner knowings. But, people can learn the skills to re-establish those lines of communication with Nature. It's not hard, it just takes some patience.

Ms. Alexander pursues studies in the new sciences. She inquires into the fields of spirituality and consciousness. As Dr. Conroy continues to evolve Tree Whispering and the Green Centrics System, Ms. Alexander continues to listen for developments. More often than not, she hears some insight or discovery from Dr. Conroy that parallels the works which she studies.

They have a working agreement: Ms. Alexander shares information about her studies only after Dr. Conroy discusses his insights. He prefers to be unbiased. He wants to remain free of any knowledge of other people's discoveries. In this way, his knowledge comes directly from his experience with trees and plants. Dr. Conroy's approach has benefits. By protecting his exposure in this way, he makes independent, new discoveries and can open up new doors of thinking. Dr. Conroy's work with trees and plants often shows the practical application of another's theoretical work. Additionally, Dr. Conroy and Ms. Alexander say it is a pleasant surprise to find that there is sometimes congruence or parallel thinking between his discoveries and other people's works.

GUARDIANS OF TREE WHISPERING

Dr. Conroy and Ms. Alexander call themselves guardians of the principles of Cooperative BioBalance and of the teachings of Tree Whispering. As teachers of Cooperative BioBalance and Tree Whispering, they happily share the skills. As champions, they travel and speak tirelessly. As stewards, they protect the purity of the principles and practices from anyone who might misunderstand or attempt to misuse the skills involved.

Basia describes teaching: The first thing we do is tell people that *coming from the tree's point of view* is possible. We are like pioneers in a new land saying, "Follow us. It's safe." Then, we advocate that having a more enlightened kind of relationship with trees, plants, and all of Nature can enhance the quality of people's lives. Usually, on their own, students see how taking respectful actions toward all plants is good for themselves and sustainable for the planet.

Some people think that our techniques will help them make the plant grow a certain way, make the crop yield more, or make the tree do what they want it to do. That is not true! Usually, those people cannot let go of their desire to dominate Nature. We believe in partnership and cooperation with Nature. We caution students against any attempts to control or manipulate trees and plants. Control and manipulation never works anyway, in the long run. It always backfires on people because of the way that it throws living systems out of balance.

Dr. Jim reveals what he has learned: For years, I have been listening to trees and plants, learning how to come from their points of view. To do that, I have had to check my ego at the door. In other words, I have had to set aside my own personal point of view. I have learned to ask the plants and trees what is best for them and to have humility in doing so.

I have also had to come to terms with letting go of my investment in advanced education and a corporate career. My formal training consisted of indoctrination in the scientific mindset and instruction in methodologies for controlling and manipulating plants. In developing Tree Whispering and Green Centrics, a major lesson for me was to let go of my human-centric agenda. I had to liberate myself from my training. What I thought was right turned out to be often wrongly used. What I was taught should be done may not have been in the best interests of the trees and plants. I did a full turn-around; I left the corporate world and struck out to do what I felt and still feel is a higher calling.

Dr. Jim protects while welcoming: Cooperative BioBalance and Tree Whispering have come to me as gifts from a higher power and I am their guardian. I want to share them with you and–at the same time–protect the **Green Beings.**

For those people who would misuse the skills or disregard the value of the tree's or plant's Life Force, or attempt to dominate and control trees, plants, and Nature with this knowledge, I say: "Put down this book. Do not take my class."

For all of you who share a love and respect for trees and plants, for any of you who desire to honor these life-giving Green Beings, I say "Welcome. Come and learn the most respectful and loving ways to enter a tree's or plant's world. It is an honor to be your guide."

Dr. Jim says: The trees actually do know best. The Plant Kingdom arose long before humanity upon this planet. They have mastered mutual communication and co-existence in communities. They know what is right for their own health and what should be done to help them. Homo sapiens are relative newcomers on Earth so we should learn from our elders.

You can touch, heal, and communicate with Green Beings. And, they want to touch, heal, and communicate with you, too. The trees and plants are waiting for you to communicate with them.

Chapter 3: Messages from Trees and Plants

INTRODUCING MESSAGES FROM TREES AND PLANTS

*Dr. Conroy and Ms. Alexander understand that some people readily accept the idea that trees, plants, and all of **Nature** have a kind of capacity to **communicate**, while other people are not sure about this. They—as Tree Whisperer® and The Chief Listener—intend to assure everyone that trees and plants have the ability to transmit information. They declare that communication–as a two-way activity–among people, trees, plants, and all of Nature is not only possible but also is available to anyone. More information is in the Appendix.*

*Dr. Conroy and Ms. Alexander lay the foundation of understanding that **Green Beings** and all of Nature's organisms are not only physically living Beings but also partners on Earth and wise teachers in Spirit. Green Beings are both **intelligent** and creative.*

In this chapter, expect to

- *be amazed by stories of trees' and plants' intricate and ingenious physiological evolution.*
- *become informed about science's inroads into a new perception of plants as intelligent and having signaling and behavioral capability.*
- *read actual messages that come from trees and plants through various people's relationships with them.*
- *encounter your own attitudes, beliefs, and concepts about exchanging communications with Green Beings.*
- *learn that messages from Green Beings fall into four general categories; read stories that fit each category.*

Dr. Conroy and Ms. Alexander say that people can receive their own messages from trees and plants. The model that Conroy and Alexander suggest is proposed in this chapter. Practical methodology—how-tos—for exchanging communications with Green Beings will be offered in the following chapters.

MESSAGES RECEIVED BY THE TREE WHISPERER

Dr. Jim Conroy, The Tree Whisperer,® admits: Yes, trees and all kinds of plants communicate with me. I experience their communications in various sensory or emotional ways. Sometimes they talk in the sense that I hear their communications as words. They may say, "It hurts here."

Usually their communications to me are brief and succinct, because a short message may be all I need to know in that moment in order to perform a healing technique with them. Other times, they have more to say.

Dr. Jim adds: If I feel an impulse from a tree indicating that it has a longer message of importance for me or for other people, I will pick up my pencil and begin to write. While receiving its message, I feel a lot like a United Nations language translator who can hear one language being spoken while simultaneously speaking words in another language. However, the tree's language is not always in words but often in impressions.

Basia explains what happens when she translates: Translating communications from Nature is easier than it may seem. Intuition plays the greatest role in the process. The most important things I do are trust my intuition and let go of any expectations. In Chapter 4, we will explain the process of receiving communications so that you can do it—if you want to.

Dr. Jim describes: Many trees have spoken for the whole Plant Kingdom. In sharing their three main messages with you, let me alert you: they speak in their own way. As you read, you will discover that they express themselves in more awkward ways than you and I might normally say things. Be prepared to read not only the words but also the meanings within the words.

FIRST MESSAGE FROM THE TREES AND PLANTS

> WE ARE ALIVE.
> WE ARE LIVING BEINGS AND VALUABLE
> ASSETS TO PEOPLE
> AND TO THE PLANET.
> WE WANT TO BE HONORED.

We are alive! We are a life form, a Life Force, and valuable assets to humans and all of the planet. We want to be honored for our contribution to humans and as a part of all of Nature. We have a far different form than humans but, like people, have a Life Force that keeps us alive. This Life Force and life form needs to honored.

We contribute so much to humans. However, most humans take us for granted. Since we can't yell or bark at them, they cut us down or pull us out without even a nod of respect for the Life Energy. And some have not even given any respect for disrupting our whole ecology or community.

We are also a valuable asset to all other living things. We are food for the animals and insects; we are home for animals, insects, and organisms. Just as humans want to survive, so do the insects, the animals, and the microorganisms want to survive. We give them a place to do just that.

SECOND MESSAGE FROM TREES AND PLANTS

When our fluids are pulsing and we are making food for ourselves,

> WE ARE WEAK. THUS WE ARE OPEN TO HURT FROM INSECT BEINGS AND DISEASE BEINGS.

we are growing. Growing is what we want to do; it is what we need to do. To grow, so many things must happen inside of us in the right order and in perfect timing. This is like making music with many instruments. We are healthy on the inside when our song is strong. Then, we can live together with some insect Beings and some disease Beings. All can co-exist.

We live through many seasons, but we are sometimes hurt on the inside by many things that people do not see. When our friend , Water, visits us not enough or too much, we become weak. When our friend, Air, brings too much or not enough of Fire's hot breath, we weaken. In so many ways, most of us are becoming weak.

© Basia Alexander

When people look at us, we might look healthy to them, but we are hurt on the inside. Many times our leaves are lush, green, and bountiful. We have plentiful branches and are actively growing. If you look at the ends of our branches, you can see the new growth. We sparkle in the sun and shimmer in the wind. At other times, we look lush and sparkle in the sun, but we are not healthy on the inside.

We hurt on the inside. Our pulsing of fluids may be blocked, which slows down the way we bring water and nutrients from the soil. If our flow of fluids are blocked and we are not bringing up water and nutrients from our friend, the soil, then our food-making ability isn't operating correctly and we are not producing enough food to feed ourselves. If we are not producing enough food and our currents of fluids are blocked, then the food is not getting where it needs to go to keep us healthy and growing. One by one, our parts and inner workings break down. At first we look the same as when we were healthy, but we are weak.

We call for help from the community of similar surrounding trees or plants. They do what they can to help. But sometimes, they, too, are weak and cannot help.

The insects have learned to listen closely. They hear our cry for help to our nearby tree friends . Insect Beings take advantage of our weakness. We become food for their lives. Disease Beings come as well. We are weak and cannot resist their efforts to use us for food or for other reasons. You see, when we are healthy, we can co-exist with insect Beings and disease Beings. We all need to live. But when we are weak, the evenness of co-existence goes out of balance.

When people come along, they think that we are weak because of the insects eating us or the diseases working on us. They use various liquid, stinging things to kill the insects that are eating us or the diseases that are using us. Little do they know, they are also killing the insect Beings and disease Beings that would help us as well as killing the ones that would not bother us at all.

When these stinging things are used on us or around us, they make us even weaker. We have to break down the stuff, taking precious energy that we don't have because we are weak.

Then, it gets worse. Those liquid stinging things kill the first insects and diseases, but more come. They are stronger. We are weaker. They eat us, use us. People use even more liquid, stinging things, then we get weaker and weaker. We cry for help, but only more insect Beings and disease Beings hear us.

And so, the spiral continues.

Do the people hear us? Not usually. The people don't realize that our defenses are low. The people don't realize that our pulse of fluids, our ways of making food, our ways of storing food, our ways of growing, our flow of energies, all need to be healed. Sadly, the things people put on us don't heal us. Sometimes the things do the opposite and make us worse.

THIRD MESSAGE FROM TREES AND PLANTS

Our inner music plays as a beautiful song when all of our thousands and thousands of inner instruments are tuned and playing together. It is a joyful and divine sound.

But, we weaken with insults from our surroundings. Discord and dissonance reign when we are weakened.

> OUR HEALTH CAN BE RESTORED WITH PEOPLE'S HELP, BUT ONLY IF THEY COME INSIDE OF OUR WORLD, SEE OUR LIVES FROM OUR POINT OF VIEW, AND HEAL OUR INNER CURRENTS, OUR ENERGY FLOWS, AND OUR SONG.

Our health needs to be restored. If we are weak because our inner pulse of fluids, our food-making abilities, or our energy flows have broken, does it not make sense to our friends, the humans, to correct or heal those inner operations rather than to give us more of what we do not want? People can help us, but only if they come into our world. We ask:

© Basia Alexander

please come from our point of view. The more you get to know us, feel our Life Force, and experience our world, the easier it will be for humans to restore our health in the ways that matter to us—in ways that work for us.

Touch us. Communicate with us. We can share this healing as a cooperative task. We are eager to offer messages to people. We want people to arise as our partners!

A HEALTHY-LOOKING TREE SAYS, "FIX MY OUCHIE"

Dr. Jim smiles: When you go to the doctor, you might say to him or her: "It hurts here," or "I feel awful." You might ask, "Gee, Doc, can you fix this body part or that system?" Many trees and plants talk to me in the same way. Requests for help are the kind of messages that I usually get. A Copper Beech tree in central New Jersey, asked me: "Fix my ouchie."

That Copper Beech is one of my favorites; it's so big and majestic! It's an example of the kind of *cooperation* and *coming from their point of view* that the trees and plants request.

That Copper Beech is also a good example of what I call a **healthy-looking** tree. Ones that look good on the outside aren't always really healthy on the inside. As The Tree Whisperer, I regularly watch over this tree. It always looked healthy, but one day I squeezed between the tree and the garden house and– uh-oh! I found the dreaded bleeding canker.

My doctorate is in plant pathology, so please let me interrupt my story for a moment to tell you about this disease. Bleeding Canker is caused by the Phytophthora organism. It's not a very strong organism by itself and normally lives in the soil. Thus, it is everywhere. If it affects a tree, then the tree is already somehow stressed or in **decline**. Even with the appearance of health, when Phytophthora shows up it means the tree's internal functionality is compromised in some way. It could kill the tree. What I have learned since earning my doctorate is that the commonly accepted use of products for Phytophthora only adds stress to the tree. The tree has to not only fight the organism in its system but also use its precious resources to break down a substance that is foreign to it.

Green Centrics,™ my **bioenergy** healing approach, helps any tree become healthier so that it can naturally come into **dynamic balance** with the organism. When I am using this system, my own personal bioenergy field–which comes from my heart–and the energy field of the tree make an overlapping pattern. In science, it's called a *coherence pattern* or *diffraction pattern.[1]* I am "in the zone" like an athlete or artist so my right-brain is operating at an alpha-wave state of intuition.

Back to my story. As soon as I found the bleeding canker in the Copper Beech, I asked the tree for permission to overlap my bioenergy field with its bioenergy field. I put my hands on the tree and opened my heart and mind to connect with its **Life Force.** In my intuitive hearing, I heard the tree say, "I have an ouchie! Get rid of it. Fix my ouchie, please." I felt so sad when feeling the tree's distress. I began using my Green Centrics System immediately to find out what was happening inside of this beautiful but distressed tree.

Dr. Jim relates: My first task was to find out how the inner functionality of the tree was compromised or blocked. So, I asked questions of the tree's innate **intelligence**. It led me to understand that its circulation was blocked within the little streams of fluids going up and down on the inside. If you took botany in high school, you may remember that movement up of fluids is in the xylem, movement down is in the phloem. A tree does not have a heart to pump the fluids, but the whole tree *is* the circulation system. And this Copper Beech's circulation was blocked. I knew this because it communicated that feeling and visualization to me.

This is not just some kind of gifted diagnosis that I do. I don't just find out what is wrong. Actual healing results from this interaction, although I am reluctant to take direct credit. I feel that my conscious **intention** and concentrated attention interact with the tree's own force to live. In the Copper Beech tree, our collaboration began to free up its circulation system.

How? The simplest way I can describe it is to say that when I am in a bioenergy interface with the Life Force of the tree, it is offering information and instruction as to how it can repair itself. For example, it's like there is a bank of electrical outlets on the wall and a mess of wires on the floor. I have to find which plug goes into which outlet. Later, I'll tell you in detail how the Copper Beech and I "fixed the ouchie." It's a mutual process but the Copper Beech really healed itself.

This story shows how people can interact with trees in ways that trees and plants want: offering healing, coming from their point of view, realizing that they normally live with other organisms, avoiding use of chemicals, empathizing, understanding their needs, being attentive to them, and–well–simply loving them.

ALIVE? CREATIVE? INTELLIGENT? SPIRITED?

The following four sections in this chapter address key questions that many people have about trees and plants: Are they alive? Are their forms the result of evolutionary trial and error, or are they creative? Do they exhibit intelligence? Do they have Spirit?

Dr. Jim asks: Some people view trees and plants as things–like a chair or table. Are they alive? After all, trees don't bark like a dog. Many people think about plants as if they were only physical organisms. Prevailing attitudes hold that they have evolved through trial and error. Most people give plants no credit for showing intelligence. Plants don't have brains. Can they be intelligent?

Basia adds: Can you get a message from a tree? We say "yes!" We say that communication happens for three reasons. First, trees and plants are alive; they are living Beings. Second, they have remarkable physiological attributes that show a creative approach to interacting with life. Third, they exhibit **cognition**. Thus, we believe that they can communicate. Over and above that, we believe that trees and plants have consciousness and Spirit and want to share their wisdom with us.

TRY THIS: LOCATE YOURSELF ALONG THIS CONTINUUM
Read through the steps. Decide whether you feel comfortable doing this exercise. If you do not feel comfortable or have any concern whatsoever, do not do it.

Step 1: Identify where your ideas, beliefs, attitudes, and concepts are along this continuum:

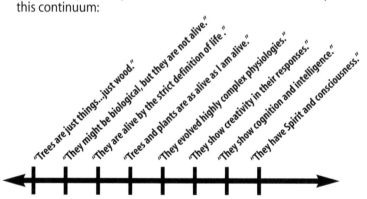

Step 2: Make a note in your *Tree Whispering: Trust the Path* notebook about where your ideas fall along this continuum.

Step 3: If the statements don't resonate with you, write down your beliefs or attitudes about the aliveness of trees and plants.

Step 4: Ask yourself: **"Am I willing to shift my attitudes or beliefs?"**

Step 5: Ask yourself: **"What would happen in my life if my beliefs changed?"**

Step 6: Ask yourself: **"Would I allow my beliefs to shift further toward the right side of this continuum?"**

Step 7: Write any additional notes or reflections in your *Tree Whispering: Trust the Path* notebook.

Dr. Jim suggests: Don't pass up the chance to ask yourself these questions. Your honest answers may surprise you. Your answers to these questions–your current attitudes and willingness to change–will determine whether you will really enjoy this book.

TREES AND PLANTS ARE ALIVE, ARE LIVING BEINGS

High-school biology or botany books itemize plants' parts and functions. See how similar their attributes are to those of mammals.[2]

Life Attributes of Mammals	*Life Attributes of Trees/Plants*
❑ *Breathing*	❑ *Respiring carbon dioxide through stomata under leaves*
❑ *Growing, cells multiplying*	❑ *Growing: cells multiplying, leaves appearing, branching occurring*
❑ *Eating*	❑ *Producing their own food through photosynthesis*
❑ *Reproducing, bearing young*	❑ *Producing fruit, going to seed*
❑ *Sleeping*	❑ *Going into dormancy*
❑ *Moving around on legs*	❑ *Moving parts: roots, trunk, branches, and leaves*
❑ *Organizing into systems: circulation, respiration*	❑ *Organizing into systems: circulation, respiration*
❑ *Adapting, ability to change and respond*	❑ *Adapting, ability to change and respond*
❑ *Metabolizing in networks, converting matter and energy into cellular structures*	❑ *Metabolizing in networks, converting matter and energy into cellular structures*

Dr. Jim emphasizes: To us, there is no question about the aliveness of trees and plants. They are alive, living Beings.

TREES AND PLANTS ARE CREATIVE

Basia offers: If you were to consider trees and plants only from the perspective of the vitality of their physical attributes, the ways that they have evolved, and their physiologies, they show great creativity in their vitality. The Plant Kingdom—through its patience, fruitfulness, and inventiveness—has mastered innovative responses within itself and with its surroundings.

Dr. Jim explains: There are many parallels between plants and people, but people can't directly convert sunlight into food. Trees and plants *eat* sunlight through their complex interactions.

© Basia Alexander

A tree–much like the sunflower seedling shown to the left–grows, branches, and leafs out by itself. It feeds itself by taking resources directly out of the earth and air, then converting those resources plus sunlight into sugars. A plant's leaves unfurl like solar panels unfold. Solar panels generate electricity; plants' leaves generate food, which is energy for the plant. As soon as the plant begins to feed itself, all of the intricate systems like circulation, uptake, and growth interact dynamically as a dance of life.

Plants have a reciprocal agreement with microorganisms around their roots. The plant feeds the microorganisms, and the microorganisms feed the plant. In this arrangement, there is a full system operating that starts at the microorganisms and the roots and goes through the parts and functions in the plant all the way to the leaves, which are producing food for the plant. Leaves, while producing food, also serve to accomplish at least two different gas-exchanges at the same time. In photosynthesis, they intake carbon dioxide and output oxygen. In respiration, they intake oxygen and output small amounts of carbon dioxide.

I feel that the following examples show a full range of plants' expertise and effectiveness: their evolutionary creativity and their creativity in moment-to-moment responses to stimuli.

EXAMPLES OF CREATIVITY IN THE PLANT KINGDOM

The Carbon Cycle: *Plants produce some carbon dioxide by their chemical processes of respiration but use it up through photosynthesis. The result is a net production of oxygen.[3] This surplus of oxygen results in the air that humans enjoy breathing.*

Evolution: Dr. Mark Moffett, award-winning National Geographic *contributor, has said that the philodendron is a favorite plant. In a 1994 interview, Dr. Moffett said he photographically documented its snake-like behavior in jungles and rainforests. He explained that as a seedling grows on the forest floor, it sends out shoots to find a tree trunk. The vine loses its roots in the soil. It remains about two yards long and moves through the trees. It moves by elongating stems to travel in shadows and slows down to enjoy the sun in the canopy by producing larger leaves.[4]*

The glasshouse plant, Rheum nobile, is part of the rhubarb family and lives at an altitude of 14,000 feet (4,000 meters) in the Himalayan Mountains. It makes its own greenhouse so it can live in the extreme cold and ultraviolet exposure of the high altitude. Its outer bracts become translucent so light can get through. It grows about 5 feet tall, and its roots are the size of a man's arm.[5]

Heliotropism is a response to blue light. It means the motion of flowers or leaves to follow the sun. The motion is performed by motor cells in a flexible segment just below the flower, called a pulvinus. The motor cells are specialized in pumping potassium ions into nearby tissues, changing their turgor pressure. The segment flexes because the motor cells at the shadow side elongate due to a turgor rise.[6]

© Basia Alexander

Dr. Jim waxes poetic: The definition of heliotropism sounds so dry. But, have you ever seen a whole field of sunflowers facing east in the morning? It is awe-inspiring! Later in the day, like a whole army, they have turned west. Even more amazingly, by the next morning, they are facing east again. See a field of sunflowers at least once in your life!

Defense: *Plants may not be able to run away from a predator, called herbivores, but they have developed elaborate defense strategies.*

- *Plants avoid herbivores by growing in a location where they are not easily accessed by herbivores. Some plants change seasonal growth patterns. Another approach diverts herbivores toward eating nonessential parts. Sometimes plants enhance their ability to recover from damage. Some plants encourage the presence of natural enemies of herbivores, which in turn protect the plant. And, while most plant defenses are directed against insects, other defenses have evolved that are aimed at vertebrate herbivores, such as birds and mammals.[7]*

- *In her paper entitled* "The Myriad Plant Responses to Herbivores," *Linda Walling, PhD, of the University of California at Riverside, explains that feeding insects induces the plant to create an array of volatile chemicals as a mechanism of defense. Further, she says that the blend of volatile chemicals provides cues to attract other insects that would be parasitic to the original attacker.[8]*

- *In* "Airborne signals prime plants against insect herbivore attack," *the authors of this study showed that compounds called "green leafy volatiles (GLV)" warn a plant's neighbor about insects that are attacking. GLV are suspected to play a key role in plant-to-plant signaling and plant-insect interactions.[9]*

TREES AND PLANTS HAVE INTELLIGENCE

All self-organized systems are, in fact, intelligent. They have to be. For they must continually monitor their environments, internal and external; detect perturbations; decide on the basis of those perturbations what the likely effect will be; and respond to them in order to maintain self-organization.[10]

STEPHEN HARROD BUHNER

Basia proposes: Please consider that trees and plants are not only alive and creative but also intelligent. Trees and plants fit the scientific criteria for showing cognition. Plants have learned and adapted in order to live in their environments. They have also shaped their environments. After all, ecosystems are massive **feedback loop** systems of life interacting with life.

SCIENTIFIC EXPLANATIONS OF INTELLIGENCE IN THE PLANT KINGDOM

Physicist and director of the Center for Eco-Literacy in Berkeley, California, Fritjof Capra, in his book The Web of Life *calls cognition the process of life. He says that all living organisms—plants, animals, or humans—are self-organizing systems that interact with their environments through mental-type processes. He describes cognition as the process of knowing and says that it does not require a brain or a nervous system. In an example about bacteria, he notes that they can sense chemical differences in their surroundings. Bacteria can swim toward food and away from poisons. Something comparable can also be said about trees and plants.[11]*

Scientific researchers have been surprised, since the 1990s, to discover that their plant subjects—thought to be passive and without the benefits of human-type senses or brains—can do something that has been considered within the sole domain of mammals: communicate. As the second decade of the twenty-first century dawned in the scientific community, a more dynamic notion began to take root about plants as living Beings that have abilities to cope with new situations. There is evidence that plants have adaptively variable behavior; in other words, they show intelligence by any dictionary definition.[12]

Examples of plant intelligence research from the mid-2000s include:

* *Consuelo M. DeMoraes, at Penn State University, studies a parasitic plant, the Dodder. She shows that it can detect volatile chemicals released by a potential host and then grow toward it.[13]*

* *Plants engage in self-recognition and can communicate danger to*

their clones or genetically identical cuttings planted nearby, says Richard Karban, PhD, University of California at Davis, and Kaori Shiojiri, Kyoto University, Japan. Sagebrush can respond to cues of self and non-self without physical contact. Plants seem to be able to warn others of impending danger by emitting chemicals.14

• *Plant cells and neurons have similarities, says University of Bonn, Germany, scientist Frantisek Baluska. Tip-growing plant cells, such as root hairs and pollen tubes, resemble neurons extending their axons.15 Many scientists have revived the discussion started by Charles Darwin: The root apex may be considered a "brain-like" organ with a sensitivity that controls its movement through soil.16*

• *Austrian philosopher, Gunther Witzany, expert in biocommunication, has developed a "theory of communicative Nature." He says life is different from nonliving matter by language and by the use of signs. Plants communicate using both chemicals and physical influences as signs. They communicate on at least three levels:*

(1) within and among their own cells,

(2) among themselves and their own species as well as other plant species,

(3) between themselves and other species, such as microorganisms, fungi, insects, and animals.

He calls this true communication because the signs–sometimes the same signs–are combined by using rules of syntax and are exchanged in situational or behavioral contexts for differing meanings.17, 18

• *The mission statement of the scientific Society for Plant Signaling and Behavior reads in part:*

> **The goal of this field is to illuminate the structure of the information network that exists within plants. Plants are dynamic and highly sensitive organisms that actively and competitively forage for resources both above and below ground. Plants accurately compute inputs from the environment, use sophisticated cost-benefit analysis, and take action to mitigate diverse environmental insults.**
>
> **Plants are also capable of refined recognition of self and non-self, and are territorial in behavior. This view sees plants as information processing organisms with complex, long-distance communication systems within the plant body and extending into the surrounding ecosystem.**
>
> **Our Society was originally founded in 2005 as the Society for Plant Neurobiology to reflect these views of plant function. In**

> *May 2009, the Society voted to expand its view and change its name accordingly.*
>
> *One goal of establishing a community for Plant Signaling and Behavior is to provide a venue for all interested biologists to explore complex plant behavior utilizing all levels of experimental approach. Among our symposia participants have been molecular geneticists, biochemists, electrophysiologists, physiological ecologists, community ecologists, mathematical modelers, plant designers, and even philosophers. Plant Signaling and Behavior will use the lens of integrated signaling, communication, and behavior to integrate data obtained at the genetic, molecular, biochemical, and cellular levels with physiology, development, and behavior of individual organisms, plant ecosystems, and evolution.[19]*
>
> SOCIETY FOR PLANT SIGNALING AND BEHAVIOR

Dr. Jim asks: What do you think about intelligence in plants? Merriam-Webster's definition of intelligence includes this phrase: "the ability to apply knowledge to manipulate one's environment."[20] Some people may say that the plant's interactions with their environment are just mechanisms, just natural evolutionary steps that have happened as a result of eons of reproductive trial and error.

I say, "Hogwash!" Have they asked the plants? I have.

I believe that plants are intelligent. But, people sometimes react defensively when I use the word *intelligent* because they define it while they are coming from their human point of view. Because people are naturally human-centric, they tend to see themselves as intelligent, and exclude others from having intelligence. They correctly believe that intelligence involves reasoning, thinking, and understanding. I am not suggesting that plants and trees have the same reasoning capacities as humans do. I am suggesting that–in their own world–they have even greater capacities and advanced skills.

Ask them. Trees and plants are *telling us* they are intelligent.

Basia gives credit to Dorothy: From her 2006 book *Call of the Trees*[21], we are honored to be able to quote the message from the Golden Conifer received by Dorothy Maclean. In this message, the Golden Conifer is telling us directly that it is intelligent.

THE GOLDEN CONIFER SAYS, "OUR INTELLIGENCE IS"

© Mary Moosey

We are happily established here, but are always glad to make the conscious contact, for our intelligence IS.

We ourselves are very much alive. Unawareness of this fact on the part of humanity seems an inexplicable waste.

Why do you go around in little water-tight worlds of your own as if you were the only intelligence, when all around you our world is bursting with awareness, full of the knowledge and truth that the Creator gives us and which would be of inestimable value to you?

Now, for instance, you hear the rain and just consider it as water coming down making a noise and quenching the thirst of plants. You simply accept it as an inanimate thing, or part of a process, and you miss all the joy of the Spirit of Rain with its broad intelligence and great role in all Life. You miss that which rain could impart of Oneness and flexibility to change and flow with the life of the Creator in the moment. Rain could be an example for all time and beyond, but you cut out all these mysteries and remain in narrow ruts.

We do not want to have a preaching aura with what we convey; we simply want to share with you and make you realize the abundant, bounding, integrating life, which is all around you in our worlds, which is always there and always has been, and with which you could be communing to a great betterment of this and every planet. You and I both have the equipment to share and can be joyous together as we each fulfill the roles which the Creator has for us. The same One Life flows in our veins, and the more we recognize and act on this fact, the more will all worlds come together in unison. This coming together is of the plan; for, in truth, we are all children of the One, all part of the One Life, all here because we are meant to be here.

You wonder how awareness of us fits into your everyday living. WE CAN ONLY ANSWER THAT FROM OUR POINT OF VIEW. We see you going around in a world of energy of which you are very much a part, yet closing off your connections with it and concentrating on a minute part of the whole. You have short-circuited yourselves when you could be dynamos of power and great transformers. To us, you seem half-dead, when all the time you could spark here and there with all of life and join in the great, moving, shining whole of it. You are limited. You need not be — and in your limitation, you do dreadful things. When your awareness is increased, your life will be completely different — free, unfettered, and universal. We are all for you opening out to all of Life, where you will find the One who is never absent, and with us you will praise It forever. Every tree, every atom tells this story and humans could be aware of it, if they would.

We thank you for listening. May our worlds be more and more one in the joy of the One Life.

TRY THIS: HOW DO YOU FEEL ABOUT THE MESSAGE FROM THE GOLDEN CONIFER?
Read through the steps. Decide whether you feel comfortable doing this exercise. If you do not feel comfortable or have any concern whatsoever, do not do it.

Step 1: Re-read the Golden Conifer's message.

Step 2: In your *Tree Whispering: Trust the Path* notebook, write how you feel about the message from the Golden Conifer.

Step 3: Next, write what you think about the tree communicating with Dorothy.

Step 4: Write about whether you feel or think that you could get a message—whether in words, intuition, or sensations–from a tree or plant.

Step 5: Acknowledge yourself with positive praise for doing this exercise.

THE SPIRIT OF TREES AND PLANTS

Dorothy Maclean is the remaining co-founder of the original Findhorn Community in Scotland, founded in 1962. In years since, the re-named Findhorn Foundation has grown into a spiritual community, an ecovillage, and an international centre for holistic education.22

Basia briefly retells Dorothy's story: Dorothy Maclean has been communicating with trees and plants, with their intelligence, and with the consciousness of Nature since 1962 when she co-founded the Findhorn Community in Scotland. Pronounced with a short i-sound, Findhorn has long been known as the garden where the founders communed with intelligence within the Plant Kingdom and followed its advice to grow amazing and enormous food crops for their own meals.

In their original 1968 handbook, *The Findhorn Garden, Pioneering a New Vision of Man and Nature in Cooperation*, Peter Caddy, Eileen Caddy, and Dorothy Maclean explained that they were unemployed, hungry, and living in a small motor home on the sand and rock overlooking the North Sea waters of Moray Firth in Scotland. Dorothy already had a strong faith in God and meditative practices. She received and wrote Divine Guidance that would come to her.

It was the Deva–or universal essence–of the garden pea whom she first asked to engage in conversation. In short order, Peter asked her for directions from the Devas of the tomatoes, lettuces, and all the other crops they were growing in the garden. He was a spiritually practical man and wanted to implement their gardening directives immediately.*23*

Basia continues: The word Deva is a Hindu expression for a benevolent supernatural Being or a deity.*24* Dorothy explained that she used the word Deva—meaning "shining one"—rather than the English word "Angel" because of the existing Western imagery involving Angels. She did not want people to associate Devas with winged and halo-ed Beings.

In spiritually connecting with a Deva's intelligence, Dorothy describes her experience as generally feeling moved by their force of energy but not sensing any particular form. She likened them to architects who draw-up plans–one for each kind of form.

I believe that Devas (pronounced with an "ay" sound, not the long "e" sound in the word "diva") represent the intelligence of design within the consciousness of Nature. So, naturally, I call them Design Intelligences.

Dr. Jim expands the idea: In my healing work, I have a sense of the presence of a Design Intelligence within a particular tree or plant with which I am energetically connected. This is not a linear or hierarchal arrangement. The individual tree has its own Design Intelligence, which holds its unique pattern. There is also a Design Intelligence for the type of tree it is, like Maple or Oak. This is what makes a Maple a Maple or an Oak an Oak.

Beyond that, the entire Plant Kingdom has a very powerful Design Intelligence. That intelligence of Nature's design is what makes a plant a plant.

Basia explains: However, you should not think of either Devas or Design Intelligences as individual Beings, Angels, or Nature Spirits. Design Intelligence is intangible; it may be something like dimensionally overlapping vibrational patterns or formulas of energy operating and interacting in feedback loops. I believe there is a fractal-type quality to them. Dr. Jim will discuss Network Patterns–which are a similar idea–in Chapter 7.

Dr. Jim adds this distinction: I feel the Spirit of the tree that I am healing while I ask its Design Intelligence for help in accomplishing the healing. To me, there is a difference. Spirit is what makes a sunflower turn its head; is what makes a plant operate the way it operates.

At this point, this is how I believe it might work. Design Intelligence and Spirit are two distinct aspects that operate in harmony! Let's talk about a carrot. The Design Intelligence— intangible energy formula—we call "carrot" holds the design of the carrot. Design Intelligence "says" it is orange, long, and narrow, grows below the soil line, is biennial, and has other unique characteristics.

At the same time, Spirit runs all of the parts and functions in an individual plant. In addition, Spirit helps all of the energy that is being generated by the plant to fill-in the form—which the Design Intelligence is holding—called "carrot." So, the form fills in and becomes a carrot plant.

Jim chuckles: By the way, Spirit is multidimensional, nonlinear, and outside of time. Don't try to figure it out with your mind. You may feel this with your heart. You could go outside and ask a tree, if you are willing to stand quietly for a while.

Basia gushes with enthusiasm: Dr. Jim and I had the wonderful opportunity to meet Findhorn's Dorothy Maclean in 2008 when she gave a workshop at Serius Community in Massachusetts.[25] Approaching her 90s at the time, we were touched by her candid honesty, gentle approach, and clarity of vision. She radiated with warmth while she led all the students in meditations and into considering how we might address the challenges of today's ecological and spiritual environment.

FOUR CATEGORIES OF MESSAGES FROM TREES AND PLANTS

Dr. Jim describes: Messages from trees and plants tend to come in four basic categories. We will describe each category and give you an example of a message. More information about how you can intuitively receive messages for yourself will be provided at the end of the chapter and in the next chapter.

Basia adds: Now that we have shown that plants and trees are alive, creative, intelligent, and spirited, it's easy to realize that you, too, can receive messages from them.

FOUR CATEGORIES OF MESSAGES

1) *What's going on inside and out for the Green Being's health. This includes what is going on inside of its physiology and/or what the environmental conditions are that influence the tree or plant on either the inside or outside.*

2) *Instructions to humans. These are actions to take like "water, now" or "stop watering so much."*

3) *Personal messages for you. Get information that is useful in your personal life like "spend more time breathing deeply" or "bring your children to visit me."*

4) *Insights or wisdom from Spirit; timeless information or advice.*

MESSAGE CATEGORY 4: INSIGHTS AND WISDOM FROM SPIRIT

Dr. Jim comments: We are starting with category four first because trees have Spirit and a timeless purpose and may communicate about that first. I received the following message from a White Pine tree in Wayne, New Jersey. The message was not just from that one tree but also from the Spirit of all the Evergreen trees. They serve as a refuge for other life forms.

The Evergreen Tree Spirit Describes Its Purpose

I am the Evergreen Spirit.

The protector of people, places, animals, plants, and other things.

My hands wisp in the wind to fold and hold

For all those who hold the trust are told.

And may they forever know for dear

That my longing and caring is always here.

And for those who seek the protective Spirit,

May they find faith and warmth in my protective arms.

For they are the mighty ones who seek rest from the harshness of their worries.

And I am here to comfort them from all their cares.

For, you see, my purpose is to protect, for all those who seek comfort from me.

From me, the birds sing.

From me, the mountains ring.

From me, children see a king.

From me, everyone feels some soothing.

For, you see, my purpose is to protect, for all those who seek comfort from me.

I have fun, too, because while all is going on—even the wind and rain—

I have the opportunity to be dancing with a joy from my Spirit heart that is sheer magic and prancing.

I have a tune.

It is the tune of the universe that says: "I am the protector for all to see, for you see my purpose is to protect, for all those who seek comfort from me."

And may I leave you one last thought?

My arms have fingers and hands.

Maybe a little odd compared to some.

But, you see, they fold and hold, for all those who seek comfort from me.

And I, like others, keep my hands and fingers for Life,

And reach to the stars for my dreams.

So why should anyone ever doubt my truth?

For, you see, my purpose is to protect, for all those who seek comfort from me.

MESSAGE CATEGORY 1: WHAT'S GOING ON INSIDE AND OUT?

Dr. Jim reminds: My story earlier in this chapter about helping the Copper Beech with the "ouchie" represents a category one message: what's going on inside and out. You don't have to have special training to get insight into what is going on inside of a tree's or plant's physiology. Anyone can interact with the amazing maze of interactions. Just ask.

Message Category 1: An Iowa Apple Tree Calls for Help

Dr. Jim tells the story: The story of the Apple tree in Iowa shows how to-the-point a tree's communication can be. The story also shows something about how we are all connected.

The question always comes up: "Which tree in a community do I pick to treat?" It is the tree or plant that calls out to me. "How does it call?" For me, it is a matter of tuning my inner receiver to hear that message being broadcast just like you would tune an old-fashioned radio to the station using the dials.

The owner of a small and young Apple orchard in Iowa showed me a particular sick tree even though many trees in her orchard needed help. She expected me to treat that tree. But, my inner antenna was picking up "help me" from another tree. The owner was confused and said, "I want this tree treated." All I could say was, "But, this one is calling."

As I started to do my healing work on the tree that called out to me, I bent down low to the ground to touch the soil area. My hands were near the base of the trunk. As I touched the area, I felt something under my fingers. There was a bump under the turf right at the base of the tree. I pushed back the turf and soil. There it was: a nylon rope starting to strangle the tree. The rope was left over from the support ropes when the tree was originally planted a few years back. It had slipped down and was now very tight around the trunk. It would have killed the tree by cutting into its cambium layer and stopping movement of fluids.

The owner jumped up and ran to the house to get a knife. We cut the rope, feeling great relief. I completed the healing treatment on that tree. Then, I moved and spread the healing treatment to all the trees in the orchard community. The following year, the whole orchard put on tremendous new growth. The lesson for me from that experience was to always listen carefully and find the tree that is calling. I can't follow the suggestion to simply treat the tree that looks bad. It has to be the one that calls to me.

Basia alerts you: I talked with many Tree Whispering workshop graduates in preparation for writing this book. I hope you will enjoy their many stories and advice which are scattered throughout this book. *Detailed information about graduates quoted in this chapter can be found in the Citations.*

Category 1–What's Going On Inside and Out: Stories from Graduates

Alana DuBois, Robbinsville, New Jersey, massage therapist, Reiki and energy-medicine instructor: I was walking around a nature park with my family. A young Maple caught my attention and communicated to me through my intuition, "Snake!" I jumped, but there was no snake there. I didn't understand why the tree would say that to me, but I put my hands on it and said "thank you" to it anyway. As I walked farther along the path, I saw a low stone wall that meandered in and out of the field in a serpentine fashion. I laughed out loud because the tree had been my tour guide.

MESSAGE CATEGORY 2: INSTRUCTIONS TO HUMANS

Dr. Jim on providing what the tree needs: Conventional wisdom suggests that we use our human knowledge to determine what is needed by the plant. How about using our human knowledge to ask the right question of the tree or plant? That way, you can really know what the plant needs. Helping trees and plants is not a cookie-cutter approach. Each one is individual, much like humans.

Category 2–Instructions to Humans: Pruning in an Ornamental Garden

Dr. Jim recalls a visit to Seattle, Washington: I was visiting an arboretum in Seattle, Washington. One area had trees and plants that were sculpted into various shapes and figures.

My tour guide, who knew about my work, asked me, "What do the plants think about being sculpted like this?"

I replied, "I will ask them."

So I did. I put my hands on various plants and asked them, "How do you feel about being sculpted into these shapes?" I found their answer most intriguing.

PLANTS IN THE ORNAMENTAL GARDEN SAY

*We don't mind too much that the humans cut us back into
shapes and sizes. It is like a haircut for us. Overall, the
humans are caring to us as best they can from their point of
view. However, if the humans would ask us how we should be
shaped and cut—if they would come from our point of view—
we would be far more beautiful than anything the humans
could imagine.*

Category 2–Instructions to Humans: Stories from Graduates

**Georgette Hritz, Scotch Plains, New Jersey, postal worker
and homeowner:** A friend gave me a small red Azalea bush
which I planted in my front yard. After a few years, I noticed
that it wasn't growing much. So, I talked with it, and it said it
was lonely. It wanted a companion. But, it specified that it did
not want another red one. It gave me a clear picture of a white
Azalea and showed me—in my mind's eye—where to plant the
new one nearby. I marked the spot with a stick and left to get the
companion. It's been another year and both are growing happily.

Carol Hulley, Kings Park, New York, gardener: My girlfriend
likes to hold a party once a year when her enormous Cherry tree
blooms. During the celebration, she asked all of us to touch the
tree and get a message from it. Most of the people attending had
not taken the Tree Whispering class; they reported that the tree
was happy and grateful to her for her love. That was probably
true; at the same time I got a message that was somewhat
disturbing but certainly practical.

It said, "I am suffocating and need to breathe." I looked around
and saw that my girlfriend's patio was made of bricks that were
laid too close to the trunk of the Cherry tree, covering much of
the root area. I told her that her tree needed to get air into its
roots; it needed to have some of the bricks removed. Because of
the class, I know that a tree can look great—such as having lots of
blossoms—but the next year it can start to weaken.

MESSAGE CATEGORY 3: PERSONAL MESSAGES

Basia points to the obvious: You'll know when a Being of
Nature has a message just for you. Perhaps they greet you or
something in their message rings true about your life.

Basia tells her story of the Sentinels: After an hour's hike into a state park in New Jersey, I touched two trees—randomly, I thought—as I walked between them so that I could stand on a rock in the middle of a tiny, bubbling stream. In that meditative moment, standing on the rock, I felt something jerk my attention backwards. I heard, "Welcome! We are the Sentinels. We are the gatekeepers of this stream. You have chosen to walk between us and, so, have entered our realm. You may find a magical delight in this place." So, I did. I return whenever I can to commune with them and with the Spirit of the place.

Category 3–Personal Messages: Stories from Graduates

Marise Hamm, Sag Harbor, New York, feng shui consultant: I always assumed that trees and plants were living Beings and that they can communicate if we allow it. But something totally spontaneous happened which made me realize that connecting with the energy of trees is a real experience.

I moved out of Manhattan many years ago. On a return trip to my old neighborhood to visit a friend, I walked past the small park adjacent to the Museum of Natural History. Suddenly, I felt as if a certain tree's heart jumped out to greet my heart. "It's good to see you again!" is what I felt this gnarly, old tree saying to me. I was stunned but did remember that tree from countless walks past it to the subway station. Upon reflecting, I realized that in my years away, I did a lot of global travel to wildernesses and eco-resorts to study my craft and expand my spirituality. When I walked past the tree again, I was able to spontaneously receive Nature's intelligence in a whole new way.

Carol Ohmart-Behan, Endicott, New York, author and guide of spiritual journeys to Glastonbury, England: While leading many trips, I have come to know the Oak standing above The Chalice Well and befriended a colleague in the tour business. My colleague and I had a sudden and uncharacteristic difficulty in our friendship. I sought inner peace by connecting with the Oak. Because I knew that it was familiar with both my colleague and me, I felt it reassure me. It said, "Despite his sudden actions, his caring for you is sincere. Let the situation heal. Have faith in who he is at heart." I thanked the Oak for its good advice.

A short walk away from the Oak, there is a Copper Beech on the vast grounds of the Glastonbury Abbey with whom I have a strong affinity. Every year, when I arrive with my tour group, I can sense this Beech reaching out to me as soon as I get off the bus. When the Beech comes into sight, my heart leaps with delight. Tears of joy are usually streaming down my face. At last, I embrace the massive gray trunk and am enveloped by this presence. "Welcome home," it tells me.

Liz Wassell, New Paltz, New York, copy editor, Reiki practitioner, animal and Nature communicator: I suggest that you bring a notebook and pens or pencils when you connect with the energy of trees and plants. You should record the messages you get immediately. If you are receiving words, write them. If you are inspired to draw, then draw. Just record the experience as you are getting it, without engaging the rest of your mind in that busy-talk that can squash the communication.

The Teacher Tree, Stone Ridge, New York, gave this message to Liz Wassell, who wrote it down this way:

Go sit down now. You want to know my message. It is simple. I won't use many words.

Usually, we work in pictures, but a few words from me will do.

It is a blessing to be seen. Stop that, and the world stops.

You must not feel that you fail by stopping here and there, but know that your awareness is our delight!

Madeline "Groweesha" Thompson, Boonton, New Jersey, business owner and professional counselor: In my backyard, a wonderful old tree's roots grow like spider legs around a big rock. I have named her "Grandmother Spider" and we have become friends. She calls out to me, telling me to sit beneath her and pray with her. Often, I ask her for guidance.

As my four boys were getting older, it was time for me to go back to work. I brought my concerns to her about not being there full-time for my boys.

Grandmother Spider told me "Make a small family garden at my base. Put plants here that will grow again, year after year. Put them here, around my roots and under my branches–one plant for each boy. I will watch over them for you. Your boys will grow connected to the Mother and they will be safe. You need not worry about the boys; go out to do your important work in the world."

> *FOUR CATEGORIES OF MESSAGES*
> *1) What's going on inside and out.*
> *2) Instructions.*
> *3) Personal messages for you.*
> *4) Insights or wisdom from Spirit; timeless information or advice.*

Basia concludes: The four categories of messages–what's going on, instructions, personal messages, and wisdom–are designed to be helpful to you. Of course, there can be overlap among them.

WHAT KIND OF MESSAGES CAN YOU GET?

Basia hopes to inspire: Please consider another level of intelligence—one that goes beyond the physical. Dr. Jim and I believe that people are more than physical bodies. There is a Life Force that animates people's physical, Nature-based bodies. People often call that Soul. Dr. Jim and I don't know whether each animal or plant has its own Soul, but we do believe that there is a Force of Spirit and Design Intelligence within all Life.

Perhaps you have had some unusual or extraordinary experience happen to you. Perhaps you knew something and you couldn't explain how. Haven't you received a phone call or bumped into someone soon after thinking about them? I don't believe that these experiences are accidents. All such experiences are exceptions to Western culture's decree that only rational, linear thought exists. These exceptions show that modern cultural systems of understanding and interpreting how the world works are inadequate. Such experiences show that there is an underlying force of consciousness that you can tap into at will and can communicate with.

How does this communication occur with the consciousness in Nature? Well, easily and everyday for all of us. For example, we don't only listen to what other people say, we are all masters at interpreting nonverbal signals from other people. So, it is easy to transfer those abilities into receiving and interpreting the nonverbal yet authentic, palpable living communications and messages from trees, plants, and all of Nature's Beings.

Such intelligence, or **Nature Consciousness**, can communicate in various ways that we can train ourselves to receive and

understand. Here are seven modes of communication that are
ways Nature Consciousness can communicate with people.
There may be more ways. Your particular use of these avenues
of communication may be quite unique. I feel that by
considering new or different methods of communication, you
can expand your repertoire.

**METHODS OF COMMUNICATION THROUGH WHICH PEOPLE CAN
RECEIVE MESSAGES FROM NATURE'S CONSCIOUSNESS**

• **Physical Sense** *experiences, such as tingling, warmth,
visualizations, sounds, words, fragrances, etc.*

• **Emotional Feelings**, *such as a deep compassion, love, humor, or
joyousness; also feelings of fear or thoughts that warn of dangers.*

• **Direct Perception or Intuitive Perception**, *such as inner hearing,
inner seeing, inner knowing, etc.*

• **Impressions** *during spiritual practices or personal experiences of
meditation, prayer, chanting, dreams, epiphany, etc.*

• **Impulses** *during artistry and/or creativity, such as inspiration
during painting, sculpting, singing, dancing, writing, etc., as well
as the* **beauty of the result** *of that creativity.*

• **Messages** *arriving in meaningfully synchronous ways, such as
overheard conversations, songs on the radio, signs on trucks,
books opening, sudden appearances of animals or insects, etc.*

• **Various energy vibrations or light stimuli** *that can be translated
into the spoken or written word, or other expressions.*

PREPARING YOURSELF TO COMMUNICATE

Basia talks about receiving messages: You are probably a tree
or plant lover and may already be a good listener. Perhaps you
already *secretly* talk to your house plants or the trees in your
yard. It may be a little monologue you deliver to them about how
beautiful they are or how you want them to grow. Maybe you
even issue the occasional threat to them: "Grow, or else!"
Regardless of how you talk with them, Dr. Jim and I are pleased
that you consider them to be living Beings.

We hope that the scientific information about plant cognition as well as specific Green Beings' messages we have shared with you so far awaken in you the realization that *it is possible for you* to have two-way communication with trees, plants, and Nature.

Give yourself credit for your existing communication skills. Only a small percentage of person-to-person communication comes through words. Vocal inflection, body stance, timing: These are all aspects of communication among people. You are already good at interpreting the full meaning of someone's message. If you are the parent of a baby or young child, you have an advantage: They are verbal but without language skills. So, you have had to develop sensitivities to other kinds of input in order to understand their needs. Perhaps you keep animals: dogs, cats, horses, or even birds. You know how smart they can be. They don't talk, but they may as well. You understand what they are "saying" to you.

Basia affirms and commits to you: The challenge with communicating with trees, plants, and Nature is that the message comes through avenues other than verbal language or sounds. So, you have to have an open mind, be patient, and be a good receiver. Dr. Jim and I are here to give you encouragement and specific methods to communicate with trees, plants, and all of Nature.

The Golden Conifer's lesson is that trees and plants *are very much alive, intelligent,* and happy to make conscious contact with humans.

I asked the Design Intelligence of the Plant Kingdom if It wanted to add anything.

THE DESIGN INTELLIGENCE OF THE PLANT KINGDOM ADDS:

In preparing people to receive our messages, remind them that we also have a sense of humor.

Chapter 4: Be a Better Receiver of Trees' and Plants' Communications

INTRODUCING THE CHAPTER: BEING A BETTER RECEIVER

In preparing to become a better receiver of trees' and plants' **communications**, *some scientific background about human bio-electromagnetic energy fields and plant bio-electromagnetic energy fields is presented.* More information is in the Appendix.

Later in this chapter, two personal exercises for tuning up one's sensory sensitivity and emotional engagement are explained and offered.

At the end of this chapter, the "Stepping Inside the Plant's World" guided visualization experience is offered in detail.

BIOENERGY FIELD SCIENCE

THE HEART IS ANOTHER BRAIN AND PRODUCES A BIOFIELD

Ms. Basia Alexander, The Chief Listener begins: Why are we talking about the human heart in a book about trees and plants? Because Tree Whispering® is a personal and deeply moving experience with **Nature**. When Tree Whispering with a tree or plant you don't just think about it, you interact with it. For that reason, you need both an open mind and a caring heart.

> *Far more than a simple pump, as was once believed, the heart is now recognized by scientists as a highly complex system with its own functional "brain." Research in the new discipline of neurocardiology shows that the heart is a sensory organ and a sophisticated center for receiving and processing information. The nervous system within the heart (or "heartbrain") enables it to learn, remember, and make functional decisions independent of the brain's cerebral cortex. Moreover, numerous experiments have demonstrated that the signals the heart continuously sends to the brain influence the function of higher brain centers involved in perception, cognition, and emotional processing.[1]*
>
> ROLLIN MCCRATY, PHD,
> RAYMOND TREVOR BRADLEY, AND DANA TOMASINO
> INSTITUTE OF HEARTMATH

Basia says: The heart is a brain in its own right since it has as much neural tissue as the grey-matter in our heads to which we give so much credit. HeartMath Institute research indicates that the heart has its own **intelligence**, makes choices, and then informs the brain through the rhythm of its beats so that the nervous system can act on its choices. When Tree Whispering, the heart's intelligence operates with the nonlinear logic of heart-based wisdom, not the linear logic of reason. Please see the Appendix for more information about the HeartMath Institute and more scientific detail.

The heartbrain and the "brain-in-the-head" or headbrain have a two-way conversation. When you experience compassion or appreciation, your heart beats evenly so your nervous system gets in sync with the cardiovascular system: You feel good. HeartMath research calls this a state of "coherence" between the heartbrain and headbrain.[2] We need this inner, coherent state of harmony when communicating with trees, plants, and Nature.

In addition to the extensive neural communication network linking the heart with the brain and body, the heart also communicates information to the brain and throughout the body via electromagnetic field interactions. The heart generates the body's most powerful and most extensive rhythmic electromagnetic field. Compared to the electromagnetic field produced by the brain, the electrical component of the heart's field is about 60 times greater in amplitude, and permeates every cell in the body. The magnetic component is approximately 5,000 times stronger than the brain's magnetic field and can be detected several feet away from the body with sensitive magnetometers.[2, 3, 4]

© Basia Alexander

Basia describes her first illustration: We talk about the human heart being involved in Tree Whispering because the heart generates a **biofield**.

My first illustration shows what HeartMath Institute research has proven: The heart produces a bio-electromagnetic energy field that is detectable several feet away from the body.

An initial set of research performed by the HeartMath Institute in 1998 made promising inroads into scientific proof of a mechanism that could explain how energy medicine such as the laying on of hands might work. They suggest that an exchange of electromagnetic energy produced by the heart occurs when people touch or are in close proximity. They showed that one person's electrocardiogram (ECG) signal registered in another person's electroencephalogram (EEG) when there was hand-holding and also when the two people simply sat within 18 inches of each other.[5]

© Basia Alexander

Basia describes her second illustration: What about when people are together or are touching each other? In both Western and Eastern healing arts, most people feel that an energy exchange occurs through the touch or close proximity of a caring healer or practitioner. To me, it makes sense that when you sit or stand near someone, both of your heart fields overlap. I think this is how we know whether we like a person—or not.

<u>TRY THIS: OVERLAPPING HEART FIELDS</u>

Read through the steps. Decide whether you feel comfortable doing this exercise. If you do not feel comfortable or have any concern whatsoever, do not do it.

Step 1: Sit down in a comfortable and private place where you won't be interrupted for 5 to 10 minutes. This exercise is best done with eyes closed, if you are comfortable closing your eyes.

Step 2: You have a donut-shaped bioenergy field around you. Pause for a moment and allow yourself to experience your own bioenergy field radiating from your heart.

Step 3: Imagine that you can see your bioenergy field's shape or feel its warmth.

Step 4: If you are within about five feet of another person, please take a moment to realize that both of your bioenergy fields are overlapping and interacting.

Step 5: Think about what having a bioenergy field generated by your heart means to you.

Step 6: Think about the fact that bioenergy fields can overlap. What does that mean to you?

Step 7: Jot down a few notes about it in your *Tree Whispering: Trust the Path* notebook.

THE BIOFIELDS OF TREES AND PLANTS

Basia recounts: In order to explain to you that trees and plants have biofields, I have done research into a patchwork of emerging scientific arenas: quantum physics, **energy medicine**, bio-electromagnetics along with the EM spectrum, living systems with the concept of emergence, fractal math, plant neurobiology, and network patterning–just to name a few. You can also consult the reading list at *www.TreeWhispering.com* if you want to look further into research on bioenergy fields.

In Chapter 3, Dr. Jim and I already talked about plants being intelligent. In doing so, we quoted a variety of recent scientific research. But, in order to have a personal experience, *to get to know* a tree or plant as you can through the guided visualization experience in this chapter, it helps to understand that they, like all people, produce bioenergy fields. True, they don't have hearts, but trees and plants do produce electromagnetic fields.

Cells are an example of an intelligent living system. According to Dr. Bruce Lipton, a noted cellular biologist, the membrane of every cell–whether the cell is floating on its own or in a complex living organism–has to be "smart" enough to "know" what substances to keep out and what to let in.**6**

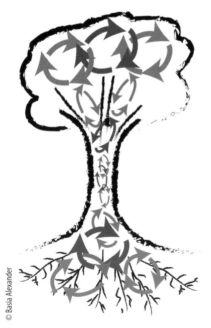

Organisms such as trees and plants are living systems. They are vastly large and complex groups of cells. They have countless interacting parts and functions operating in **dynamic balance** or stability as shown in my third illustration, on this page.

What it means to be a living system was redefined during the last two decades of the twentieth century. New criteria defining living systems were elegantly described by Fritjof Capra, in his book *The Web of Life*.**7** A brief description is in the Appendix.

© Basia Alexander

Basia explains "biofield": The term "biofield" is short for bio-electromagnetic field. Dr. Jim and I like to say "bioenergy" or "bioenergy field."

Dr. Beverly Rubik is the author of 60 scholarly papers and two books about exploring biofield science and energy medicine. Her main area of focus is research on the subtle energetics of living systems. In her 2002 paper, "The BioField Hypothesis: Its Biophysical Basis and Role in Medicine," she explains that the term "biofield" was coined and accepted in 1994 during a panel meeting at the U.S. National Institutes of Health.[8]

> *On the one hand, conventional biology provides a reductionistic, analytical view of life based on molecules and on structure/function relationships. On the other hand, the emerging biophysical view is a dynamic one that addresses the whole organism, its field interactions, and its integral flows of information in relation to the environment.*
>
> *Metaphorically speaking, conventional biology depicts life as a crystal, and the emerging biophysical view depicts life as a flame. Although both views are correct within a certain context, each alone is limited. Together they are complementary and provide a more complete view of life that offers greater potential for understanding health and healing.*
>
> *That is to say, the living state is richer and more complex than it is possible to express in a single model or metaphor.[9]*
>
> BEVERLY RUBIK, PHD

Basia continues: Dr. Rubik defines the biofield with scientific terms and with analogies. She uses one of our favorite: the orchestra. What I believe Dr. Rubik is saying in her paper is that every living Being produces a bioenergy field because it is composed of electrically charged parts that aggregate in levels of complexity—like molecules joining to make cells, cells joining to make tissues, and tissues joining to form systems. She indicates that each individual component contributes to the total biofield in the same way that each instrument in an orchestra contributes to the whole symphony. She describes the possibility that this whole organism becomes self-regulating. Without a distinct conductor, the whole orchestra plays the music in sync and in tune.

Furthermore, being in sync and in tune as a whole biofield, each component keeps its particular part going. Dr. Rubik suggests that the biofield acts as a regulator of this dynamically balanced state within an organism. She thinks that it serves to coordinate life functions in people.

Dr. Jim suggests: I believe that the Spirit of the plant runs the orchestrated parts and functions. Furthermore, parts and functions of trees and plants are tied into a system of drivers governed by the intelligence of the plant and contained within the bioenergy field.

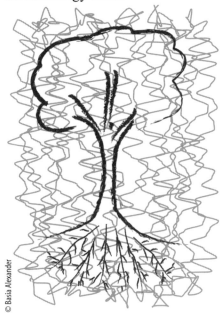

© Basia Alexander

Basia explains her fourth illustration, shown left: If people could see the bioenergy field of a tree with their eyes, it might look something like my illustration. The biofield is not only within the visible structure of the tree or plant, but it also extends beyond the confines of the form, above the canopy and below the roots. You might imagine that it is like a spherical or multidimensional vibrating envelop that is permeable and may overlap with others.

KIRLIAN PHOTOGRAPHY

When electrical voltage is sent through a photographic plate, the bioelectrical field around the object can be seen as in the photo to the right. This is often called Kirlian photography.[10]

An object like a leaf is placed on a photographic plate.[11]

© Marcin Filipiak www.NoweEnergie.org

Basia reminds: But, people do not have to see the biofield in order to sense its reality and power.

BIOENERGY FIELDS INTERACTING BETWEEN ORGANISMS

The earth's magnetic field is a very similar torus (or pattern) to what hearts and magnets emit. Like that of the heart, the earth's magnetic field is a constantly shifting, living field. All living organisms possess just such a torus, including plants.... The heart is not only concerned with its interior world. Its electromagnetic field allows it to touch the dynamic, electromagnetic fields created by other living organisms and to exchange energy....

The heart not only transmits field pulses of electromagnetic energy, it also receives them, like a radio in a car. And, like a radio, it is able to decode the information embedded within the electromagnetic fields it senses. It is, in fact, an organ of perception.[12]

STEPHEN HARROD BUHNER

Basia concludes: When your cell phone drops a call, you say that the signal was lost; carrier waves from the cell tower didn't get to your handset. You can't see those energy waves but you know they are there. Whether you realize it or not, your heart is radiating, too. And, the most amazing thing about the heart is that it also receives the broadcasts from other organisms. You may not be able to take a phone call inside your heart but you do pick up signals from other living Beings.[2, 13]

© Basia Alexander

Basia describes her fifth illustration, on this page: To me, it only makes sense that the bioenergy fields of all living systems overlap. The illustration suggests, in a very rough way, what that might look like. Scientists would call this overlapping of waves an "interference pattern" or "wave propagation." Overlapping of two or more similar waves–like drops in a pond–carries new information and causes a third pattern to arise.[14]

© Oleg Alexandrov, Mathworks MATLAB

Dr. Jim and I say that communication with Nature's innate intelligence happens in two ways: when physical bioenergy fields interact and when the nonphysical information carried in those fields is exchanged and interpreted.

EXERCISES FOR BECOMING A BETTER RECEIVER

Basia says: The trees and plants do have messages for all of us. It is up to each of us to become better receivers.

HOW TO RECEIVE NONVERBAL INFORMATION

- *Through heightened awareness of and the use of any or all of the five physical senses*
- *Through uninhibited emotional engagement*
- *Using "intuitive" perception: a blend of left-brain logic, right-brain creativity, and heart-oriented inspiration*
  - *Inner seeing...the "mind's eye"*
  - *Inner hearing...the "little voice inside"*
  - *Inner knowing...comprehending the heart's truth. Doesn't necessarily need logic or linear thinking.*
- *By asking "yes" and "no" questions while the nervous and electrical systems are in a bioenergy overlap with another living system...and allowing the answer to come.*

Basia explains: Plants and trees don't have mouths for talking. But we know that they have a lot to say to us. It is up to us to expand our skills of receptivity to get their nonverbal communications. As we just learned, trees and plants are doing something like broadcasting resonance waves or signals because they are alive. Insects have evolved acute abilities to receive information from plants. Think of the honey bee seeing a flower in ultraviolet.[15] Flowers look different to them than to us.[16]

We didn't evolve insect eyes or antenna, but we did evolve with sensitive nervous and electrical systems. Sadly, modern city lifestyles and the Western mindset of intellectual orientation have robbed us of the acutely developed sensitivities that our ancestors must have had in order to live, survive, and thrive in their wild natural environment. But, we can redevelop those sensitivities and skills.

I invite you to join me in "tuning up" your senses and engaging your emotions in order to prepare for communicating with trees and plants. You can think of turning the dial to tune to a car radio station. This metaphor may be lost on people born after about 1995 for whom everything has been digital.[17] I will try another: It's like tuning violin strings to resonate on pitch.

THE FIRST EXERCISE: INVITE SENSORY SENSITIVITY

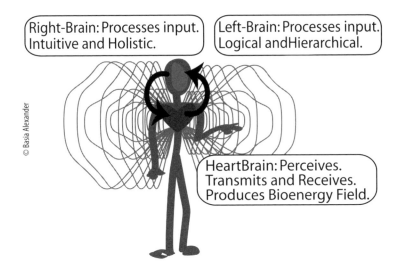

Basia invites participation: In the first short exercise, you will create an **intentional** cycle of neural coherence to pave the way for enhancing your sensory sensitivity. What does this mean?

HeartMath Institute scientists have found that when people's attention is focused on heart-based feelings, their heartbrain's electrical rhythm and their headbrain's electrical waves move in sync. They call that entrainment or "neural coherence" because the heart's nervous system and the rest of the body's nervous system are operating in sync or vibrating in harmony.*2*

In order to make this an *intentional* cycle–in other words, to take advantage of neural coherence to purposefully open the door to enhance sensory acuity–I suggest adding some proven techniques to the exercise. The exercise borrows from ancient and modern healing systems. You will do slow breathing, imagining or visualizing, touching or tapping on your body, focusing your attention on a topic and using deliberate concentration.

Basia continues: When neural coherence is combined with healing techniques, the outcome can be a shift in the **bodymind's** operation so that capabilities or skills may be improved. Understand it this way: Focusing your attention and bringing conscious awareness to what you want while involving the bodymind's automatic or "autonomic" functions creates an underlying condition so that the physical body may change.

HEALING SYSTEMS	*HEALING TECHNIQUES USED*
Acu-pressure/puncture	*Slow Breathing*
BodyTalk System™	*Imagining/Visualizing*
EFT Method®	*Touching*
EMDR®	*Tapping*
Healing Touch	*Focused Attention*
HeartMath®	*Intentional Concentration*
Matrix Energetics®	*Deliberate Focus*
Polarity Therapy	
Reiki	
Touch for Health	

GET READY FOR SENSORY ENHANCEMENT

Basia talks about the senses: Select a sense or combination of senses that you would like to enhance.

Perhaps you would like clear inner seeing, or distinct inner hearing, or greater inner knowing. Or, maybe you want deeper discovery of the world through the sense of smell. Smelling is fundamental to survival since it is the oldest sense with its center located deep inside the brain. The senses in this illustration correspond to the ancient Chinese Five Element system.

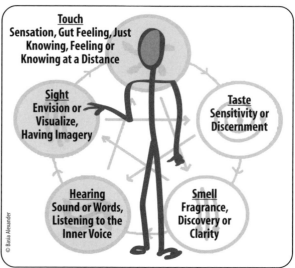

Pick whatever physical or subtle sense you would like to expand.

Your focus of attention will be on that sense during the exercise.

Basia describes tapping as the next step: Tapping your fingertips lightly on the heart and on the head will serve to involve the physical body.

I consider the heart to be central in the chest, under the sternum; not on the left side where you may hold for the pledge of allegiance. You will be using the fingertips of BOTH hands to tap lightly and rhythmically on the center of your chest.

Tapping as you breathe for two to three breaths engages the heartbrain. It's like telling the heart "now is the time to apply your leadership qualities throughout the body."

Then, tapping on the skull while you breathe for two to three breaths gives impulses to the headbrain. It's like telling your brain "wake up, pay attention." To tap on the skull, use both

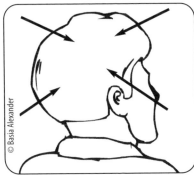

hands again, one on each side of your head.

It doesn't matter whether you tap in the front of the head, top, back, or sides. What matters is that you tap on *both* sides of the head at the same time in order to use the left-brain/right-brain or bilateral attributes of the headbrain.

Please understand that doing this tapping will not by itself cause the sense you have chosen to become sharper or clearer. What you are doing by tapping, breathing, and focusing is laying the foundation for your bodymind to go through an expansion. You are opening the door to more sensory input at the time and in the way that is most comfortable and gentle for you.

TRY THIS: INVITE SENSORY SENSITIVITY

Read through the steps. Decide whether you feel comfortable doing this exercise. If you do not feel comfortable or have any concern whatsoever, do not do it.

For your convenience, this exercise is reproduced in your Tree Whispering: Trust the Path *notebook. Audios are also available at* www.TreeWhispering.com.

Step 1: Sit down in a comfortable and private place where you won't be interrupted for 5 to 10 minutes. This exercise is best done with eyes closed.

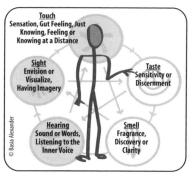

Step 2: Choose a sense that you want to enhance. (See illustration to the left.)

Step 3: Focus on the sense and take a comfortable, deep breath.

Step 4: Gently tap with the fingertips of **both hands** on the heart (center of the chest) and take 3 to 4 comfortable breaths. **Focus on the sense.**

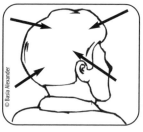

Step 5: Gently tap with the fingertips of **both hands**, each on opposite areas of the head. You may tap anywhere: front, top, back, or sides. Do this while taking three to four comfortable breaths. Focus on the sense.

Step 6: Repeat Steps 4 and 5 about five times while focusing your attention on the sense.

Step 7: Open your eyes, breathe gently, and sit quietly for a moment.

Step 8: Jot down any comments or reflections in your *Tree Whispering: Trust the Path* notebook.

Note 1: You may repeat this exercise regularly, as long as you feel good and enjoy it.

Note 2: You may or may not feel an immediate enhancement of the chosen sense. The exercise is designed to provide the foundation to the bodymind in which the enhancement can occur. The exercise will not by itself cause the sense to be enhanced.

Basia comments: People who attend our introductions enjoy this exercise. Dr. Jim and I always notice how much more relaxed people look after doing the tapping, breathing, and focusing.

THE SECOND EXERCISE: ENHANCE EMOTIONAL ENGAGEMENT

Basia asks for continued participation: Next, create a breathing rotation to bring about emotional engagement. What does it mean? It means preparing yourself to clearly and vividly feel a healthy range of emotions. Why do this exercise? To become better at offering and receiving nonverbal communications.

Emotions carry information. Parents know clearly what a crying child is communicating: fear, pain, hunger, sorrow, or even attempts to manipulate. When communicating with trees and plants, information may come in the form of emotions.

Think about giving. You don't want to just give, give, give because that empties your personal reserves. Or, constant receiving is often considered selfish and feels unfulfilling. Giving and receiving are best done in balance. It's the same way with your breathing. You can't just breathe in and keep breathing in. You have to also breathe out. It works as a pair, a rhythm, a rotation.

The breath–in and out, ebb and flow–is a good example of giving and receiving. The in and out breathing rotation parallels the cycle of giving and receiving. The best way to open the door to giving and receiving in your body is to breathe. Plenty of scientific and medical literature extols the benefits of slow, gentle, deep breathing for the body, mind, and Spirit.

We know that we breathe through either our nose or our mouth. But, in this exercise, I ask that you imagine that you can breathe in through your heart area and imagine that you can breathe out through your belly button or solar plexis area. The solar plexis is another power center of the body.

I ask that you imagine a breeze or a stream of air looping through your body: The breeze comes in through the heart and goes out through the solar plexis.

In this exercise, add the elements of imagination, directionality, and focused intention to the breathing rotation. I ask you to imagine that you are breathing in an emotion through your heart and breathing out another emotion through your belly button or solar plexis area. You can always select which particular emotions you want to invite.

Whenever you consciously engage emotions, be sure to welcome emotions that are healthy, good, and positive. For this exercise, the emotions I'll suggest are these: breathing in *courage*, breathing out *gratitude*. HeartMath research suggests that this gentle, slow breathing cycle with caring or loving emotions may increase feelings of well-being or even lower blood pressure for some people.*2 and 3*

Basia explains the emotional engagement exercise: I suggest that you first practice a few cycles of imagining that you are breathing in through the heart and out through the solar plexus. Get used to this somewhat different physical feeling. As you do this, you may hold your heart area with one hand and hold your upper belly area with the other. Better yet, you may rotate your arms, bringing your hands toward your heart as you breathe in and moving your hands away from your belly as you breathe out. It's like making circles, pulling the stream of air toward your heart and then moving the air away from your belly.

TRY THIS: Enhance Emotional Engagement

Read through the steps. Decide whether you feel comfortable doing this exercise. If you do not feel comfortable or have any concern whatsoever, do not do it.

If possible, use your nose for breathing IN and your mouth for breathing OUT during this exercise. This exercise is best done with eyes closed.

You may engage this pair of emotions: **courage** *and* **gratitude.**

For your convenience, this exercise is reproduced in your Tree Whispering: Trust the Path *notebook. Audios are also available at* www.TreeWhispering.com.

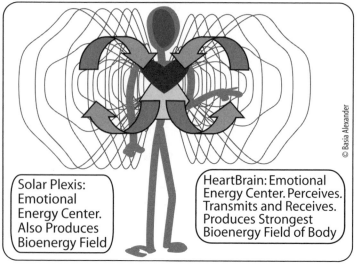

Solar Plexis: Emotional Energy Center. Also Produces Bioenergy Field

HeartBrain: Emotional Energy Center. Perceives. Transmits and Receives. Produces Strongest Bioenergy Field of Body

© Basia Alexander

Step 1: Sit down in a pleasant and private place where you won't be interrupted for about 10 minutes.

Step 2: Focus your attention on the feeling or idea of courage.

❑ *Remember a time when you felt courageous or brave. Or, recall a scene from a movie in which you felt that a character was doing a courageous act.*

❑ *Take a moment to feel courageous or brave.*

Step 3: Focus your attention on the feeling or idea of gratitude.

❑ *If there is something you are grateful for, think of that and allow the experience of gratitude to come to you.*

❑ *Take a moment to feel grateful.*

Step 4: Imagine a stream of air looping in through your heart area and out through your belly area.

Step 5: While imagining the looping stream of air, gently and easily breathe in and out for 4 or 5 breaths.

Step 6: Imagine that on that stream of air, you are breathing in **courage** through your heart and breathing out **gratitude** through your belly area.

❑ *Allow yourself to gently experience courage flowing in, then gratitude flowing out.*

❑ *Or allow yourself to simply relax and enjoy breathing in and out slowly and gently. Do this for about a minute.*

❑ *If you are comfortable and enjoy this experience, you may continue for several more minutes.*

Step 7: When you feel ready, open your eyes and sit quietly for a moment.

Step 8: Jot down any comments or reflections in your *Tree Whispering: Trust the Path* notebook.

Note: You may return to this exercise any time with any pair of positive and life-affirming emotions that you prefer.

Basia congratulates: Good work! Thanks for joining in!

GUIDED VISUALIZATION EXPERIENCE WITH A PLANT

Basia describes the experience: Now that you have enhanced your senses and engaged your emotions, you are ready to "step inside" the plant's world.

Find a house plant or go outside to be with a tree while you do this exercise. You will need to be able to look closely at the plant or tree, and to touch it on the outside and feel it on the inside. Have an attitude of open-mindedness, curiosity, fun, and patience with yourself. The more allowing you are, the easier it will be. Communication is about receiving information and impressions, not about dominating the conversation or controlling. For example, if you were with a person who spoke in a stumbling way while telling a story, you would probably be considerate and gentle as you quietly listened. Be considerate and gentle with yourself and with the plant, too, as you quietly listen.

Basia suggests what might happen: What can you expect? The exercise takes you on a journey. It's an adventure. You might feel like you are actually moving inside of the plant. You may feel physical sensations like tingling or warmth. You might envision some image in the back of your head or out in front of you. A word or phrase might come into your mind. Some information or insight might occur to you. Happiness, sadness, or any feeling in between might arise within you. A sense of movement, beating, or pulse might come from the plant. Personal memories could also pop up. Thoughts about how the plant operates or how it feels might present themselves to you. The plant may have a clear message for you.

If you think that you are making up those thoughts—you are not. You will know that the thoughts are not yours because *you cannot make any certain thought happen*. Thoughts simply arrive.

Be trusting and allowing. Maybe you are a bit analytical–not getting into the fun of it. Just remember that this is an adventure. You are stepping into a new world and can bring back a great story to tell.

Are you skeptical? That's okay. There is a place for doubt and questioning as long as you don't let it close your heart to possibilities.

Or, perhaps you hope for so much but you think that nothing is happening! Your expectations put too much stress on you. Just breathe and relax. Start from the top. You can always try it again.

If you are actually uncomfortable, then stop. Don't do anything that is uncomfortable, unpleasant, or painful for you.

A short version of the guided visualization exercise is written here. Please read it through first and then take yourself through the steps one at a time.

TRY THIS: "Step Inside the Plant's World" Guided Visualization Experience

Read through all the steps.

Decide whether you feel comfortable doing this exercise. If you do not feel comfortable or have any concern whatsoever, do not do it.

It's an adventure! You are stepping into a new world and can come back with feelings of inspiration and a great story to tell!

For your convenience, this exercise is reproduced in your Tree Whispering: Trust the Path *notebook. Audios are also available at* www.TreeWhispering.com.

Preparation: Make sure you are in a pleasant and private place where you won't be interrupted for 10 to 15 minutes.

There will be times during the exercise that you may want to close your eyes. If you are comfortable doing that, please do so.

Make sure you have a plant near you that you can touch. You may also do this exercise standing or sitting outside privately with a tree.

Have your *Tree Whispering: Trust the Path* notebook handy to write down some notes about your experiences. You're not likely to remember later. It's best to make notations immediately.

Questions will be asked during the experience. Those questions are meant to be answered privately, inside yourself. You may jot notes for answers.

Please recall this illustration showing the overlap of a person's heart biofield with the biofield of a tree.

© Basia Alexander

Step 1: Begin.

❏ *Get comfortable.*

❏ *Breathe deeply and gently.*

❏ *Turn your attention to the plant. Never mind its name. Forget anything that you may know about it.*

Step 2: Since it is a living Being, we always ask permission to make contact.

❏ *In your Heart, say to the plant, "**I would like to spend some time with you and get to know you. Is that okay?**"*

❏ *You will probably feel a sense of calm. That means you have permission from the plant. It is unlikely, but if you feel disquiet, you may move to another plant, or stop.*

Step 3: Focus your sight on the stem, trunk, leaves, or flowers. Notice even the tiniest details.

❑ *See a multitude of shapes.*
❑ *Notice how the leaves are arranged on the stem.*
❑ *Notice how they are oriented in space.*
❑ *Distinguish shades of color.*
❑ *See how light or shadow plays around them.*

Step 4: Now, very gently, touch the plant.

❑ *Feel the textures.*
❑ *Notice the shapes.*
❑ *Perceive curves and turns.*
❑ *Sense the temperature.*

Step 5: Use a soft focus and perceive the whole plant.

❑ *Be aware of any scent.*   ❑ *Capture a sparkle around the edges.*
❑ *Be aware of any sound.*   ❑ *Welcome a tingle.*
❑ *Distinguish any quality of goodness.* ❑ *Intuit an impression.*

Step 6: Ask yourself: "**How do I feel?**" and "**What do I know?**" Quietly answer those questions for yourself.

Step 7: Focus for a moment on your own body. You may close your eyes.

❑ *Around your body, notice your heart's bioenergy field.*
❑ *Notice the bioenergy field's current size and shape.*
❑ *Imagine that your heart's biofield is like the sun—shimmering with light or radiating with energy.*
❑ *Imagine that the field is increasing in size and intensity.*

Step 8: Notice or imagine the bioenergy field of the plant. You may close your eyes to do so.

❑ *Imagine that the plant's bioenergy field is also expanding. Feel it.*
❑ *Your heart's field now overlaps with the energy field of the plant.*
❑ *In that overlapping area, information is shared and exchanged, sensory experience is stronger, and emotional perception is heightened.*

Step 9: With your eyes closed, for about a minute, allow yourself in the overlap to be aware of any new information, experience, or perception.

Step 10: Step into the plant's or tree's world.

❑ *Engage your imagination and close your eyes.*
❑ *Feel as if you shrink or expand to fit the plant's or tree's size.*
❑ *Imagine that there is a door on the stem or trunk. You open it. A bright, white light shines on you, and you step inside the stem or trunk.*
❑ *There are thousands of cells all around you. Imagine reaching out with your hands and touching some cell walls.*

❑ *As you look around, you see little streams going up and down all around you. These are circulating plant fluids.*

❑ *Imagine that a tiny boat comes along. Hop in and begin moving upwards with the flow of the fluids. Continue moving upward.*

Step 11: Ride into a leaf.

❑ *You are approaching a leaf. The boat docks. You float forward, following a vein into the leaf.*

❑ *Sense light coming through the layers of cells.*

❑ *There is lots of activity: A bubble of carbon dioxide is captured. A bubble of oxygen is released.*

❑ *Sense the heat from foods being produced.*

❑ *You are inside the leaf.*

Step 12: Ask yourself: "**What do I sense? What do I notice? What do I realize?**" and "**What is important to the plant?**" Quietly answer those questions for yourself.

Step 13: Ride the sugar molecule.

❑ *Inside the leaf, photosynthesis is producing sugar molecules, which are food for the plant. Imagine that you shrink down so small you can jump on a sugar molecule.*

❑ *Ride it into the stream. Travel out of the leaf and down the stem or trunk.*

Step 14: Move inside the roots.

❑ *Imagine that the stream flows beneath the soil and you gently submerge into the root zone.*

❑ *Imagine that ahead the little stream is splitting and narrowing.*

❑ *Your molecule stops on the side of the little stream as food.*

❑ *You step off the sugar molecule. You are inside the roots.*

Step 15: Ask yourself: "**What do I sense? What do I notice? What do I realize?**" and "**What is important to the plant?**" Quietly answer those questions for yourself.

Step 16: Pick up the sponge.

❑ *Now, imagine that you have a sponge.*

❑ *Step to the stream and sop up some water and nutrients.*

❑ *Another little boat comes along. Bring the sponge with you and get in.*

❑ *Feel a surge forward as the root's pumping action pushes you upward.*

❑ *You emerge and are traveling in the brightness, up the stem or trunk again.*

❑ *Find your way to a growing point and deposit the water and nutrient-soaked sponge in a growing cell.*

Step 17: Fill the whole plant or tree.

❏ *Now, feel yourself expand and grow until you fill the whole plant or tree.*

❏ *Sense all the activity—thousands of things happening and interacting. All these interactions and feedback loops are its Growth Energy.*

❏ *Almost like a pulse or heartbeat, sense the strength of that Growth Energy.*

Step 18: Come from the plant's or tree's point of view

❏ *Feel the movement of the Growth Energy around the plant or tree.*

❏ *Perceive where it is surging.*

❏ *Find out where it might be weak.*

Step 19: Ask yourself: "**What do I sense? What do I notice? What do I realize?**" and "**What is important to the plant?**"
Quietly answer those questions for yourself.

Step 20: Enjoy a few moments being with the tree or plant.

Step 21: You have made a new friend. Ask these questions to the plant or tree and immediately write down any feelings or impressions you receive. You may hear it, see it, or feel it.

❏ *Ask: "**Do you have an instruction for me?**"*

❏ *Ask: "**Do you have a message for me?**"*

❏ *Ask: "**Do you have a lesson for me?**"*

Step 22: Exchange gifts with the plant or tree.

❏ *Breathe in any gift(s) from the plant.*

❏ *Breathe out and say "**Thank You**" to the plant for letting you into its world.*

Step 23: Leave the plant or tree.

❏ *If you are still touching the plant, slowly release it.*

❏ *Look at the plant and recognize a friend and a partner.*

❏ *Return to your own body and to your own point of view.*

❏ *When you are ready, wiggle your toes.*

❏ *Take in a long, deep breath and stretch your back and shoulders.*

Step 24: Immediately, make notes in your *Tree Whispering: Trust the Path* notebook in answer to these questions:

❏ *What was important to the plant?*

❏ *What were any messages, instructions or lessons from the plant?*

❏ *What gift did you receive?*

Step 25: Share your experience with other people.

❏ *Think of a friend or family member with whom you may share your personal experience. Imagine sharing this experience with them.*

❏ *If you feel safe, actually tell them about it. If you don't feel safe or think it would be a bad idea, don't do it.*

Step 26: Congratulate yourself for completing the exercise.

PEOPLE SHARE INSIGHTS AND EXPERIENCES

During public introductions and workshops, Ms. Alexander leads people through guided visualization exercises while they are holding small house plants brought into the meeting room specifically for the exercise or while they are touching trees outside of the meeting room.

People report all kinds of perceptions from the interactive exercise. From over 300 public introductions to Tree Whispering that Dr. Conroy and Ms. Alexander gave between 2005 and 2011, people have shared insights and experiences like these:

"Gee, the plant just told me that it breathes from under its leaves."

"I got a message! I realized that I usually think of plants as things, like sticks. The message was, 'You have to start paying attention to us. We're real!' I think I can try to do this now!"

"The plant was yelling to me, 'I can taste the plastic. Get me out of this plastic pot.'"

"This little plant has a very delicate feeling; it's very shy and likes the warmth of my hands."

"I got the message 'Trust! We are all connected–plants and plants, people and people, plants and people.'"

"The breathing in and out that we did is exactly what the plants do; they breathe the air and sunshine. I felt how light and bright it is in the leaves. I felt how dark and damp it is by the roots. I understand now how the plant brings the energy of the sun down into the soil then sends it back up to renew itself. I heard it say 'I can't wait to be planted outside to grow, grow, grow!'"

"I got a 'thank you' from this little plant for something I did for some trees on my property last summer. I'm stunned and grateful."

"I'm still learning, but when you asked us to join our energies to the plant's energy, I felt a really strong surge or connection! I think that was the overlap of biofields you talk about."

"One thing that struck me was that when you look at these plants, they look solid and static. Then, you go inside of them like we just did and you find out how much activity is going on inside of them—how elaborate their systems are. Until you actually step inside, you don't know. It gave me a much greater appreciation."

"I felt a pull, like I was as rooted as the tree. It felt good."

"This tree said that it needed water in the root system and that the electrical wires above are affecting its branches, too. It said that it liked absorbing and receiving our attention during this exercise."

"The little tree over there is focused on growing and sustaining itself. I asked it whether it was getting everything it needed. It told me, 'Well, yes, but we need love, too.'"

"In the exercise, when you directed us to go into the leaves, I went up into the top of this tree and I had the feeling that it was showing me how connected it is to the sky. For me, it was like being at the top of a tall building. And, in the roots, it was showing me how connected it is to Earth. I felt that it was looking down into its Mother. When I asked it for a message, I heard, 'We have all the answers that you need.' It was a beautiful experience for me."

"I'm an arborist, and I thought that I already appreciated trees. I have a much greater sense of appreciation now."

"I picked out this particular plant for the exercise because I recognize it as one of the oldest known species. It's a Cycad. If you touch it with your fingers, it's really tough and sharp. I had a powerful vibrating feeling in my hands with it."

"This tree was very loud saying that it needed its space. It said that it was feeling smothered in its roots. The tree also said that it needs people to honor its space when they walk by. I am personally reminded to be respectful of others."

"This Cedar told me that we all–plants and people–need to work in harmony with one another. The tree wants us to know that we all share a symbiotic relationship. It said, 'Tell people to wake up. We need to honor each other. I will work until there is nothing left of me so that I can help you.' I know that this tree wants to be of service. It only wants to give. It wants to work with us."

"On the same tree, I felt that the roots are starting to rot a bit and that it needs stability."

"I feel that both the plant and I feel empowered and energized. I had the idea that it was pushed to the back of the shelf or that something was on top of it and it didn't like that."

"I had to move around during the exercise, because there was so much dynamism around the trees. I would have danced, if I could have."

"I felt a lot of constriction in the roots of this fall cabbage plant. And,

it's no wonder. It's already September, so it is pot-bound. Even though it will not become a cabbage head, it said to me that it could be fulfilled in its short life by being planted outside even at this late date. It would be fulfilled by feeling the sun and growing for a while."

"I felt a huge spiral at the base of the plant. The gift it gave me was beautiful: I felt that fresh, green fragrance that you smell outside in spring."

"I've had plants in my home all the time, but now I feel more interactive. My relationship has expanded to a partnership."

"I'm going to check out the trees at the nursery for good vibes so that I can buy a companion tree for my prize Japanese Maple."

"We had the chance to connect with four trees tonight. Each one is different. They are individuals!"

"It surprised me that this little Marigold had as much Life Force in it–to my feelings–as the big tree over there did."

"Thanks to this exercise, I know why the Lemon tree in my greenhouse is so happy! We love it so much. My grandmother brought a slip over from Europe and planted it 80 years ago. We respect this tree. When we want a lemon, we approach it, ask it if we may have a lemon, then leave. When we come back twenty minutes later, there is usually a lemon on the ground for us. I will continue to do the 'stepping inside of its world' exercise and thank it for its bounty."

"Doing this exercise was challenging for me. I don't know if I felt anything. I'm afraid that my expectations are too high. Somehow, I think that I have to have the same experiences as other people, so I'll miss the truth of whatever I might be able to experience myself."

"For a moment, in the exercise, I was becoming the tree and forgetting about myself. It's like, for that moment, everything in the world wasn't about me! It was a revelation and great relief."

ADVICE FOR BECOMING A BETTER RECEIVER

Basia encourages: Yes, every person's experience is different. Many of our students want to give you advice and tell you some stories about how they have developed their perceptive abilities to become better receivers of communications from trees, plants, and other Beings of Nature. In the next chapter, read what they have to say, but honor your own experiences first of all!

Chapter 5: Advice for Expanding Perceptions and Developing Intuitive Skills

How to Be a Better Receiver of Communications from Nature's Beings

Ms. Basia Alexander, The Chief Listener, begins: Welcome to all **Nature** lovers. I have a question for you. Do you take your walks in the woods or through a park to be with a human companion? to be with your own thoughts? or to be with Nature? All these purposes are commendable. As a Nature lover, if you go on your walk to have an experience with the Beings of Nature, do you want to be even more aware of their vibrant lives and their wisdom? I believe you do. Please let me assure you that you don't have to be born with some special gift. Anyone and everyone can be conversant with Nature's Beings.

When you tried the *Stepping Inside Their World* exercise in the previous chapter, did you feel that your experience was fully successful? partially successful? or were you discouraged about even attempting to go through it? That exercise is designed to assist you with expanding your perceptions and to further develop your intuitive skills.

This chapter is unusual in that it is filled with insights from people who have taken Dr. Jim's and my various workshops and classes. Each of the students tells a story or talks about how to be a better receiver of **communications** from Nature's Beings. The people who speak in this chapter have all done the *Stepping Inside Their World* exercise. Most have had an enjoyable–even revelatory–experience. They report that their awareness of plants' and trees' beauty has intensified. They tell us that, overall, they have become more receptive, with sensitivities effortlessly amplified and appreciation expanded. But, let them tell you themselves. As they speak, their nuggets of advice are seen as *italic* type.

Detailed information about graduates quoted in this chapter can be found in the Citations.

Please read this chapter as if you were listening to a series of people introduce themselves at a networking meeting. Or–better yet–imagine that you are sitting in a large circle at a Native American council where each member gets to speak only when he or she receives the talking stick that is passed around the circle of people.

I will give the talking stick to Lori, and she will introduce herself, say where she is from, and say her occupation. She will tell her story or offer her advice to you. Then, she will pass the talking stick to Leo, and so, it will go on around the circle.

Lori Myrick, East Windsor, Connecticut, energy therapy practitioner: The more I practice awareness, the more my own feelings open up. I often ask questions of the trees, and their answers come in song. I suggest that people *go out, sit under a tree, breathe and relax, listen and feel.* Most importantly, *be patient.* Let thoughts come and go; *be quiet.* Try *touching* the tree–touching helps in the beginning. Pick one tree and *visit* it often. It will feel more familiar each time. Simply *have fun*!

I sometimes feel a profound energy moving from beneath the earth, up to the sky, and through the tree, giving me the sense of connection to a greater Spirit. I know that we are all connected and need to honor and respect what Nature has to teach us. I know that it needs us, too.

It doesn't matter if I spend five minutes or a few hours, I often begin to laugh and feel playful. The joy I feel is powerful, whether I know exactly what the trees are saying or not. But, I think that they must say funny things to me.

Once, leaving a grocery store, I looked at a White Birch and suddenly cracked up laughing. My niece, who was with me, asked me what happened. I explained to her that the tree just told me something funny but I didn't know what it was. There is a lightness of heart for me that I love.

Leo G. Kelly, West Haven, Connecticut, arborist and master gardener: I don't know about whether my perceptions or awareness has expanded, but I do know that the workshop changed my life. I had an arborist's degree but never worked in the field. After retiring, I took the workshop and immediately felt empowered. Dr. Jim and Basia suggested to all the students that we *get involved with the trees* in our towns. I did! I brushed up my arborist's license, then I got the town to create a tree commission. It wasn't long before I got myself appointed as the tree commissioner.

As the tree commissioner, one of my main goals is to have people look at and touch the trees. I think people can feel close to trees while they are doing a tree inventory in the town. Volunteers gather data about the size of our town's tree canopy and its health. Knowing such data can help the town save money. But, the most important thing is that the people get out, touch the trees, and get to know them.

So, I am positioning myself for the time when I can bring up what I learned even more. I want to save trees through this awareness that Dr. Jim and Basia teach. It's my mission. People who used to joke with me are starting to change their thought processes. People are calling me for my advice because the word is out that I will give sincere advice about the care of their trees. They know that one of my tools is feeling the energy of the trees. They have seen me take out my little "cheat sheet" from class.

People are looking for other options. They love the trees and they are starting to accept my actions more. They enjoy hearing that this tree energy is–in fact–there. The majority have told me that they believe it.

Mike Nadeau, Sherman, Connecticut, holistic land care practitioner: I will look at trees that are in my care on clients' properties. I walk up to them, but before I touch them, I state my **intention** quietly. I say, "I'd like to come inside. I'd like to listen to you." Then, I'll touch the tree with fingertips of both hands, then with my forehead or with my nose. Sometimes I feel electric impulses. I feel the pulses coming to me and then going back into the tree. Sometimes I don't ask questions; I just sense what I am feeling.

I remember what Dr. Jim said: "Forget everything. *Forget the botany and the physiology that you know.* Forget all the learning and just listen to the tree." To me, forgetting equates to humility. Humility is tough for me because I am proud of what I know. But, as Dr. Jim tells me to do, I come from the tree's point of view to hear from the tree, not me. I do my best to live my life from the spiritual aspect. I want to learn the deeper, more spiritual version of this work from Dr. Jim and Basia.

Alana DuBois, Robbinsville, New Jersey, massage therapist, Reiki and energy-medicine instructor: As a sensitive healer with people, I develop my perceptions with trees and plants in the simplest way I can. I try to *feel like I am talking on the phone*: a connection gets made and I hear the tree or plant speak.

Robin Rose Bennett, Hewitt, New Jersey, author, visionary herbalist, and renowned teacher: I've had the very good fortune to visit some of the world's oldest trees. Tane Mahuta is one of relatively few remaining kauri trees in New Zealand and is thought to be over 2,000 years old. I stood near the "Lord of the Forest," as it is called, and felt linked to ancient wisdom and deep peace. To stand in the presence of such an old Being is beyond words, but I'll do my best to describe the sensation. It was a heart-to-heart, or perhaps it's better to say, Spirit-to-Spirit link. It was a merging, as if we were sharing our innermost Spirits with one another.

The Fortingall Yew in Scotland is thought to be the oldest tree in Europe, at least 3,000 years old and it was in full flower when I was there! The tree is huge, nearly a block long, because its branches ascend and then go back down into the earth to become roots for new tree growth. Sadly, there is a barrier around the tree because it had been vandalized. It's hard on the trees when they can't be touched. If you are with a tree that can't be touched, *take time to share your love with it energetically.*

Making that connection is a process of *emptying yourself,* of allowing the personality to fall away. *Sharing breath* is the best starting point. Be as *quiet in the mind* as possible and *open your heart. Let go of the desire* for anything in particular to happen. You can imagine a figure-8 or an infinity sign of breath and energy going back and forth between you and the tree.

Dorrie Rosen, RLA, New York, New York, Plant Information Specialist, New York Botanical Garden: Trees and plants may not be "talking" to me, but they are expressing their essence of Being. I *appreciate* that trees are living, breathing organisms that are crucial to and enhance our world. In my work, I have learned how to help plants thrive. After the workshop, my relationship with all plants has deepened and I have found that trees can teach me, too. Now, a stronger connection with trees will truly allow the healing process to take place.

Chuck Winship, East Springwater, New York, Maple syrup farmer: As a Maple syrup producer, my sense of taste has to be a sharp perception. I've taken many technical and aesthetic college courses, too. I know a lot about trees. But more than that, I like to *go to a quiet place to just be in their presence.* They are a lot more than just a pile of wood. I sense their needs. I feel what they like and don't like. Between the visual and the touch, I can determine their general state of health.

Since taking the workshop, I have a better awareness, too. Before I go out to run a new lane of pipes, I think about how it will affect the trees. Then, in the back of my mind, I believe that I communicate–I tell them–what I am going to do. I think that puts us into better harmony. I have a sense of how to appreciate their position and what they are trying to accomplish.

I suppose you could say that we have a partnership; we are equals. It's like we say to each other, "I'll take care of you and you feed me." I think that I have a knack for nurturing plants that comes from a *deep appreciation* of them.

Cheryl Smith, PhD, University of New Hampshire, Extension Professor and Plant Health Specialist (plant pathologist): I think a lot of people are hesitant to believe they can receive messages from trees. They wonder, "Am I putting my own thoughts in?" I would advise you to *slow down, allow your own Spirit and your energy some freedom. Believe in your energy and the path it may take.* It will only give you more energy and freedom.

Try participating in practices that expand awareness of body, such as Native American rituals or yoga. It might feel a little strange at first, but awkwardness is okay. Just get through it. *Don't be embarrassed. Welcome the gift of the moment. Share that part of yourself with other people. See a bigger picture.*

The best part for me is giving voice to a Being who can't speak for itself. We exist in a world with many other Beings, we all need to work together, to listen to each other, all of us.

Sylvia D'Andrea, New Jersey, graphic designer and homeowner: My advice for people about being better receivers of communications from trees and plants is simple: *Keep an open mind. Have no distractions. Be present in the moment;*

don't have an MP3 player stuck in your ear or don't be talking on your cell phone. *Your "now" presence is required to be with Nature. Be mindful of where your focus is directed.*

David Slade, Guilford, Connecticut, arborist and business owner: I've climbed and worked with trees most of my life, but that first evening in the workshop was an amazing expansion of my conscious awareness of trees. We touched Maples first. I was present to my Maple's subtle twisting movements with a deeper understanding of what was happening for the tree than ever before. *I realized that I had always been looking at trees, but not seeing them.* All of a sudden, the Maple's movement became visible to me. It was very peaceful and beautiful. I felt an intimate connection with the tree.

I'd always seen trees move in different ways based on the forces involved or from the way that I would move them as an arborist. But, this was very different. I feel that the way the tree was moving with a light breeze was something that was always there but I'd never seen before. I was seeing how the wind and the movement in the canopy translated into the trunk. It was surprising that there was a sort of a twisting motion. I'd never perceived that before, but it made perfect sense. It was Divine in its beauty and its trueness to its growing conditions.

You are asking me whether my perceptive abilities have expanded since then. [Pause] Yes!! Yes!! [He chuckles.] They must have! There has been a lot of change in my life lately, so I think that I have more ability to ground myself to the earth and feel these changes and movements inside of myself; whereas before, I might not have been in touch with how I was feeling.

Maria Petrova, New York, New York, professional graphic designer and energy medicine healer: While growing up in Bulgaria, my family helped on my grandfather's farm on the weekends. Being out in Nature was always about the task–such as berry picking or potato cultivating–which was often done with a sense of duty and exhaustion. My family had anxiety about whether the crops would grow correctly in order to feed us. I never had a joyful relationship with Nature, so I never thought of myself as very perceptive with the Beings of Nature.

In my practice of energy healing, I am sensitive to the energy field of the human body. I also know that Nature is alive, but until the Tree Whispering workshop, I never knew how conscious trees and plants are or how sensitive they are to our presence. I had a breakthrough with my receptivity; I felt a oneness with the earth to a degree I had never felt before.

I apply the same perceptive approaches to making energy connections with trees that I do with my clients. I love to lean against my favorite tree–a Gingko in the West Village area of New York City. I go into the connection with the Gingko or with any other Being without high expectations–*without any expectations* at all. I respect the other by asking permission. I encounter the Being knowing–within it–there is a unique consciousness and **Life Force**.

While energetically connected, my physical sensations have to feel good to me. I must be comfortable so that my partner– whether a tree or a human client–can feel comfortable, too. Then, I like to be *playful*! I start to wonder and ask myself questions such as, "what would happen if...." I let the ideas come, and they usually make sense and feel good. Then, I *apply trial and error*. The more I work with the ideas, the more I know whether they are right or wrong by whether the energy-feeling I have is stronger or weaker. At the end of our time together, I feel so energized and light.

Madeline "Groweesha" Thompson, Boonton, New Jersey, business owner and professional counselor: How do I develop my perceptions of trees and plants? I open myself up to knowing trees in a way that I don't already know them. I open myself up to possibilities of greater awareness because I know that I am not limited. Then, I make sure that I feel anchored or grounded. I give in to my curiosity since I have a deep desire to know.

My personal affinity is with trees. Sometimes I think I am a tree. By going to the Tree Whispering workshop, I experienced trees with the other students as a group. By *being together*, I felt a stronger current. It was freeing for me to see that each person was finding her or his own way of connecting and no way was wrong. One might have shoes on, another had shoes off, one might be touching the tree while another was touching the ground, one might be hugging a tree, while another stood away and left some space. At the same time, being in the group gave me a sense of belonging and way to feel the sensations of connection more strongly because all the attention from all the students was focused more strongly.

Developing perceptive abilities or intuition is like developing a natural resource: It exists but lays dormant until it is found. We use our ability to connect with people and things all the time, we're just not consciously aware of that. We sense things and feel things all the time, we often take that for granted. When we make efforts to *connect consciously* with the Life Energy of a tree or plant, we find our dormant intuitive skill.

I talk with a lot of people. I think that some people get confused or discouraged about expanding their intuition and perceptive abilities. Often people's beliefs about what is possible create a barrier that doesn't let in anything they can't see, touch, or feel. So, people lose the connections to their imaginations and childlike wonder. Think of how a child uses his or her imagination. It's *okay to be like a child* again–one who talks with plants, trees, butterflies, or bugs. That innocence is in everyone; it is going to connect to the purity of the Nature Being. Everyone can enjoy this connection through imagination.

Your intuitive sense *uses imagination;* it uses *specific metaphors* that you—and only you—are going to understand; it uses the concepts to which you already personally relate. In this way, the intuitive sense aims you toward the information you will need. At the same time, it's important for you to *have good, personal boundaries.* You need to know what to allow into your body, mind, and Spirit. You need to keep out what is not good and what does not serve you. *Be discerning.*

So, there is both interconnectedness and individuality. Both our bodies and the trees are wise guides. They teach us how to grow through our challenges and be fully connected to the Source.

Ann St. Germaine, Eatontown, New Jersey, educator, writer and photographer: I have a growing awareness that there is a lot more to the trees than just what I see with my eyes. When I am with trees, I start to *feel these little thoughts* about them. I am drawn to the silhouettes, lines, angles, and colors that trees display before me. As I take my daily walk through the park nearby, I ask myself, *"What lessons can I learn from the trees today?"* And, a beautiful lesson always comes. I hear their messages in the wind.

Aged trees that stand tall, erect, and branching widely over tender saplings, teach me the importance of elders who guard, protect, and shade their young from harm. Broken limbs that fall onto the branches of neighboring trees can remain there for years, just as people support their weakened and failing loved ones for as long as it is necessary. I learn patience from passing the same familiar trees year after year. Just as children pass through phases of growth and maturity, the trees bud every year with new life, flower with enthusiasm, transform from deep greens to golden autumn shades of russet, and endure winter's cold and darkness with noble tranquility. There are life lessons and wisdom all around, encircling me as I walk.

Just *looking at the differences* between trees standing side by side illustrates how every living Being is an individual with its own characteristics. The varied texture of bark is like my unique fingerprint, none exactly like another. As my stance differs from that of others, so too does the stature of trees show marked contrasts. An oak can stand upright like a soldier on guard duty, the white birch can bend low like an elderly grandmother, and the evergreen can bow with a sweep of its boughs like a princess swinging her gown. I find that the more I *pay attention* to trees, the more I appreciate them and respect them for what they add to my life, and I am grateful for their presence.

Dwight Brooks, Katonah, New York, arborist, horticulturalist, organic land care teacher: Since the class, I don't think that my perceptive abilities have changed, but I think that my willingness to have them change has increased. That's a big step for me. When I think about myself before the class, I was taking trees for granted. I saw them as objects, even though I knew they were living Beings. One of the big gifts is that I don't cut trees down anymore. My thinking is "who am I to decide to cut down this living tree?"

I am concerned about putting human traits onto plants; it's called anthropomorphizing them. I think putting human traits onto plants is my brain putting a label on the experience. Being human, our language and thinking is limited to what we know. So to describe something we don't know, we have to use language about what we do know or understand. It's paradoxical. And yet, we have to use the tools we have and do the best we can to describe our impressions from trees. Is it perfect? No. But, it works, and as long as we *have the awareness that our experience may be more than our words can actually describe, that's the key thing.*

Leslie Ashman, Reston, Virginia, project manager and Gaia Consciousness advocate: My sensitivities and perception of plants' energies has expanded since the Tree Whispering workshop. Sometimes I feel an energy field or a vortex rising up from trees. Perceiving that field is a little like seeing the heat waves shimmering and coming off of an asphalt road.

But I don't use my visual perception as much as I use my hearing. Trees talk to me in the rustling of their leaves and movement of their branches, sending messages about themselves and the planet; and in receiving them, I, too, enter into partnership with them, as we are all connected in Gaia.

In connecting with trees' root systems, I understand much more fully how trees stand for us, marking time, generating oxygen while observing our actions, and holding energy in their roots and in the soil from which they are fed. They are helping us, and we are partners. For their gifts, they respond profoundly to simple acknowledgment and a little care.

Judy Perry, Maine, artist and landowner: I have been looking at and painting trees for 15 years. Since the Tree Whispering workshop, I am much more able to see and appreciate individual trees. I do not see them as a group anymore. My reverence for trees has deepened as I now see and appreciate these lives all around me and on my property.

What do I do to perceive a tree? *I go up to a tree to meet it.* Within minutes, I can feel the tree's energy, usually in my heart or solar plexus and sometimes I feel a pulsing in my hands. Learning the Tree Whispering techniques gave me a good structure for this practice. *I greet the tree, ask permission, check-in with it, and then I have information.*

In my experience, every tree has a different energy, which is constantly changing just as I constantly change. I now see my relationship to the trees and my painting in a new way. I am not the same person that I was when I first painted the Pines or the Maples. And when I return to those images, I bring a different energy and the trees are different, too. It is the energy of the moment that comes through in my paintings. It makes a big difference in my paintings to feel connected to the trees, to stand next to them rather than look at them from a distance.

Painting, for me, has been a great way to develop a relationship or connection to Nature and to trees in particular. People often tell me their own stories of trees. Usually, they have important memories about their connection to Nature or a special tree. For so many of us, trees bring us back to our childhoods.

Carraig "Rocky" Romeo, Princeton, New Jersey, businessman and Druid: The guided visualizations in the workshop gave me a good foundation and the confidence to develop my perceptions. I have since expanded my perceptions by *being totally open and nonjudgmental.* Now I let myself be open enough to receive whatever is conveyed to me. I do this by not expecting myself to get a certain thing. I try to be really open.

And, I believe that the trees have messages generally. You know, you can't judge a book by its cover; you can't tell what is going on for a Being on the inside by what you see on the outside only. So I realized that I had to *be forgiving* about getting messages from the trees, especially if I sensed that there was a difference between its appearance and its inner health.

The best way to get better at perception is do it more often. I play the trumpet. Even though I know what notes to press, if I don't play often, my lip muscles aren't strong anymore. It's the same with this. *Practicing* builds up the perception.

Joan Lenart, North Haven, Connecticut, gardener and homeowner: I don't feel an energy connection through my body, but I know that I communicate with my trees and plants. I think of it more as talking to someone. Then, I pause and hear an answer. My advice is about going back to basics. Keep your eyes open. *Be aware* of what's happening as you go for a walk in the woods. Pay attention beyond the little circle just around you. When you are with a plant, *tell it what you appreciate about it.* Tell it how beautiful and beneficial it is. I tell my plants that I am trying to provide a good environment for them. For example, when tidying up my yard, I pose a question then explain what I would like to do. I sometimes modify my actions in order to be careful and considerate to the plants.

Sally Malanga, West Orange, New Jersey, business owner and tree protector: I don't think I can tell anyone about how to be a better receiver of trees' communications because I don't think that I'm a very good receiver. I just deeply appreciate their company and the scenery they endow. When someone says that the view is beautiful, it's all about the trees. Occasionally it's about the mountains, but the trees clothe the mountains.

I am passionate about saving trees. I feel that as living Beings they deserve to live and have a right to stay in their place and grow. Also, they provide housing and food for many other creatures.

Mary McNerney, Lincoln, Massachusetts, attorney: It seems to me that our biggest stumbling block is self-doubt. We have a great capability to negate our innate intuitive abilities. We have also tuned out [our senses] in order to manage in this fast-paced world. If we were open all the time, we would be overwhelmed. But, I think that when we *approach Nature with the intent to ask It about Itself,* feelings and words will come forth. And, if we do it enough, then the doubt is eliminated. Please, let me add that in a group setting, insights received are often confirmed or buttressed by what other people received.

All people are immersed in a sea of information that comes to us through the nonlinear mind. And, as humans, we have the unique capability to draw upon that subtle knowledge and to add to it our logic, our book-learning, and our intentions.

We become empowered to *go—with conviction—into action.* We get information, then our very next question has to be, "What do I do with this information?" Moving into action is the joining of intuition with logic, knowledge, and even insights from others for the betterment of all. In taking action steps, we use all of our abilities; we can make any combination of conventional and nonlinear, heart-oriented steps.

Jeff Dawson, Napa, California, horticulturalist: As a professional in tree and plant care, developing the heartspace is the most important aspect for me. The heart is a perceptive tool. As I learned from Dr. Jim and Basia, the HeartMath Institute has done leading-edge research into the ways the human heart works as a receiver of Nature's communications.

I use meditation for developing my conscious connection into the heartspace. Then, I connect with trees, the soil, and the landscape. Using the mind only, I wouldn't have the ability to reach deep into Nature. The best information does not come through thoughts and mind; it comes through feelings. The greatest percentage of my work is done through feelings and then I interpret those into thoughts that my mind can use.

My advice is to *recognize the consciousness in Nature.* The concept of Nature Spirits has arisen from the recognition and the individualization of the consciousness in Nature. Recognition and connection to the consciousness of the trees and plants allow me to do my work. Then, the miracles happen.

Anonymous, painter: I love to paint trees. In order to paint, I have to *turn off the busy-body brain*, the dialogue in the head. I take the tree's point of view and *step out of the way.* Sometimes, I think I am more tree than human. I hope that I convey something through my art and that trees are the vehicle. The trees speak better than anyone.

Carol Ohmart-Behan, Endicott, New York, author and guide of spiritual journeys to Glastonbury, England: I have a fairly well-developed intuition, and the workshop gave me tools to build upon what I already had for myself. I took the processes to heart, practicing and enjoying the results. It helped me to explore an interactive dialog with trees and plants. The guided visualization helped me *form a structure* for such a dialog.

I employ my listening skills all the time when I am out in wild Nature. I practice gratitude for living Beings and all of Nature. I would advise people first to *see the possibility of it,* then to *have confidence* while being *open-minded and open-hearted. Follow up with gratitude.* People need to know that this communication can be done simply, easily, and that it enhances daily living.

Cathy, New Jersey, acupuncturist and herbalist: Native Americans call trees "Grandmother" or "Grandfather." I was taught herbalism by a Cherokee medicine priest. Now I routinely communicate with the herbs I offer to clients to be sure that the herbs resonate with the client's body.

My Cherokee medicine priest teacher taught me to deeply honor and respect trees. He explained that he would ask a tree if there was anything he could do for it, and then he would give it a sacred offering. The tree would engage, or not. Not all trees respond to all people. If his invitation was accepted, then he explained that communication would begin.

I was learning how to meditate while I happened to be sitting next to an old, gnarled Cottonwood. The tree took me inside of it. I went into the center of the trunk. I was on a journey. My consciousness went up and down simultaneously. I heard the vibrations of the leaves. It was like hearing a million tiny violins all playing together, yet I felt that I could hear each one individually. Then, I went into the roots and heard this amazing gong sound. After that, I was inspired to continue meditating. Basia and Dr. Jim gave me a similar opportunity to journey by teaching me to step inside the plant's world in their way.

The most important piece of advice is to *trust*. Trust that it is our gift and our birthright as humans to be able to communicate with trees and plants. The ability is within all of us.

Gerry Verrillo, Guilford, Connecticut, arborist: When I went to clients' properties, I would go to give the answers, as if I had them all. Now I go to *receive answers* from the trees. Rather than thinking I will pry information from these majestic and mysterious tree Beings, I simply *stand or kneel, holding the tree, and wait* for the information to be given as a gift.

Before taking the workshop, I wouldn't be thinking about trees as Beings, but, now, there is no going back. I crossed a threshold. Now, working at my profession feels so much wider and gentler; I have more patience. Dr. Jim's and Basia's heart-centered approach simplified my relationships with trees, with the earth, and with other Beings.

As I started to use the Healing Whispers™, I'll confess that I struggled with questions about my ego. I wondered where the balance was between feeling selfless in my healing efforts with trees and wondering whether I was giving myself too much credit. The advice that guided me through was "stay heart-centered."

I realized that doing Tree Whispering is all about connectedness. It's about sharing the mystery of life. It isn't about the ego. It isn't about waving my hands around and healing something. It isn't about justifying my years of formal education or my investment in my profession. Doing Tree Whispering is about receptivity—allowing something to come and allowing something good to be given back. When I kneel with a tree, I'm receiving more than I am giving. I am there as a fellow citizen of Earth, an equal Being, sharing a unique moment of communication with another Being. As long as I keep that innocence and purity, then trying to take too much credit won't be an issue for me.

I use a little secret to *expand my trust in my heart*. It is based on the tapping exercises Basia showed us in the workshop. [The tapping exercises are detailed in Chapter 4.] I tap on the center of my chest while I *give* my heart energy-center *permission to be* and permission to have its own say. Then, I tap between my eyebrows and tell my heart's energy to be uppermost while it links with my headbrain. I do this tapping back and forth from heartbrain to headbrain many times, asking them to work in conjunction. It helps me settle down. I am grateful.

Ilona Anne Hress, L.C.S.W., C.M.T., Rev., Madison, New Jersey, spiritual healer: My advice is to *develop conscious conversation* with the Kingdoms of Nature. We humans are made up of the Kingdoms of Nature. If we allow ourselves to activate the connection between the Plant Kingdom and our bodies, it is much easier to communicate and have a harmonious understanding about how good life can be.

It goes like this. If we are willing to honor the fact that the Plant Kingdom lives within our bodies, because we survive by eating plants; if we are willing to recognize that we are made up of the elements–the Mineral Kingdom–that form the earth that we stand on; if we are willing to recognize that we are mammals–we are of the Animal Kingdom; then we know that we *inherently have the ability to connect* with these kingdoms of Nature. This has to be a conscious recognition that we are comprised of these Kingdoms; we are not beyond them.

When we ask for a conscious connection with the Plant Kingdom within us, it will automatically reach out on its own terms and connect with the plant or tree we are sitting with. Then the conversation will appear in the unique language of the specific Kingdom. Allow that "Plant Kingdom" part of your

Being to connect with a plant; energetically, you have that inherently within you without having to think about it. Just observe the process. Don't try to figure it out. It just takes patience and attention. You're learning a language that is already being spoken inside of you.

Another thing is to learn about how the Classical Four Elements cooperate on your property. These are realities as well as metaphors to give you insight. For example, know how Fire energy from the sun works with the Air energy of the wind. Learn about how Water energy is involved in the way Earth energy is oriented so that your property drains properly. Find out if the Air energy can help standing water to evaporate away from a particular tree. Is the whole property congested and muddy or is it vibrationally clear so that Fire, Earth, Air, and Water can take in the higher frequencies to support the Life Force energies of the plants–and of you! All must be in balance.

Alexandra Soteriou, Passaic County, New Jersey, energy healer and business owner: When I was communing with a tree during the workshop, I believe that I briefly saw the tree's chakras. It was a circular rainbow of vibrating luminous color; it was so beautiful! They were very different from human chakras that I see in my healing work with people. Thanks to Dr. Jim's and Basia's teachings, I have been able to clearly feel trees' emotionality. As a citizen of our green environment, I aspire to be a comforter and healer for these gentle giants.

Jude Villa, Martha's Vineyard, Massachusetts, professional landscaper and designer: Just by touching them, I feel the energy flow in trees. I don't know if this ability has increased, but I think I have more of an awareness of it. I have always worked with the land, but now I am noticing the trees as individuals. Touching the trees fills me up; it's a real spiritual connection. When I really connect, I can focus and breathe. It fills me up mind, body, and Spirit. It's like a meditation, but I don't like to just sit. So, connecting gets me away from all the stuff in life and helps me be clear.

Melanie Buzek, Cornville, Arizona, physical therapist, energy-medicine practitioner and educator: I practice and teach a healing system that is fundamentally based upon communicating with the innate **intelligence** within the human body. We honor that intelligence by always asking for permission prior to performing a session. Developing one's perception skills and being a good receiver of communication in complementary energy healing means *acknowledging that all life has consciousness*. As part of my teaching duties, I show others how to hone their intuitive skills to receive "yes" and "no" answers when working with a client to determine which body areas are priorities to focus on.

Georgette Hritz, Scotch Plains, New Jersey, postal worker and homeowner: Even though I grew up in the country and always loved trees, I am more aware now of sharing energies with trees. I think the most important thing about feeling a tree's bioenergy field is to *believe in the impressions you are getting*. I advise people, "Trust that you didn't make it up." I figure, if you get impressions from people when you meet them, why not get an impression from a tree when you meet it?

Believing in my impressions was validated for me during the second workshop I took. It was held in a hotel. The lobby had an island of tropical plants inside the atrium. I remember that I had the impression that the tall palms didn't want us to touch them because–all day long–people brush by them without thinking or saying "excuse me." Later, another student and I compared notes and discovered that we both had the same impression!

Anonymous, PhD psychologist: I have known the land I now live on for over 50 years. I feel like I am an ambassador for all the living things here, especially the trees. I do my best to treat all of the life forms with respect.

When I was in graduate school, there was little credence given to the mind-body connection. But, things have changed. Now we know that giving up focus on self and opening the heart in communication with other Beings results in benefits for a person that can be measured as reduced inflammation, less anxiety, and less distress.

So it works both ways: by helping trees I feel like they are helping me. For example, Wild Rose taught me to relax and release tension in myself as I pruned it. As long as I was open to it and calm, the wild rose allowed me to trim with my clippers. I worked a branch at a time, often standing in the middle of sprays of canes with big thorns. I didn't get cut. I learned to work with it. It enhanced my patience. I am very fortunate to be in a position where I can spend time with trees, feel their strength and beauty, and communicate with them. I also am very fortunate to have found teachers who understand my experiences with trees.

Linda S. Ludwig, USA, divine healer and business owner: The best way to tap into your intuitive gift is to imagine the possibilities. *Set the intention that your intuition will expand, let your imagination take over, and have fun with it.* Some like to use journaling to bring information through and others use meditation. By practicing journaling or meditation daily, you will more quickly connect to the Divine, all knowing, aspect of yourself.

I receive information from the level of Divine Source in client sessions that enables me to offer a high degree of service. This approach works when communicating with any conscious Being–human, animal, insect, plant, or tree. When you have a question, the best way to receive information is to wonder about the question and let it go. Trust that you will receive what you need. It is, however, important to ask from your heart field and not your ego.

Adaela McLaughlin, Haverhill, Massachusetts, professional gardener and landscaper, and long-time Tree Whispering student: My key memory from the Tree Whispering class at the Omega Institute is from the first evening. Basia led us in a guided visualization where we touched a plant and imagined feeling what it would be like to be inside of its leaves and roots.

Then, Dr. Jim led us outside to put our hands on the majestic White Pines at the entryway. I've been a gardener for many years, but I never before felt this. Suddenly, I could *feel my hands go inside of the tree,* like I've heard about psychic healers doing with people. My hands were inside of this tree, touching the Life Force of this tree. Now, *I visualize this happening and practice it* more and more. Tree Whispering has opened my eyes and my senses to what is possible to perceive. I really do love plants and I am grateful to be with them so much.

Danielle Rose, Northern New Jersey, author, newspaper columnist: Western culture dictates that if something doesn't conform, we shouldn't pay any attention to it. So, sometimes we prevent ourselves from hearing correctly; we hear what we want to hear, not what we need to hear. I used to resist, but now *I accept perceptions as they come.* I simply recognize the fear and get past it. Letting go of cultural training and my own resistance is important for self growth and for connecting with all the other Spirits out there–both human Beings and Nature Beings. When I let go, the limiting things I believe go away. I allow what I feel to come to me and accept that it is okay, that it is right.

Carol Hulley, Kings Park, New York, gardener: My Japanese Maple is a favorite. When it was young, it looked small and roundish so I gave it a name: R2-San. Acknowledging the tree with a name is a kind of recognition for it. So, I find that I pay more attention to it.

Sadly, a big branch from another tree fell and sheered the back off of it. I knew it would be stressed so I communicated with it to try and help it. As I was doing the techniques from the Tree Whispering workshop. I heard it say, "I want to grow, to grow tall, be bigger." I was shocked because the words "grow" or "tall" would not have been my thoughts about what the tree would want. I treasure this tree, and I am so happy that it is now several inches taller.

I have many big trees here, but I decided to give my full attention to just R2-San, my Japanese Maple. When I sit under it and commune with it, I am closely surrounded by its leaves. That way, it's my size so it feels like a size I can handle; it's like being able to start painting with little paintings rather than big ones. And, since Basia reminded me that trees operate in community, I figure that it shares my healing ministrations with the others. I feel good that I am taking really good care of it and that it is healthy.

Debbra Gill, New York, New York, holistic nutrition and wellness director for an international children's art project: As a child, if I was upset, I would go to my favorite tree and feel better. I also wrote poetry while sitting beneath its branches. I seemed to get phrases; ideas would just pop in. Now, I'm sure that the tree was helping me. If you have a *favorite tree from childhood*, I would recommend that you return to it. Perhaps you can reclaim some of your childhood wonder. It may be happy to see you again and give you fresh insights and inspiration just as my childhood tree did.

My family's symbol is the Red-Tailed Hawk. When my mother died in early February several years ago, I returned home to the tree the hawks used for nesting to seek some loving support. As I was hugging it and crying, a Red-Tailed Hawk landed in the tree and made chortling sounds to comfort me. After a while, I opened my eyes and there, near the ground, a feather was stuck upright in a crack in the bark of the tree. That was an amazing gift, a sign of new life from both the tree and the hawk.

Tchukki Andersen, Billerica, Massachusetts, arborist: I used to get clearer messages as a young person. Now it seems that if a message doesn't show up on a flaming billboard, then I think I'm not getting it. But I know that's not true. So, I have to be aware that if I'm not getting a "wow," then either the tree doesn't communicate that way, or I'm not open, or there is nothing to say. I have criticized myself for losing touch, but I have to realize that people change and, so, *forgive myself.*

I know that all I need is a little practice because I did just fine in perceiving tree communications when I was in the workshop. Since then, a fellow student and I get together periodically to practice the Tree Whispering techniques. A lot of the information we get from a tree is the same. It validates both of us to know that we are doing it right and getting very similar responses. When we get something different, we evaluate each other: Maybe one of us is not entirely tuned in or maybe we interpreted the tree's message differently. Overall, we find it mutually supportive to connect to the same tree simultaneously.

Liz Wassell, New Paltz, New York, copy editor, Reiki practitioner, animal and Nature communicator: Being perceptive? Well, we have to get over our constant second guessing of what we believe our first impression was all about. In the classes I've taken, I realized that exercises and techniques are there–partially–to *distract* our overly busy egos from telling us that we were crazy. So, I say to you, "*Trust* your first impression always."

I suggest that you *bring a notebook and pens or pencils* when you connect with the energy of trees and plants. You should *record the messages you get immediately.* If you are receiving words, write them. If you are inspired to draw, then draw.

Just record the experience as you are getting it without engaging the rest of your mind in that busy-talk that can squash the communication. That inner chatter can suppress the belief that this communication is really happening—and can stop the communication, too. We all have those thoughts, wondering if we are crazy or wondering what will others think of us. It's natural. But you want to distract yourself from the inner chatter and just receive the experience and record it while it is happening. Writing it down will distract the ego part of the mind from the wonderful flow of direct information that is happening.

Basia concludes: The talking stick has come fully around the circle now. I am deeply grateful to all of our graduates for the advice and stories they have shared. I hope that you are inspired.

Chapter 8, called "What You Can Do," will have specific suggestions, lessons, and exercises for touching, healing, and communicating with trees, plants, and all of Nature's Beings.

Chapter 6: How Trees and Plants Really Operate

A Tree or Plant Is Like an Orchestra

Dr. Jim Conroy, The Tree Whisperer,® explains: When trees and plants are healthy, their interior parts and systems are functioning together like an orchestra playing beautiful music.

ORCHESTRA	TREE OR PLANT
❏ *Has instruments—violins, oboes, trumpets, drums, etc.*	❏ *Has parts—roots, leaves, and stems containing "pipes" called xylem and phloem, which carry the water, nutrients, and sugars.*
❏ *Organized into sections —strings, horns, woodwinds, etc.*	❏ *Organized into systems—uptake of water and nutrients, photosynthesis, circulation, etc.*
❏ *Each tuned to the same key—B flat, C major, etc.*	❏ *Each tuned to the same goal—"get healthy" or "be strong."*
❏ *Each instrument interacting, playing to the beat, and in sync.*	❏ *Each of thousands of parts and multiple systems interacting and coordinating with all other parts and systems through chemical signals and energy impulses.*
❏ *A conductor coordinates the action.*	❏ *The whole tree—as a whole living system—coordinates its own action.*
❏ *A unique piece of music is the organizing principle of the interactions— Beethoven's* Fifth Symphony, *Tchaikovsky's* Swan Lake, *etc.*	❏ *Nature's blueprint—original, innate design intelligence as well as the DNA of the tree or plant—serves as the organizing principle for the interactions. Each species has its own blueprint or song.*

Dr. Jim points to tree stress: An orchestra that has lost the beat or is out-of-tune sounds discordant. Similarly, a tree whose parts and systems are not operating in self-reinforcing **feedback loops** or are not synchronized will be sick; its **internal functionality** will be **compromised**. What can cause a tree's operations to become compromised? We offer a list of 12 stress factors.

12 TREE AND PLANT STRESS FACTORS

1. Current conditions: too hot, too cold, too wet, too dry, poor lighting, flooding, standing water, drought, etc., or some combination of the above.

2. Multiple-season and multiple-year stress factors that are additive: summer drought followed by extremely cold winter and/or a cold and wet spring followed by extreme heat. Other factors include lightning hits, splitting, etc.

3. Human factors: root loss when transplanting, originally planted too deep, "volcano" mulch piles, piling soil at base, digging around base, construction, changes in land grade or topography, improper pruning, bands left on trunk, compacted soil, removing autumn leaves, hit by car, abuses like carving, "topping," road salt, etc.

4. Poor soil composition, fertility, or drainage.

5. Competition from unwanted plants, called "weeds."

6. Animal damage: chewing, digging, rubbing, eating, tunneling, urinating, climbing, etc.

7. Excess or inappropriate use of any product (such as harsh fertilizers or protective sprays) or invasive techniques (air spading, harsh pruning).

8. Pollution of soil, air, or water.

9. Global or local environmental or climate changes: rainfall amounts, season length, insect/disease survival, composition of local ecosystem (invasive or nonnative plants, diseases, or insects), average temperatures or higher nighttime temperatures, level of water table, etc.

10. Any combinations of the above nine factors.

11. Biotic stress factors: direct interactions with harmful insects and diseases, which usually come *after* other stress factors weaken the tree's or plant's inner functions.

12. And, the vicious cycle continues! Uncorrected inner functionality or physiological imbalance opens the door to more additive dysfunctions inside the tree or plant, then more insects and diseases are attracted, often leading to decline.

STRESS FACTORS COMPROMISE INTERNAL FUNCTIONALITY

Dr. Jim asks: Which comes first–insects and diseases or weakness in the tree's health? I say that it is weakness in the tree's inner health that generally calls forth insects and diseases. When a tree is sick, it sends out a signal that attracts them.

Many people think that diseases and insects cause weakness in trees and plants. They do, but it is additive. That is, the internal workings of the tree or plant were initially weak, which attracted the insects or diseases. Just like you and me, if we are run down, then we are more susceptible to catching a cold.

Many companies would have you believe that the "bad guys"– insects and diseases–attack otherwise healthy trees or plants so that their products would be the superheroes. Except for some very aggressive and sometimes nonlocal insects and diseases, it is the weakness in the tree's health that comes first.

What are the stress factors that weaken a tree's or plant's inmost health and deplete strength from its vitality? Please see Stress Factors on the facing page as I comment on a few points.

Extremes in the environment are the most common stress factors. Here, I mean too hot, too cold, too wet, too dry, or some combination. These are additive over seasons and years. Many people think that when rain finally comes after a hot and dry spell, the trees will absorb water and be fine. Healthy trees might do that. However, to a tree that is already stressed, heat and dryness cause additive damage.

Even with the best of **intentions**, people often do the wrong things. Trees and plants may be planted in poor soil or in the wrong place. People plant too deep or pile mulch too high over the roots–cutting off precious air and promoting rotting bacteria. When doing construction around trees, even some professionals will regrade the land, thereby burying the trees under too much soil. More than an inch or two is actually too much. In an attempt to give a transplanted tree bracing, bands and ties might be left on too long. These will choke a tree's flow of fluids. People forget–or never realize–that a tree is alive. Just like a person, a tree or plant needs to breathe, to drink water, and to live in a clean, bright place.

Stress factors can create a vicious, downward cycle.

ABCDE Internal Functionality Flow Diagrams

Box 1–Healthy Tree or Plant

Normal flow of functions
in self-regulating
feedback loops.

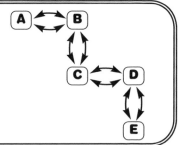

Box 2–First Stress

First stress compromises
internal functions, but the
tree or plant compensates.

The tree looks okay but is
thinning and has smaller
leaves or is browning and
has few needles.

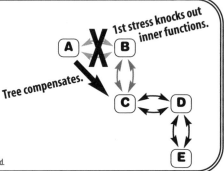

Box 3–Second Stress

Second stress compromises
more internal functions, but
the tree or plant
compensates again.

The tree looks sick. It is very
thin on top and dropping
small branches.

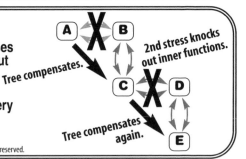

Box 4–Third Stress

Third stress compromises more
inner functions and knocks out
the compensation(s). The tree is
trapped. It cannot grow. It is in
decline.

The tree probably looks very sick
and has lots of dead branches and
ancillary complications. However,
it may appear healthy but still be
in this stress/decline condition.

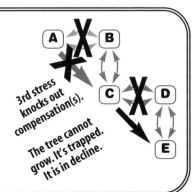

HOW STRESS COMPROMISES INTERNAL FUNCTIONALITY

Dr. Jim explains the ABCDE Internal Functionality Flow Diagrams (to the left): Trees get stressed, too. What happens to the trees when some stress factor comes along? In the series of diagrams on the left, follow the progress of stress factors as they knock out functionality. The tree can compensate for a while–years in some cases–but systems such as uptake of fluids or photosynthesis may continue to break down until the tree goes into **decline** and dies.

It is really as simple as ABCDE to understand how stress compromises internal functionality. The diagrams on the facing page show the flows and blockages of functionality inside of a plant or tree as I perceive them. These diagrams are representative of the challenges I am dealing with when I restore functionality.

A normal flow of functions inside of a tree or plant consists of countless interacting feedback loops as seen in the tree illustration on the right. I have simplified these processes to show a series of five self-regulating feedback loops in the ABCDE diagrams to the left.

© Basia Alexander

In Box 1, to the left, see how A↔B↔C↔ D↔E flows. Function A flows to function B, B flows to C, and on. An intrinsic flow like this is representative of a healthy tree with a full, lush canopy.

Then, an initial stress occurs as shown in Box 2 to the left. Let's say a long hot spell and drought in summer disrupts the ratio of water, nutrients, and sugars in the circulation system. Perhaps a cold, cloudy, and wet spring slows down photosynthesis. The affect of the stress factor is shown as an X knocking out the feedback loop between A and B.

A healthy tree can compensate for the blockage between A and B by using other interactions to get to C. The diagram represents this as an arrow between A↔C. The loss of A↔B takes an energy toll. Even when conditions become favorable again, it may not be able to re-establish the A↔B feedback loop by itself.

The inner function may be lost. The tree or plant has lost **Growth Energy** but it still appears relatively healthy.

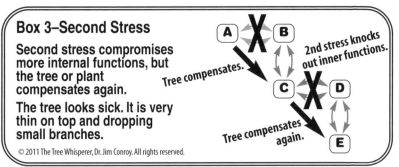

Box 3–Second Stress

Second stress compromises more internal functions, but the tree or plant compensates again.

The tree looks sick. It is very thin on top and dropping small branches.

Tree compensates.

2nd stress knocks out inner functions.

Tree compensates again.

A second stress occurs as shown in Box 3 repeated on this page. If it was hot and dry, maybe the next major stress is cold and wet. Or perhaps it is human or animal damage. Since stresses are additive, the tree's feedback loops represented by C↔D are blocked as shown with an X. The tree or plant must then compensate for this disruption of feedback loops with other interactions to accomplish C↔E. Even if conditions become favorable again, the tree or plant probably won't return to the full flow of health.

Dr. Jim gives an example of a tree with the effects of two stress factors: A tree with two stressors usually looks sickly or thin or has dead branches.

Environmental conditions between 2005 and 2011 in the Northeast United States have stressed Dogwoods and Sugar Maples. Their internal condition and subsequent inner compensations look like Box 3 as seen above.

The Native Dogwood, seen to the left, shows the thinness in the canopy from multiple stress factors.

© Jim Conroy

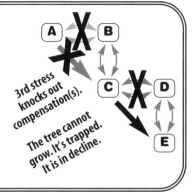

Box 4–Third Stress

Third stress compromises more inner functions and knocks out the compensation(s). The tree is trapped. It cannot grow. It is in decline.

The tree probably looks very sick and has lots of dead branches and ancillary complications. However, it may appear healthy but still be in this stress/decline condition.

3rd stress knocks out compensation(s).

The tree cannot grow. It's trapped. It is in decline.

A tree's real misfortune happens with a third stress, as seen in Box 4 repeated on this page. The nature of the stress factor doesn't matter at all.

If the third stress factor knocks out operations where the tree has already compensated, then the tree goes into a spiral of decline. The tree is trapped. It can no longer compensate for the new disruption. It will stop growing. It is headed into decline and will likely die unless its inmost functionality is restored.

EXAMPLE: STRESS COMPROMISING INNER FUNCTIONALITY

Dr. Jim continues: Let me give you an example of how stress factors compromise inner functionality. I'll use the situation of climate extremes. Let's say there is a sequence of three stress factors: too hot and dry in summer, too wet the next spring, and then too cold the following winter. That's just the kind of thing that will send an older American Beech tree into decline. I have found that decline generally happens for Beeches because their circulation of fluids is compromised. In other words, the flow of fluids in the tree's essential pipes–called xylem and phloem– becomes clogged.

As a result of the circulation being compromised, less water and nutrients are absorbed by the roots. So, less water and nutrients flow up to the leaves to be available for photosynthesis. Without the proper amount of water and nutrients, there is less photosynthesis. Less photosynthesis means less food is produced by the tree for its growth. Then, *because* circulation is compromised, whatever food is produced doesn't travel to the growing points, or wherever it needs to go, such as the roots for storage. Also, less food means less fuel to support the tree.

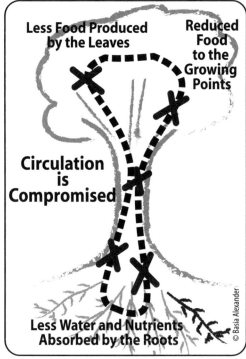

Less Food Produced by the Leaves

Reduced Food to the Growing Points

Circulation is Compromised

Less Water and Nutrients Absorbed by the Roots

© Basia Alexander

With less food being produced by the tree, and a compromised circulation system, now less food, water, and nutrients are able to get to the growing points, such as leaf buds or roots tips.

Less growth along with continued degradation of circulation and photosynthesis then starts a downward spiral. See illustration.

Other interior systems will be compromised, too. For instance, there will be an imbalance in the ratio of nutrients, sugars, and water. I call this the "plant chemistry." There will be reduced or stagnant cell division, which will stunt growth.

RESPONSES TO STRESS–HOW TREES COPE

Dr. Jim answers a key question: How do trees and plants cope with stress? They have amazing and sophisticated chemical and physiological responses, which they muster to cope with both the abiotic (nonliving) and the biotic (living) stress factors.

However, mustering these responses takes a toll. They use precious energy to compensate. Think of how a train dispatcher operates. He or she has trains rolling, trains waiting, and trains needing to cross paths. Also, if one of the switches goes down, trains have to be rerouted. The dispatcher has to prioritize.

Trees cope by rerouting and reprioritizing their dwindling resources. The rerouting itself takes fuel and energy from the tree. Sometimes they will sacrifice an older or an upper branch; they stop sending resources to it so that they can use their declining resources more efficiently on newer or closer-in tissue.

Dr. Jim informs: The use of products–anything from fertilizers, bug killers, or fancy growth regulators–have unanticipated negative consequences for trees. If you were standing in their roots, coming from their point of view, as I do, you would realize that a sick tree must use part of its precious energy resources to chemically break down those products. From the tree's or plant's point of view, products may have some temporary positive effects–like knocking down populations of aggressive insects–but they are not the answer to restoring health. And, very often the insects or diseases rebound with a vengeance because the tree is weaker than it was before. The tree's or plant's inner health needs to be restored.

THREE OR MORE STRESS FACTORS CAN LEAD TO DECLINE

Dr. Jim teaches: I want to add some comments to what I described about decline in the ABCDE diagrams. Stresses are additive for trees and plants. In other words, if a tree or plant is already in poor health or is stressed, another stress factor worsens its physiological health. Three or more stress factors lead to a condition called decline. A single additional stress factor after several stresses usually tips the balance. The tree is trapped; its interior processes can no longer compensate and cannot operate to support the life of the tree.

For a tree, the outsiders–the diseases and insects–move in after other stress factors weaken a tree. Most people usually only see the insects and diseases; they focus on the later stages of the whole weakening process. They don't see the initial compromised operations that invited the insects and diseases in the first place. So, believing in a quick fix, they throw on a fertilizer or a pest-killer, hoping that the tree will get better.

The parts, interior systems, operations, and **dynamic balance** of functional interrelationships within the tree or plant need to be addressed in order to truly restore health and vitality. We can do this easily inside of trees and plants through **bioenergy** healing interactions with their **biofields**. Connecting these bioenergy interactions is what we teach in our classes and will continue to explain in this book. When people help trees and plants regain health with the techniques of Tree Whispering®, they, themselves, usually feel good, too.

A REAL EXAMPLE

Dr. Jim and the Larch: A Larch tree is a kind of Evergreen. This one in Fair Haven, New Jersey, is easily fifty feet tall. To the casual observer, it looked great. But, in my intuitive listening, I could hear the tree say, "Help me. I am hurt."
It was pushing out sap in three places.

If a tree has *not* been recently injured, but begins to leak fluids through its bark, that is a sign that circulation is not running properly. If the fluids can't flow up and down, the tree pushes them out. When the circulation system is blocked, the tree pushes sap out through a path of least resistance–old pruning holes, old injuries, or cracks in the bark.

I would like to outline how this Larch's functionality was compromised; however, please remember that every tree is different! So, what I say about this tree applies only to it.

When first learning Tree Whispering, you would not need to determine the level of detail I am talking about in this example. Tree Whispering is a simple version of Green Centrics™, which is the system that I perform. However, both are permission-based and priority-based systems. Chapter 7 will give you insights into how I determined these findings and do my healing.

FUNCTIONALITY COMPROMISED AND SPECIFIC PROCESSES WEAKENED OR NONFUNCTIONAL FOR THE LARCH, WRITTEN IN PRIORITY ORDER

1) Circulation in the tree was not operating properly. Since fluids could not move properly up and down in the tree, they were being pushed out or were leaking out of the bark in three places.

2) Specifically, movement up of fluids in the xylem was not occurring.

3) Connection between soil and roots was crippled.

4) Downward movement of fluids in the phloem was blocked.

5) *The right reactions were not taking place to convert food (made by photosynthesis) into usable components.*

6) *The process of photosynthesis was operating at minimal levels (due to circulation issues) and needed to be maximized.*

7) *The process of photosynthesis was detached from the process that balances plant chemistries in the sap, therefore allowing the sap to block the circulation system.*

8) *The flow of Growth Energy (which prompts and regulates growth) around the whole structure was unevenly distributed.*

9) *Life Energy was in a downward spiral leading toward decline.*

Dr. Jim concludes: These were only the first of the Larch's many dysfunctions. Do they sound like typical tree-care diagnoses? I think not. But, these impaired processes were very real–especially from the Larch's point of view.

Wouldn't it be wonderful to heal those weakened inner processes and return health to operations that are broken? It's possible. It's also possible to return dynamic balance and synchronization of inner operations within the whole tree or plant.

Conventional tree and plant care can neither identify these kinds of problems nor heal the Larch's inner malfunctions as Tree Whispering and Green Centrics can.

MYSTERY-PUZZLE OF DIMENSIONALITY FACTOR

Dr. Jim gives an insight: There is a mystery here. I call it "the puzzle" or "the puzzle of dimensionality factor." This may be complex to understand because it is not linear. Reading and speaking are linear processes. As you read, try to go outside of sequential, linear thought since the puzzle of dimensionality is a comprehensive, "whole-istic," and integrated view.

When I do my bioenergy healing on a tree or plant, I do *not* do a transfer of healing vibrations or make a linear connection of parts and functions. In fact, a tree's life processes are not linear. When a tree is in decline, there are a myriad of compromised parts and functions. There is also an array of connectivity patterns that have to be repaired in a certain specific order so that the repair of intrinsic operations can be made. As a human, I can't solve this puzzle-mystery. I have all the knowledge from my doctorate that is useful to understand a linear pattern. At the same time, I'm working with other Powers for the nonlinear part of the processes, which result in the healing.

A person can only receive and understand the priority order of the functionality healing patterns from working with and interacting with the bioenergy of the tree. It is unique to each tree and each situation. This is where the intuitive aspect of the work is key. Healing cannot be done with the logical left-brain. The puzzle must be completed in the pattern that is requested by the tree and the condition it is in at the time it started into its cycle of decline. You may reference Box 4 of the ABCDE Internal Functionality Flow Diagrams in this chapter, but please understand the unique and individual process of working with each tree. If this explanation doesn't make sense to you yet, it may by the time you finish this book. Or, you can ask a tree.

WHAT DOES A STRESSED TREE OR PLANT LOOK LIKE?

Dr. Jim talks about tree survival: A tree or plant under stress is trying to sustain itself. It is pulling its Growth Energy in so it can support at least some growth processes and continue to live. It will let go of some leaves and branches since its Life Force cannot sustain them. This explains why a large tree under stress has a thin canopy and many dead branches at the top. It can only sustain growth in the lower part of the structure.

All photos this page © Basia Alexander

WHAT STRESSED TREES MAY LOOK LIKE

All photos this page © Basia Alexander

When evaluating whether a tree is stressed or in decline, follow these guidelines, listed from less to more severe:

- *Lackluster look or drooping leaves*
- *Not flowering or fruiting as it did previously*
- *Yellow or curling leaves*
- *Less or smaller leaves overall*
- *Dropping leaves before autumn or not leafing out with others in spring*
- *Thin canopy of leaves, especially in the upper crown of the tree*
- *Signs of insects or diseases*
- *Lots of small, dead branches, especially in the upper crown of the tree*
- *Larger dead or falling branches*

Dr. Jim gives an insight: Whatever the many stress factors, the tree goes into a state of decline. Its Life Force is pulling in and it begins to consume its own resources, since it can no longer get sufficient nutrients from the soil, and produces few sugars from photosynthesis. A big tree can no longer sustain a large canopy. It can only sustain itself as a smaller tree. Therefore, there are dead branches and/or small leaves at the top. The Life Energy can only support so much structure, so upper parts whither away.

Trees operate by working together in a tightly knit community. See Chapter 9 for more about community. For now, I'll say this: When trees pull their Life Force inward, that protective reaction serves to disconnect them from the biofields of other trees. They fall out of community and therefore lose the valuable protection and nurturing they would otherwise get from other trees.

© Basia Alexander

The majestic American Beech, like this one, and so many other trees eat themselves up and die from the top down.

"HEALTHY-LOOKING" TREES AREN'T ALWAYS HEALTHY

Dr. Jim warns: Don't be fooled by trees that are well established or that seem to have lush canopies. These trees may look good on the outside but aren't always healthy on the inside. How would you know? Sometimes there are telltale signs like the bleeding canker on the Copper Beech tree in New Jersey that I mentioned in Chapter 3.

Here's another Beech Tree that looked very healthy but was not. This was not surprising because many Beech trees on the East Coast of the United States are weak. The property owner did not allow chemicals or invasive techniques to be used. Therefore, she had already engaged me to work on other trees on her property. One day, I found a telltale clue–bleeding canker spots–on the Copper Beech that indicated compromised processes inside the tree. After my bioenergy healing treatment, the tree was strengthened and able to heal itself, and the bleeding canker cleared.

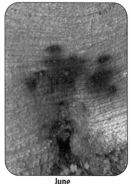

| June | September | November |

All photos this page © Basia Alexander

While some species have their particular telltale signs of inner weakness, such as bleeding cankers, many others do not. It can be a real problem in observing a tree's health. How would you know if a tree looks healthy on the outside but is really sick on the inside? Well, you could ask the tree's innate **intelligence**.

THE IDEA GOES UNRECOGNIZED: STRESS COMPROMISES INTERNAL FUNCTIONALITY

Dr. Jim explains: When I explain to an audience that stress compromises inner functionality, they understand it immediately. It tracks with their experiences with their own bodies. Like trees, people are sometimes ill but show no telltale signs. When people are stressed, they are more likely to catch a cold or the flu.

However, the idea–stress deteriorates the functionality of trees and plants–goes generally unrecognized in conventional tree and plant care. One reason professionals sometimes don't recognize the idea is because there are no instruments for evaluating inner operations *as a whole*. Existing professional tools and methods can, at best, measure one or two systems. Such tools cannot accurately or comprehensively check whether the *whole* tree's parts and systems are working properly and in sync.

This idea may not have been taught in schools or professional trainings, so it is often unrecognized as a problem. Since there is no cookie-cutter solution, the idea of stress compromising natural functionality is generally ignored.

Dr. Jim emphasizes: *Even if* the idea of stress compromising inherent functionality were well-known, there are no products that can repair all the feedback loops. Even if complex interrelationships of physiological malfunctions could be detected–there are no products that can balance the totality of their interrelationships.

At the same time, I believe that products can be useful, and I recommend using products to *keep* trees and plants healthy when they are *already* healthy. However, in spite of people's best efforts, trees and plants become stressed. When stressed, a tree's health is compromised and it compensates. Products cannot open up blocked circulation, cannot improve cellular division, cannot start movement up or down when it has been blocked, cannot coordinate food production with growth, or bring dynamic balance and synchrony to all of these functions *as a whole*.

It's not that somebody hasn't yet developed the perfect products. Products are not the answer here. Products won't ever be able to restore a whole tree to health or its inner functionality to dynamic balance. There are just too many variables involved in healthy dynamic balance.

One of my goals is to inspire people to have a new kind of personal experience with Nature. I hope that you will expand your relationship with trees and plants by learning to take their perspective. If you can come from the plant's or tree's point of view, you might recognize how delicate their interior workings are and how badly stress factors as well as certain products can imperil the delicate balance of their parts, systems, and functions. It is my hope that when you come from their point of view, you may not be so quick to put products on your trees and plants without asking them.

ADVANCEMENT IN THINKING IS NEEDED

CONVENTIONAL THINKING	NEW THINKING
❏ *Doesn't recognize the internal functionality of the tree because there is no way to address it.*	❏ *Addresses the internal functionality of the tree while coming from the tree's point of view.*
❏ *Applies products to the outside of the tree.*	❏ *Reestablishes operations within the tree with holistic, bioenergy healing techniques.*
~~AND~~	*~THEN~*
❏ *Comes from the human point of view, with the hope that the tree heals itself on the inside.*	❏ *Suggests practices and products for the outside of the tree to KEEP the tree healthy.*

Dr. Jim tells a story: I met arborist Paul O'Kula of Long Island, New York, at a trade show. After explaining how sick and stressed trees recover their health when I treat them with my professional-level Green Centrics bioenergy healing system, he said: "This is a dream come true." He expressed his frustration with watching trees die after doing the best he could do for them. Clearly, he became an arborist because he loves to work with and to touch trees.

Paul went on to say, "I was trained to look at the outside of trees. I can learn a lot about a tree like that—but I can only do so much to help it from the outside. I'm tired of having to cut down trees.

Sure, there's money in cutting them down, but I'd rather help the trees live."

This arborist was ready for something new. He wanted something that would save the beautiful trees that he and his customers love. I told him that he would have to change his way of thinking.

Dr. Jim continues: I made a play on the phrase "can't see the forest for the trees." I told Paul that he couldn't see the *tree* for the leaves, roots, trunk, soil, and pests. I suggested that he begin by putting himself in a tree's place, imagining or feeling what is going on both inside and outside of it. He told me he would look with an open heart first and then with a professional eye.

Paul went on to take the Tree Whispering workshop in two successive years. He put in the extra effort because he wanted to expand his experience and to apply the techniques as correctly as he could.

Paul O'Kula, Long Island, New York, arborist, business owner, and long-time Tree Whispering student, said: In the two Tree Whispering classes I took, I had a genuine experience of "getting in touch" with the bioenergy of the trees. I realized that my professional tree care training was never really about the inner workings of the tree itself. Now I can see that my training was done from a different mindset.

Dr. Jim says we have to come from the tree's point of view. To me, this means "being" the tree and finding out from the tree what it is going through in its life. I used to think I was a good arborist–figuring out what I should do for a tree. I thought I had all the answers. But now, I realize I can ask the trees and they tell me about their health. Now, I can do an even better job as an arborist.

DECLINE IS REVERSED BY HEALING INTERNAL FUNCTIONALITY

Dr. Jim says: Paul is talking about the shift in attitude that changed his professional actions. He already knew that trees are living Beings. But, he had to have the experience for himself of a tree's Growth Energy shifting direction when its internal processes were restored.

As I said before, a tree in decline is pulling in its energy. Generally, it dies from the top down because it can't sustain its size. Diseases and insects are secondary to the tree's inner weakness. Its internal functionality is degraded and impaired, like an orchestra playing out of tune and off the beat. But, natural operations can be healed.

Dr. Jim continues: Tree Whispering is a permission-based and priority-oriented system. First and foremost, we ask permission from the tree or plant to do a session. It is very, very rare not to get permission, but it does happen. Occasionally, a tree is so sick that it **communicates** to me that I should leave it alone. So, I bless it and just let it be.

When I do a healing treatment, I ask about the highest priority for healing inside of the tree. The tree's own Growth Energy or Life Force knows how its functionality is compromised and tells me about that when I am "in the zone" with it. I go through a sophisticated checklist of yes/no questions. The tree itself as well as some unknown Power—possibly including the Nature Deva or Design Intelligence—that exists in every living Being, communicates to me the highest priority feedback loop that needs healing.

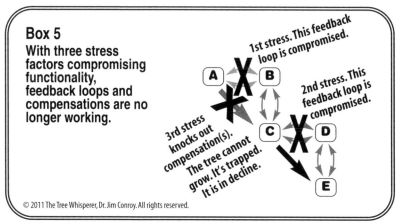

Box 5
With three stress factors compromising functionality, feedback loops and compensations are no longer working.

1st stress. This feedback loop is compromised.

2nd stress. This feedback loop is compromised.

3rd stress knocks out compensation(s). The tree cannot grow. It's trapped. It is in decline.

In Box 5, above, the highest priority probably would be to perform the first step of healing the feedback loop between A and B.

This is the mystery-puzzle of dimensionality in action. It initially involves finding the most limiting functionality factor in the tree or plant. Then, once that most limiting factor is restored, it is necessary to also restore all of the other supporting, ancillary feedback loops.

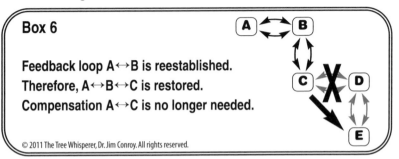

Box 6

Feedback loop A↔B is reestablished.
Therefore, A↔B↔C is restored.
Compensation A↔C is no longer needed.

In *Box 6,* above, when the feedback loop at A↔B is healed and reestablished, the blocked compensation between A↔C is no longer needed. Also, the feedback loop between B↔C is functional. Therefore, functionality A↔B↔C is reestablished.

Now, the second priority would be to perform the step of healing the feedback loop between C↔D.

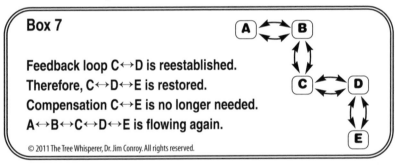

Box 7

Feedback loop C↔D is reestablished.
Therefore, C↔D↔E is restored.
Compensation C↔E is no longer needed.
A↔B↔C↔D↔E is flowing again.

In *Box 7,* above, when the feedback loop at C↔D is healed and reestablished, the compensation between C↔E is no longer needed. Also, the feedback loop between D↔E is functional. Therefore, functionality C↔D↔E is reestablished. There is a return to healthy, normal flow of functionality in the tree.

A↔B↔C↔D↔E is flowing and installed in functionality. Dynamic balance is reconnected and restored.

RESULTS FOR THE TREE

Dr. Jim asks: What are the results for the tree? Instead of feedback loops degraded and impaired inside the tree, as shown by Xs through the circular arrows in the diagram on the left of this page, dynamic balance and complete flow is restored.

Decline can be reversed because interior functionality can be healed. The illustration on the right of this page shows circular arrows, indicating restored feedback loops of functionality.

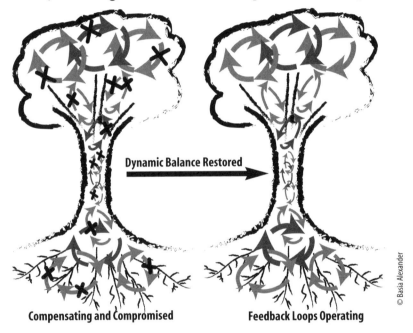

Dynamic Balance Restored →

Compensating and Compromised   **Feedback Loops Operating**

© Basia Alexander

You won't see an explanation, such as this one I have given you, if you look into many botany textbooks. My descriptions and diagrams may be somewhat unconventional. However, they are true to the experiences that I have when I heal trees and plants.

In Chapter 7, I describe, step-by-step, how I heal trees.

Chapter 7: The Five Heralds-
Healing The Tree Whisperer's Way

Dr. Jim Conroy, The Tree Whisperer,® offers encouragement:
In Chapter 4, you had a personal experience of overlapping your
bioenergy field with the **biofield** of a tree or plant. You came
from a plant's or tree's point of view; you stood in its roots and
felt the sunshine on its leaves. With that experience, it should be
easier for you to understand what I do to heal trees. In this
chapter, I explain how I heal trees and plants at my expert level,
and as the creator of the Green Centrics™ system.

In the next chapter, you can learn to do a simple, easy, and
effective healing technique yourself. You may not interact at the
level of botanical knowledge or experience that I do, but you
will see that you can feel connected with **Nature** at a deep—
even spiritual—level and can have the confidence to offer
healing energies to trees and plants. What will be important is
that you make the attempt. *Trying* counts because it shows that
your heart is in the right place and your **intentions** are good.

Ms. Basia Alexander, The Chief Listener, defines "the zone":
Dr. Jim will talk about doing his work while being in the zone.
Being in the zone is simply having inner quiet and focused
attention on something. An athlete doing his or her sport, and
doing it with total immersion, is in the zone. While you meditate
or pray, you may be in the zone. If you read this book around
distractions, you may be in the zone.

The Five Heralds
BE the Tree
ASK the Tree
HEAL the Tree
SAVE the Tree
LOVE the Tree

BE THE TREE

Dr. Jim describes his experience: I use the
phrase "get in touch" when I talk about
connecting with the **Life Force** of trees and
plants. Anyone is capable of getting in touch
with the Life Force and **Growth Energy** of
trees and plants through a hands-on technique involving
touching it and being willing to have a sensory or emotional
experience. The experience may involve a feeling of expanded
awareness such as visual perception of colors or imagery,
hearing a sound or words, or smelling a fragrance. The
experience can be a combination of multiple senses at once.

The first step for me is to *bond* with the Life Force and biofield of the tree or plant. When I touch the trunk of a tree, I may feel roughness on my fingertips, but I really feel tingling sensations or have a perception of movement. I get into the zone by allowing myself to relax into the sensations of being near the tree. I may look at the tree with my eyes or may have visual images or symbolism in my mind's eye, but I don't need to see the tree. I could be taken to a tree blindfolded and I would be able to find out what its health issues were.

As the bond strengthens, my hands feel like they are slipping inside of gloves as I touch the tree's bioenergy field. I feel its unique bioenergy signature somewhere inside my heart or in my gut. Sometimes I can hear words or the tree's song. I often smell its fragrance directly from the trunk. I sink into a meditative state—sometimes alpha sometimes beta brain waves—even though my eyes may still be open. During the experience, though, I am fully aware of what is going on around me.

I must pause to point out that this is a sacred experience for me. Being with a tree in such an intimate–even spiritual–way is often too great for words. Yet, I want you to have an idea of what it is like for me.

Dr. Jim continues: By this point in the session, I am aware of my heart's biofield. It's a bioelectric and magnetic field generated by the heart in a donut shape around every person's body. At the same time, I am aware of the tree's Life Energy. A tree produces its own biofield because it is also alive. It may not have a heart, but it has living cells and a circulation system that moves water, nutrients, and sugars. If a plant's leaves were attached to a polygraph (a lie detector), bio-electromagnetic readings would result.[1]

When the plant's field and my field overlap—as when the ripples from two drops of water in a pond overlap—I start to receive information from Nature's innate Intelligence within the tree. I get insight into the condition of the tree's health through the overlapping fields.

I ask the tree for its permission to be connected with its Life Force or Growth Energy. Then, I ask permission to interact with it. Asking permission is simple courtesy. Imagine approaching and asking someone to dance but without the fear of rejection, that's what it is like for me. Most trees have never had a person ask them to interact so it may take a moment for the tree's bioenergy to shift and register my request.

After the request is registered, I may have a sensation of tingling or an awareness of movement. Trees do move by themselves. Many times, I have had my hands on a big tree that has a fence leaning on it. I've heard the fence creak when there isn't even a puff of wind. There is a shifting of weight as Life Energy flows through the tree. Also, I may feel some emotion. The emotion is often associated with the health of the tree. For example, a tree in **decline** will have dead limbs or branches near the top; the tree can no longer support a large canopy so it dies from the top down. That is the visual sign. But, energetically, I would feel that tree's sickness from the inside-out as a sensation of Life Force being held in it.

I am getting all this information about the tree's health through my own body's antenna–like a radio receiver. Then I interpret all the sensations and information through my right-brain's intuition, my left-brain's logic, and my heart's wisdom. I feel merged with the tree. Sometimes, I feel as if I have stepped inside of the trunk. I know who the tree is as an individual life form. I do not lose myself but rather am fully aware of myself and the tree together. At this point, I am BEING THE TREE.

Dr. Jim describes: When my bioenergy field connects with the tree's or plant's bioenergy field, I experience an actual convergence of the two biofields. This is when the exchange of information begins.

Now, and only now, can I start my question-asking process. Think about this: You wouldn't rush up to strangers and start asking them about their arthritis or their sex life without getting to know them first. BEING THE TREE is getting to know it.

As discussed in Chapter 6, stress factors **compromise** inner operations; a tree loses its flow of functions and its operations break down. A tree has a certain kind of *knowing* about this. So, specific information about a tree's loss of inner functionality is available to me from its biofield. Since I am in a bioenergy overlap with a tree's field already, all I have to do is ask my Green Centrics pattern of questions and concentrate on my perceptions in order to access information from the tree.

ASK THE TREE

The Five Heralds
BE the Tree
ASK the Tree
HEAL the Tree
SAVE the Tree
LOVE the Tree

Dr. Jim describes his process: Treatment of a tree or plant to restore its health is a more targeted and purposeful exchange of **communication** than simply *being* the tree.

Tree Whispering® and Green Centrics are permission-based and priority-oriented systems. First and foremost, I ask permission of the tree or plant to communicate with it, to enter its world. I also make a specific request for permission to do a healing treatment. This is not casual or fanciful questioning. Asking for permission is the first step of building an equal and cooperative relationship with any Green Being.

I feel a tree's answer in my gut, my heart, or my mind. "Yes" means yes, go ahead with the questioning process. "No" means either "Do not treat me" or "Check into your own state of concentration." Usually a "no" means that I, myself, am "out to lunch." It may mean that I need a drink of water, or my attention is lacking, or my energy field is imbalanced. I need to correct my own situation or not treat at that time. Once I have had water and refocused myself, I ask again.

Once I have permission from the Green Being, I begin my Green Centrics question-asking process. I developed this advanced questioning technique specifically for all trees and plants, since I know something about botany. I use the full range of that knowledge to ask questions about what intrinsic parts, systems, or functions are compromised or not operating in sync.

Rarely–perhaps six or seven times since I started–has a tree said "no" to treatment because it didn't want to regain health. Most Green Beings have a natural force to live. But, occasionally, a tree is so sick that it communicates to me that I should leave it alone. So, I give it a blessing and let Nature care for it.

Dr. Jim cautions: What I *don't* do is expect to get a predictable answer based solely on my professional training. Professional training teaches that identifiable conditions require certain answers or prescribe certain actions. Since what I do is beyond conventional diagnosis, I have no preference or agenda when I approach a tree. More than that, I have learned to check my ego at the door. Therefore, I respect a "no." Hearing "no" does not challenge my personality, and I am not afraid to hear it. I know that trees are *not* like petulant children. "No" is a piece of good information that leads me to be more creative and insightful because I have to keep asking more carefully worded and deeper questions until I get a better understanding. A "yes" leads me to the next phase of questioning or leads me to clarity. Sometimes a "yes" or "no" doesn't initially fit my idea of the way I think it should be, but later on in the process, it all becomes clear. I must trust the path.

My initial goal is to find out about the tree's loss of inner

functionality. The Green Centrics questioning system leads me not only to the parts and functions that are compromised but also, and most importantly, to information about how those parts and functions have stopped interrelating. All living systems have complex **feedback loops** as illustrated to the left. So, when one thing stops working–as shown with Xs–countless others are impacted.

Dr. Jim continues: By asking the tree, I have discovered how elegant and complex the inmost workings of any living Beings are–including humans. All living Beings operate in interacting feedback loops that are called Network Patterns.

In the illustration below, the complex feedback loops inside of any living Being are represented symbolically as dots connected to other dots. To add accuracy, the dots are encircled in three patterns to show how more complex layers of interactivity between feedback loops may be grouped.

Network 1

Network 3

Network Patterns in 3 Dimensions

Network 2

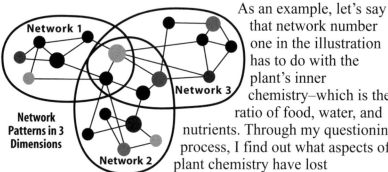

As an example, let's say that network number one in the illustration has to do with the plant's inner chemistry–which is the ratio of food, water, and nutrients. Through my questioning process, I find out what aspects of plant chemistry have lost functionality. Similarly, network number two may have to do with blocked circulation of fluids in the xylem and phloem. Then, I may find that network number three indicates halted cellular division in the growing points.

Do you notice how these patterns overlap and interact? Everything is connected; one nonfunctional part or system failure impacts nearly every other part or system. It can take a while for me to ask all the questions that identify the unique combinations of malfunctions or disturbances as represented by these patterns.

This is not classical diagnosis because I am not trying to fit a symptom with an already identified label or problem. Each tree is different and has different combinations of deterioration or breakdown in its natural interactions. So, I ask a lot of questions.

The Five Heralds
BE the Tree
ASK the Tree
HEAL the Tree
SAVE the Tree
LOVE the Tree

HEAL THE TREE

Dr. Jim gives some background information: Alternative, complementary, and ancient human health-care systems have a few things in common. For instance, many systems are less focused on finding causes of problems and are more focused on restoring usefulness and functionality. Most systems use interactive techniques. The participation of the patient in his or her own healing is vital, rather than prescribing a "magic bullet." All these approaches recognize that the "patient" is a whole, interactive, living Being, not a collection of parts. As a living whole, the person is seen as more than flesh and bone; he or she is understood as having mind and Spirit associated with both illness and recovery.

It is the **holistic** and spiritual thinking behind indigenous and complementary methodologies that originally inspired me. The techniques interested me because of their simplicity and their general lack of reliance on substances. Instead, these approaches rely on practitioners' use of their deep understanding of their system and their grasp of the whole situation for the patient. The practitioner uses his or her own focused attention or intentional concentration while moving, touching, or tapping on the patient's body. When I studied and practiced the BodyTalk System,™ I appreciated that healing occurred through deliberate application of consciousness.

I adapted various healing techniques to work with trees and plants. Here is the best way I can explain the mystery of how the healing occurs for me: Information that I gather from asking a lot of questions gives me a grasp of what is happening inside the tree. I use my system along with my background knowledge of botany. I touch and tap on the tree's trunk, leaves, or roots while concentrating my consciousness and holding a clear vision of the specific rearrangements of network patterns needed for healthy operation. When I am tapping on parts that are not energetically connected, I use my focused intention to shift the bioenergy field. Then, with continued tapping and hand movements, the various parts and aspects become reconnected and synchronized.

Dr. Jim elaborates: With all that having been explained–in truth–I am really the "pass-through" for the healing to occur. I do not feel that I do the healing; I feel that the healing occurs through me.

No healer can really explain the full extent of what he or she does. Usually, it is because the healer–in his or her ego personality–is not present. It seems paradoxical, but people who call themselves healers are usually operating as the vehicles for a metaphysical or spiritually based occurrence. When I am treating a tree, my consciousness is deeply engaged in concentrating on details, but I feel as if "I" step aside and become a pass-through so that the true healing can occur. I am not giving the tree vibrations or energy as is done in certain human healing systems. Likewise, the tree is not giving energy to me.

I witness the tree's bioenergy—and even a spiritual type of energy—connecting like lightwaves overlapping. These lightwaves run through the whole tree. As all of the network patterns come together, I have a sense of all the parts, systems, and functions operating in sync. The **dynamic balance** inside the tree has been restored. As the lightwaves begin to weave and interconnect, I can feel the whole tree become fully operational. Then, I know the tree is working again and on its way to healing itself.

COPPER BEECH TREE SAYS "FIX MY OUCHIE"

Dr. Jim reminds: Remember the Copper Beech tree that had a bleeding canker "ouchie" in Chapter 3? Let me describe how that healing session occurred.

I asked the tree for permission to connect with it. I put my hands on it and opened my heart and mind to connect with its bioenergy flow and Life Force. In my intuitive hearing, I heard the tree say, "I have an ouchie! Get rid of it. Get rid of it, please." The feeling was so sad.

As I settled into the feelings and sensations of BEING the Copper Beech, I ASKED the first set of questions to the tree's natural Intelligence. It became clear that the circulation was blocked. Initial blockage was in both xylem (movement up) and phloem (movement down.) Also blocked was the uptake of water and nutrients in the roots, as well as the movement of water and nutrients throughout the tree.

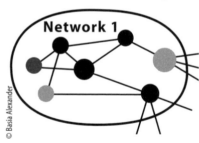

That bioenergy process could be illustrated as a network pattern. You might think of this as websites interlinked on the Internet. Notice that a few of the lines extend outside of the circle in this illustration. Those will link to other network patterns.

In order to HEAL THE TREE, I used a series of hand-tapping procedures and intentional focus techniques to reconnect the pattern of functionality at the bioenergy level of the tree's Life Force. I believe the connection is made, first, in bioenergy or multidimensional levels and then is imprinted into the physical. It happens so fast it is like a spark. The energy melds into the physical. As I do this tapping, the first network pattern is connected within itself. These hand-tapping and intentional focus techniques are just like ones employed by various human **energy medicine** systems that alternative practitioners use in their practices and in forward-thinking hospitals all over the world.

Circulation in the Copper Beech was going to open–I could feel that. But first, a related compromised process had to be repaired: the "plant chemistry" or the ratio of water, nutrients, and food

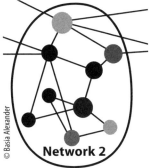

represented by Network 2. The ratio was out of balance. As uptake and circulation slowed, the chemistry was not flowing, almost like sap thickening. I don't know if the fluids actually become thick, but that is what it feels like to me. It's my perception. As it thickened, it further slowed down the uptake and circulation processes. The network pattern of feedback loops in this system needed to be reestablished. Once again, a series of hand-tapping and intentional focusing techniques were used to get the chemistry balanced in the tree.

Now, activity in the tree was starting to get going. HEALING began fast for this Copper Beech—as I stood there. Trees are not burdened with the psychological baggage that some people carry that slows their healing. Trees start to heal on-the-spot. As the circulation started to move in the tree, the start of adequate uptake of water and nutrients began. This helped the fluids begin to return to balance in the tree. And the reverse is true, too. As the fluids were returning to proper ratio and were no longer excessively thick-like, then the circulation was able to begin to flow more smoothly.

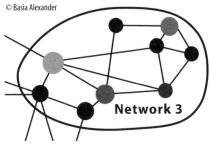

Dr. Jim continues: I ASKED the tree's innate **intelligence** and discovered that a third function or network pattern had to be healed: cellular division. Let me recap to put this piece of the treatment into perspective. As circulation had slowed, uptake of water and nutrients also slowed. The fluids became thick and were out of balance. Therefore, cell division slowed. It makes sense, doesn't it? Everything is connected to everything else. Because less water and nutrients were moving into intercellular spaces and because ratios of water-to-nutrients-to-carbohydrates were wrong, the cells were not getting what they needed to divide and grow. Cell division makes growth possible in trees and in people, too. Areas of cells all over this tree were "hardening off." This means that they were no longer able to actively divide. Since the process of cell division had slowed down, the tree was not growing. Such a slow-down can lead to death for a tree.

Dr. Jim continues: I worked with the younger, healthy cells that were not "hardened off" and were still able to divide. The feedback loops of functionality in that network pattern were reconnected. I made sure that they had sufficient resources in order to begin to divide again. I made sure that the right ratio of chemistry in the fluids was moving into the intercellular spaces and across the cell membranes. All this was done through ASKING step-by-step questions to the Intelligence of the tree at every point and HEALING with proven techniques.

A three-way pattern was now connected with everything working in all directions. Clear circulation and balanced plant chemistry helped to drive cell division. Rapid cell division helped pull fluid movement into intercellular spaces, thus helping to keep plant chemistry balanced and circulation moving.

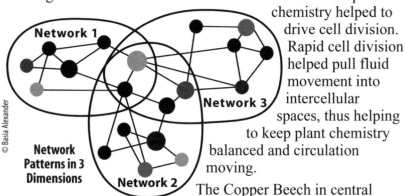

The Copper Beech in central New Jersey had a few more network patterns that had broken down. These had to be HEALED in similar ways. The last process was to bring the tree into overall dynamic balance. In other words, all the network patterns had to be overlapping and working in sync.

What happened for the Beech tree, from its point of view?

Systems were repaired.

Cells began to divide again.

Dynamic balance was restored.

The Growth Energy and Life Force of the tree shifted from their "pulling in" patterns to a "pushing out" pattern. The tree continued to heal itself because it was growing again.

What about the Phytophthora disease? As the tree became healthier, the disease cleared. A healthy tree naturally resists diseases and insects. The canker spots stopped bleeding and began to fade. Together, the tree and I "fixed the ouchie."

Dr. Jim pauses, then slowly continues: You might be asking "Is he some kind of superbeing that he can do all this'? Well, I am the pass-through. What I have is an extensive knowledge of botany and tree physiology. I use this knowledge when I communicate with the tree and let it tell me what systems have broken down and where health is lost. I hold that in my consciousness. I ask the tree about how these systems ought to be working. I hold the concepts of correct or healthy functionality and make the connections in my consciousness.

Then, I step aside. I become the pass-through. HEALING occurs. I don't know who or what does the healing, but I know that the process works.

The Five Heralds
BE the Tree
ASK the Tree
HEAL the Tree
SAVE the Tree
LOVE the Tree

SAVE THE TREE

Basia adds a philosophical note: Is it unusual to talk about a tree's life or SAVING that life? I don't think so. People will say, "Oh, the tree in my yard died." If it died, then it must have been alive. It had its own life as a part of Nature. I believe that each tree is valuable not only by human standards but also as a living part of Nature. So, if a tree's living systems can be returned to functionality, there is an opportunity for each of us to help a partner on the planet, and in doing so, help, and even save ourselves.

Dr. Jim continues: I don't like to say that I "saved" the life of a sick tree. I don't usually like to take credit that way. I am just happy when a tree lives and recovers. But, I will accept acknowledgment for kick-starting the process. It's like kick-starting a stalled engine but in this case, the stalled engine is the interior workings of the tree. Just as a person might say, "I have the flu; I don't have the energy to hold my head up," a sick or declining tree doesn't have the energy to sustain itself in its full form. It is pulling its Life Energy in and down.

During or after a treatment, a bioenergy shift occurs inside the tree. I feel it as an upwelling of Life Force. My students can often feel it, too. The healed tree is operating with serviceable feedback loops in dynamic balance, so the Life Energy changes direction—up!

All the pieces come together. The tree says, "Wow! Now I can grow!!!" Fragrances come to me from the bark. Things shift, shimmy, and shake. I'm standing there! Everything happens at once! The Life Energy just takes off! It's like fireworks! Once that shift occurs, it's only a matter of time before the result is visible in the tree.

I cannot explain what happens any more succinctly because I do not fully comprehend it. And, I don't believe that modern science has approached an understanding at this level of operation of living systems yet, because this process is too dynamic and happens too quickly. I believe that the human ability to grasp this process is not sufficiently mature yet. Even these words are inadequate. But, I know that I can feel it and that it works. You can, too.

The healed tree or plant is now operating in sync within itself. Its dynamic balance has been restored. The tree wants to grow again.

Healing drives growth. Growth drives healing. The engine is running again. The beneficial cycle of SAVING THE TREE has begun. Once the bioenergy is shifted to an upward pattern, it is only a matter of time until the results show up. People have to remain calm and patient; they must give the tree a chance to begin the healing↔growth cycle and have wonderful, new green shoots or leaves show up in the physical dimension.

The Five Heralds
BE the Tree
ASK the Tree
HEAL the Tree
SAVE the Tree
LOVE the Tree

LOVE THE TREE

Dr. Jim emphasizes: If a tree in decline is trapped inside of broken and blocked feedback loops, it will die. Tree Whispering means helping the tree out of that trap. The pure connection I feel with a tree during the healing process is best described as a profoundly humbling feeling of LOVE. My appreciation of the complex and beautiful ways trees and plants operate has expanded exponentially since I started my tree-healing work. My gratitude for the Spirit that trees contain goes beyond words.

CANADIAN GREENHOUSE WITH MALAYSIAN TREE

Dr. Jim recounts the tale: Basia and I were teaching a workshop in Toronto, Canada, one spring. To practice some of the techniques, we led the students to a botanical garden's greenhouses. All were warmly welcomed by a wonderful woman I'll call Barbara–that's not her real name. She told all of us that she already lost one tree and another was in bad shape. She didn't care about the garden's protocol at that point. She begged us, "Could you do *anything* to save this tree?"

The tree was from Malaysia, as a part of their tropical collection. I touched it and found that there was still life in it. "Never too late to save a living tree," I told her. In the previous months, the Malaysian tree had undergone four major stress factors that Barbara and I could identify.

First, in the middle of winter, the building's heating system went out. During the repair, the weather became bitterly cold, too cold for this heat-loving tree.

Second, she explained that it was customary to spray a very weak alcohol solution on plants for insect control. The botanical garden will not use commercial insecticides to avoid any risk to visitors. But, someone on her staff mistakenly added too much alcohol to the water. Alcohol would sting your skin; think about how it might feel directly on the tree's leaves.

Barbara and I determined that the soil this Malaysian tree was planted in was not of optimal quality nor native to it. Poor soil made a third stress.

The fourth and last stress was a stress borne of love. The staff really wanted the tree to survive. Everyone watered it—a lot. Overwatering is as harmful as underwatering.

Dr. Jim reviews: I have already talked about the fact that stress is additive in trees and that three or more stress factors can lead to decline. Let's review how that happens. When the first stress factor occurs, a plant's natural feedback loops compensate. This compensation is usually not visible in the tree's outer appearance. It would be like taking a simple round-the-block detour when you're driving through town. It slows you down, but you easily resume the trip.

The second stress factor comes along for a tree. It continues to compensate. Now, the effects of that compensation are sometimes visible. For example, in the Northeast of the United States, in two successive years, the weather was unusually warm through December and early January and then the temperatures plummeted. Sugar Maple trees and the Dogwoods had dramatic reactions to those two difficult winters. Most became thin and weak; the Dogwoods didn't bloom much the next spring because they had already used most of their buds in January.

By the time the third or fourth stress factors come along, the natural processes inside of a plant can no longer compensate. The third or fourth stress factors block the compensations already in place. They compromise the compensations that already occurred. The tree can't adapt to this additional stress and starts to decline, looking sicker and sicker.

Since the tree or plant is weak, maybe insects or diseases come along to take advantage of it for their own necessary life purposes. However, at this point, insect or disease control methods may be senseless. Insect or disease damage is secondary to the main problem: inner weakness, compensation in functionality, and compromised systems. At this point, the tree is trapped and can no longer compensate. It needs to find a clear path around the blocked feedback loops, but it can't. Then, it eats up its own resources, has no more food left, and dies.

The Malaysian tree was a picture-perfect example of a tree in severe decline. It is possible to save a tree in decline. But I am giving away my story.

To save a tree in decline, here's the formula: repair the inner functionality. But, surgery can't be done on a tree's circulation like a stint implant or heart bypass can be done on a person. That's why my hands-on bioenergy healing techniques fit so well with trees and plants. When inherent functionality is healed–repaired–there is a reversal of the "eating itself up" downward flow of energy. Whatever energy is left, turns upward to renew operations and kick-start growth. The compromised parts and systems that *can* work again, *do*. Then, as I said before, growth drives healing, which then drives growth which then drives more healing and on and on. Full functionality is restored along with the necessary Growth Energy to give the tree a chance to be healthy again. It can survive and thrive.

From my vantage point inside of the tree, the HEALING is like repairing a spider's web. Imagine a spider's web with a big hole in it. Then, imagine that strands can be taken, one by one, and put back into the right place. The challenge is in teasing the jumbled strands apart and reconnecting them into the right places. People often ask me how I heal trees. The talent is not in making the so-called healing connections. The art is in identifying which ones go where.

Dr. Jim continues with the story: And so the Malaysian tree in Toronto was healed as a demonstration for the students in that workshop. Of course, everything had to happen in priority order. Its xylem and phloem needed repair. Then, the ability of the tree to get water and nutrients from the roots up to the growing points or leaf buds was restored, while reestablishing the tree's ability to produce food.

At this point, something took me by surprise because I was actively explaining what I was doing to the students.

Luckily, I was still holding the tree. In my deep sensory perception, I felt the tree shift its energy upward. That reversal from pulling in Life Energy to pushing out Life Energy happened and I felt it immediately.

The tree wanted to grow again!

That reversal or shift of Life Force always happens if a tree is in decline. It just doesn't always happen on cue or while I am standing there. Sometimes students feel it too when they are practicing the techniques. A tree that is going to survive will change the direction of its bioenergy flow. Then, it will grow again!

I gave Barbara a couple pieces of practical advice: "Don't water it so much," and "Be patient."

Dr. Jim tells how it turned out: I left Toronto with great

satisfaction. Because its energy had shifted upward, I knew that the tree would survive.

What I didn't know was how long it would take for the tree to begin to put on new growth.

Several months later, I headed back to

Toronto without even a phone-call. I knew the Malaysian tree survived.

When I got there–sure enough–it was flourishing. The skeletons of its few sick leaves were still there among the lush new canopy.

Barbara told her side of the story. She said it seemed to just sit there for many weeks, then all of a sudden, she said it went "Whoosh." She threw her arms apart!

"New leaves came out like crazy," she said. "It began to flourish once again and we were all so happy!"

Now, she had a different problem. However, this problem was a lot less serious. She was worried that as winter was approaching, she would have to trim off some of the leaves that were touching the glass so that the whole tree would not be injured by the cold. I figured that was a nice problem to have after almost losing that tree.

That is proof: It's never too late to save a declining tree or plant. Remember, it still has Life Force in it. Never give up.

Dr. Jim looks forward: You can use the Five Heralds yourself. Just go outside and put your hands on a tree.

Start with BEING THE TREE, as I do. That experience will lead you quickly and directly to LOVING THE TREE.

If you want to ASK, HEAL, and SAVE it, please read on.

You might also consider taking one of the Tree Whispering workshops for the full experience and to learn the specific techniques involved.

Chapter 8: What You Can Do

VALIDATE YOURSELF

Ms. Basia Alexander, The Chief Listener, says: Graduates, or people who hear us give our introductory presentations, often approach me and describe their feeling of relief in knowing that their childhood perceptions or adult encounters with Nature are authentic and credible. Some people talk about being scolded as a child for saying that they talked with trees. Other people share that, as adults, they talk to plants secretly. They tell me that–after meeting Dr. Jim and me–they feel newly inspired to accept the truth of their experiences or to approve of themselves.

I believe that these people may have been unfairly judging themselves. They may have been influenced by historical or cultural biases concerning character and intelligence–possibly related to their own competence or intelligence or trees' and plants' natural **intelligence**.

Basia asks: Is there a chance that you may be unfairly judging yourself? If so, what can you do to feel good about yourself and validate your personal and deep connection with Nature? How have other people affirmed themselves in the face of doubt?

Detailed information about graduates quoted in this chapter can be found in the Citations.

Chuck Winship, East Springwater, New York, Maple syrup farmer: Taking the Tree Whispering course validated what I always felt when I went into my Maple forest. I sense their needs. I feel what they like and don't like. My book-learning and personal experiences were definitely verified.

Leslie Ashman, Reston, Virginia, project manager and Gaia Consciousness advocate: In the Tree Whispering class, my chief impression was feeling affirmed; I knew that the inklings and intuitions I had previously in my life were true.

I used to sense swirling energy going up above trees. I thought I was different, weird, and even wondered whether feeling that swirl of energy was really real. But, being in the class with Basia, hearing Dr. Jim talk about his perceptions, being with the other students, and connecting with the trees was a really great confirmation of my perceptions and feelings. I felt deeply validated by the class.

But, more than that, I knew I was feeling the right things. There were no questions any-more inside of me. Being sure about my own perceptions opened up changes and new freedom in my life. I have been rewarded for every step I have taken while trusting my intuitive perceptions; I know I am truly held within Spirit and by Gaia–our **Mother Earth**. I have been guided to a new life doing healing work at Civil War battlefields and bringing others to heightened and profound awareness of our shared experiences on this planet. My new work celebrates how we are all Divinely supported by Gaia.

Lori Myrick, East Windsor, Connecticut, energy medicine practitioner: Sometimes I feel that trees say funny things to me and that gives me great joy. On one occasion, I felt the presence of someone walking down the path and seeing me giggling with a tree. I said to myself, "Oh well, it's silly to be self-conscious." I realized that it *didn't matter to me whether someone saw me or what they thought of me.*

It didn't matter because I received so much joy from the tree. Feeling that joy overpowered any self-consciousness. It was greater than any judgment that I or anyone else might have of me. Then a thought came to me, "How wonderful it could be to have that person experience it, too. " I realized later, *the thought was actually a message from the tree.*

Jude Villa, Martha's Vineyard, Massachusetts, professional landscaper and designer: When I bring new plantings to a client's property, I touch those plants all the time. If someone sees me, I don't care. I just tell them that I am getting to know the tree. Touching helps me prepare the trees to be planted.

Carraig "Rocky" Romeo, Princeton, New Jersey, businessman and Druid: I used to be skeptical that a tree may or may not have anything to say, and I was judgmental of myself. I decided to *stop criticizing myself.* I realized that I had to *be forgiving* about getting messages from the trees.

Anonymous, PhD psychologist: Twenty years ago, I did meditations with trees and plants in similar ways to those that Jim and Basia offer now. Taking their workshops changed my life because I was already doing this privately and they were talking about communicating with trees and plants publicly. I felt validated.

Cheryl Smith, PhD, University of New Hampshire, Extension Professor and Plant Health Specialist (plant pathologist): To ask a plant a question is a bit unusual in my professional field. And, I believe in multiple approaches to solve a problem.

For example, when I was a graduate student, my advisor asked me, "You don't believe in taking herbs, do you?" I said, "Absolutely! Chinese and Native American medicines have been around for millennia. And, many modern drugs are based on chemicals found in plants."

"But, you're a scientist!" he countered. I explained that being is scientist is exactly why I should explore something new. Part of the scientific method is to find out if something works. I don't believe I should just debunk things because they are different. Test and see if it works. Use what you believe in.

SUGGESTED KINDS OF SELF-VALIDATION
- *Tell your own truth. Give yourself permission to be as you are, not as someone else wants you to be.*
- *Forgive yourself for a perceived transgression.*
- *Examine existing beliefs, then author new and more supportive beliefs.*
- *Approve of yourself. Praise or acknowledge your own qualities. Accept that your behavior is authentic to your inner inspiration.*
- *Take actions based on your beliefs. Be confident and persistent, even in the face of disagreement.*

ACCEPTANCE FROM OTHERS

Ms. Basia Alexander, The Chief Listener: On a similar note, people have told me that—while they have a special, personal connection with the Beings of Nature and they feel good about it and themselves—having such a Nature connection seems to set them apart from other people. They have worried about being thought of as strange, different, or even crazy.

Do you have these kinds of concerns?

Since it's only natural to want approval or acceptance from others, the situation could be an uncomfortable dilemma for you.

You may feel boxed in: Eager to share your wonderful experiences with trees, plants, or other Beings of Nature, while at the same time afraid to let other people know what you do and how you fear their disapproval.

I am here to assure you that we—all of us who **commune** with Nature, yet may feel a bit concerned about acceptance from others—don't have to be concerned anymore. Attitudes are changing!

Most people already accept the truth and wisdom of whispering with dogs, horses, babies, and even angels. Mainstream media are full of such shows. From there, it is a small step to accept the truth and wisdom of whispering with trees, plants, and all of Nature's Beings. In our years of talking with a broad range of people in various professions, Dr. Jim and I have seen more open-minded attitudes. People now believe that touching, healing, and communicating with trees, plants, and all of Nature's Beings is plausible, is feasible.

Soon, whispering with trees, plants, and all of Nature's Beings will be commonplace. We—all of us who commune with Nature, who feel good about ourselves, and who cultivate skills of sustainability—represent the "new normal" in Western culture. The "new normal" means being confident in one's perceptive abilities while trusting and acting on the information that comes through those perceptions. The "new normal" means that participating in a partnership or cooperative relationship with a houseplant, a tree, the forest, one's garden, or crops, is just the sensible and ordinary thing to do.

Basia asks: How have other Nature lovers made the transition from feeling concerned about being thought of as strange to feeling confident about being accepted and appreciated?

Cheryl Smith, PhD, University of New Hampshire, Extension Professor and Plant Health Specialist (plant pathologist): I told my sister and brother-in-law that I would talk to a tree on their property and offer it some assistance. I got some good-natured teasing from my brother-in-law, but there was no intent to criticize. Sharing with family members might be hard for some, but it's important to let those close to you know what you believe (and it may help open their own awareness).

In my goal to incorporate talking with trees into my work, I think I can make use of those skills to find out more about what is going on with trees in **decline**. I have shared that I've taken a Tree Whispering workshop with some of my colleagues and with the students I teach. That inspires others to come forward and say that they talk with plants, too.

Gerry Verrillo, Guilford, Connecticut, arborist: I decided to *share* what I learned about communicating with trees with certain clients. I'll admit I was afraid of what they would think of me. But I told myself, "Have the courage. Don't be ashamed. Speak out!" The clients were actually grateful! They were relieved and happy that I was doing their tree care from a feeling point of view, rather than an intellectual, analytical, clinical, or mechanical point of view. A couple of clients said that they wanted only me to do their work from that point on; they said they would trust only me.

Basia has some hints about receiving acceptance from others: What can you do to feel good about your connection with Nature when you are around other people? A big step in confidence is simply starting a conversation with your friends about trees. If people are talking about the environment or about children in Nature, try this. Ask them whether they have a favorite tree or if they remember a special tree from their childhood. You will start people talking about how much they love trees–just like you. You'll be amazed! You will find many others like yourself. It's fun!

Second: Show this book to family or friends. Having a book in your hands will prove to them that there are other people–such as Dr. Jim, me, and the people we quote–who feel the way you feel, do the kinds of things you do, and stand behind you.

Third hint: Let your plants and trees do the talking for you. Their vigorous health and radiant beauty show other people that you must be doing something right. When they ask you about your secret, tell them that you whisper with your trees and plants. Send them to *www.TreeWhispering.com*. Then, they may appreciate the results that you create with these valuable and powerful processes.

Another hint: teach and inspire others. Explain that because you are free of the biases and conditioning about how things *should* be done for plants, you are enabled to *be more creative.* Since you know you are a sane and rational appreciator of Nature on this small planet, suggest that they might learn as you do from **Mother Nature's** wisdom. Invite them to join you in making a difference by contributing to solutions.

Lastly, preserve your dignity by forgiving others who may be hostile and accusatory toward you. Remain silent. Dr. Jim and I have talked with such people. There are those who feel that leaves are such nuisances to rake that they want to cut their trees down. There are other people who are so entrenched in their ways, so afraid of anything that is different that they are not at all interested in changing their relationship with Nature. Others are so critical of ideas that don't fit their mindset, their training, or their religion that they cannot cope with the ideas or practices suggested in this book. Some are just negative about change. I suggest that you do as Dr. Jim and I do: be quiet. Then extend compassion and forgiveness to these disconnected souls and let them go on their way.

Basia concludes: Try as anyone might, no one can force change on another person. The biggest breakthrough regarding approval from others is taking steps toward *not needing* others' approval. Give yourself validation, know your inner truth, and approve of yourself. It may take guts to admit that you talk with trees or commune with Nature, but most people will respect you for your candid admission. Even if they look at you funny, will you care? Not if you know you're not alone.

KNOWING YOU'RE NOT ALONE

Basia suggests: Having a larger perspective can help. Millions of people around the world are just like you in their enjoyment, caring, respect, or love for trees. They, like you, have a special sensitivity to the **Life Force** of trees and plants. Consider that you have something in common with many other people.

TRY THIS: IMAGINE BELONGING
Read through the steps. Decide whether you feel comfortable doing this exercise. If you do not feel comfortable or have any concern whatsoever, do not do it.

For your convenience, this exercise is reproduced in your Tree Whispering: Trust the Path *notebook. Audios are also available at* www.TreeWhispering.com.

Step 1: Sit down in a comfortable, private place without interruption for 10 to 15 minutes. This exercise is best done with eyes closed.

Step 2: Groups go by many names. Use this list or find your own words that represent "belonging," "acceptance," or "compatibility" to you.

❑ *Family*	❑ *Friends*	❑ *Association*	❑ *Community*
❑ *Relations*	❑ *Companions*	❑ *Club*	❑ *Neighborhood*
❑ *Tribe or Clan*	❑ *Fellowship*	❑ *Team or Crew*	❑ *Congregation*
❑ *"My People"*	❑ *Kindred Spirits*	❑ *Co-workers*	❑ *Convention*
❑ *Cousins*	❑ *Sister/Brother*	❑ *Partners*	❑ _____

Step 3: For a minute, allow yourself to feel an emotion of self-appreciation and self-acceptance as a member of such a group.

Step 4: When you are ready, change the scene. Imagine that you are standing or sitting in a town plaza, a field, a forest, or a hotel ballroom. There is a bright light or the sun is shining on you. It is very comfortable, pleasant, and easy for you.

Step 5: Imagine that there are other people there. These people are just like you in their respect and caring for trees, and plants, and Nature. You like them. They like you. All of you appreciate and honor Nature.

Step 6: Imagine enjoying yourself with these people. Everyone is smiling, making greetings, and honoring everyone else. It's a very safe place.

Step 7: Imagine that more people, who are like you, arrive.

Step 8: Imagine being comfortable, happy, and excited that hundreds, thousands (or even millions) of people who are just like you, are in this place. All of you are celebrating your appreciation for the Plant Kingdom and kinship with trees, plants, and all of Nature.

Step 9: Imagine that your favorite tree, other trees and plants, as well as other Beings of Nature come to this place.

Step 10: Imagine that the trees, plants, and other Beings of Nature are rejoicing together with you. It is a very safe place.

Step 11: Take a few moments to deeply enjoy and find pleasure in your feelings of acceptance and belonging with these groups of people and Beings of Nature.

Step 12: Change the scene any way you want to, if that will give you more pleasure and more sense of belonging. Enjoy yourself.

Step 13: When you are finished, jot notes about your experience in your *Tree Whispering: Trust the Path* notebook.

Dr. Jim talks about Trafalgar Square: In London, Trafalgar Square is a well-known meeting place. Especially before the time of cell phones, everyone chose this enormous plaza as a place to meet. Basia and I want to provide a Trafalgar Square of

YOU CAN DO THE 5 HERALDS AS DR. JIM DOES

BE THE TREE

Ask for a connection with this other life form. Settle into the overlapping connection with it in a sensory and emotional way; experience its way of life. A harmony occurs called "coming from the tree's point of view." This step is transformational for both you and the tree.

ASK THE TREE

It's only respectful to ask. Asking leads to partnership.

Play "20 Questions" and feel the Green Being's "yes" or "no" responses within your body or intuition. Let a "no" response be a guidance system to lead you to a better way. The more knowledge you have, the better questions you can ask. By asking the Green Being questions, you strengthen and/or expand your connection or bond with it; you get more information about it and about yourself.

HEAL THE TREE

Restoration of internal functionality occurs in the bioenergy interactions between a person's healing intent and the tree's natural programming to be healthy. Techniques include Healing Whispers®.

The act of healing trees and plants is often a healing experience for people, too.

SAVE THE TREE

Healing of internal functionality drives growth. Growth drives healing of internal functionality. Be patient. Be observant. The tree is SAVED.

LOVE THE TREE

Love is always there. It does not come last in this process. When a person comes in contact with the Life Force and bioenergy of another being, there is a beautiful experience of purity. At the point of connectedness, the balance of purity flows back and forth. That purity flowing back and forth is LOVE.

sorts. This will be a comfortable place for you to remember that you're not alone and to find out what other tree and plant lovers are doing. Please go to *www.TreeWhispering.com.*

Dr. Jim predicts: Basia and I have a vision for the future of relationships between people and the Plant Kingdom. We foresee transformations occurring within people's attitudes and beliefs so that there is peace between people and Green Beings. Peace comes from such a shift in people's consciousness.

There will be changes in the ways that people think about the value of trees and plants and in the ways that they behave toward the whole Plant Kingdom. We call this a **paradigm shift**. A paradigm shift occurred in people's beliefs about the shape of their world starting in 1492, when Columbus crossed the Atlantic Ocean. People came to realize that the world was not flat, but spherical, and that the planet circled other heavenly bodies. Their world was no longer the center of the universe.

How do you shift to a new paradigm in the twenty-first century? There are five steps, called the Five Heralds, that you can use personally to cross the bridge to a new relationship with the Plant Kingdom.

CROSSING THE BRIDGE TO A NEW LAND

The Five Heralds
BE the Tree
ASK the Tree
HEAL the Tree
SAVE the Tree
LOVE the Tree

THE FIVE HERALDS: BE THE TREE

Dr. Jim tells the origin of the Five Heralds: In early 2010, I did some soul searching about how I might improve the work of healing sick trees. I asked my Spirit Guides and asked the trees: "How can I be more effective?"

The answer that came back was "BE THE TREE." At the time, I laughed because I didn't understand its profound meaning. But, I put the instruction into practice every day that year when I went out to interact with a tree or plant. The meaning has become crystal clear to me. Now, I "AM" the tree whenever I do my healing work. The first step across the bridge–or the first of five Heralds–is BE THE TREE.

I say "tree" in the Five Heralds because it is an easy word to say, but I mean any member of the Plant Kingdom.

What BE THE TREE means is to be connected in a sensory and emotional way with the **bioenergy** field of a tree or plant.

To BE THE TREE, the most important thing is to fully accept whatever you feel and experience when your senses and emotions are overlapping with the bioenergy of a tree or plant. Let me reassure you that the sensations and emotions associated with this experience will become clearer for you in time.

Mike Nadeau, Sherman, Connecticut, holistic land-care practitioner: When I am *being* the tree, I get a better connection with the tree. Then, whatever I feel informs my actions. Most of the time, the actions I take seem unorthodox compared to what I would normally do. Even though my business is set up to apply all kinds of organic and compost-type goodies in the ground, I may find that the tree is too sick to respond to them. Many times, I find out that providing companion plants is what the tree really wants and needs.

Paul O'Kula, Long Island, New York. arborist, business owner and long-time Tree Whispering student: Dr. Jim says we have to come from the tree's point of view. To me, this means *being* the tree by getting connected with its bioenergy, and finding out from the tree what it is going through in its life.

TRY THIS: BE THE TREE
Read through these 4 options first and decide whether you feel comfortable doing any or all of the exercises. If you do not feel comfortable or have any concern whatsoever, do not do it.

For your convenience, this exercise is reproduced in your Tree Whispering: Trust the Path *notebook. Audios are also available at* www.TreeWhispering.com.

OPTION 1: Review the "Stepping Inside Their World" guided meditation exercise in Chapter 4.

OPTION 2: Create a Breathing Connection Cycle

Step 1: Put your hands on the tree. Close your eyes if comfortable doing so.

Step 2: Imagine a stream of air coming into your heart area from the tree and going out your belly area back to the tree. This stream of air creates a connection cycle.

Step 3: On the incoming stream of air, imagine the Life Force and bioenergy of the tree connecting with you.

Step 4: On the outgoing stream of air, imagine your Life Force and bioenergy connecting with the tree.

Step 5: Continue to make the cycle of connection: the tree's Life Force coming in at your heart area and your Life Force going to the tree from your belly area.

Step 6: Breathe in and out easily and gently. Allow yourself to enjoy this connection cycle for several minutes.

Step 7: Acknowledge that your connection allows you to BE THE TREE.

Step 8: Thank the tree for allowing you into its world. Jot any notes in your *Tree Whispering: Trust the Path* notebook.

OPTION 3: Transmitting and Receiving Cycle

Step 1: Put your hands on the tree. Close your eyes if comfortable doing so. Breathe gently and easily for about a minute while holding the tree.

Step 2: Imagine that the tree is a transmitting tower. Imagine that it is sending out something like radio waves in all directions.

Step 3: Imagine that you are a radio receiver. Imagine that you can tune in and receive the tree's waves.

Step 4: Imagine the reverse. You are a transmitting tower and the tree is a radio receiver.

Step 5: Imagine that the tree and you are making a circular, two-way transmitting and receiving cycle.

Step 6: Breathe in and out easily and gently. Allow yourself to enjoy this connection cycle for several minutes.

Step 7: Acknowledge that this connection allows you to BE THE TREE.

Step 8: Thank the tree for allowing you into its world. Jot any notes in your *Tree Whispering: Trust the Path* notebook.

OPTION 4: Put Yourself in the Tree's Place

Step 1: Put your hands on the tree. Close your eyes if comfortable doing so.

Step 2: Breathe gently and easily for about a minute while holding the tree.

Step 3: Imagine your feet sinking into the earth and growing roots. Do this for about a minute.

Step 4: Imagine standing with your arms stretched up toward the sun. Imagine your fingers growing leaves and absorbing the heat and energy of the sun. Do this for about a minute.

Step 5: Imagine the sun on your face, the breeze in your hair, and rainwater soaking up from the earth. Do this for about a minute.

Step 6: Breathe in and out easily and gently. Allow yourself to enjoy this connection cycle for a few minutes.

Step 7: Acknowledge that this connection allows you to BE THE TREE.

Step 8: Thank the tree for allowing you into its world. Jot any notes into your *Tree Whispering: Trust the Path* notebook.

Danielle Rose, Northern New Jersey, novelist and newspaper columnist: I used to get angry with myself for not sitting still with my trees. My solution is to go on *moving meditations*. I walk through the woods with my young daughter strapped to my back and the dog on the leash. While moving, I allow myself to receive strong images from the trees and plants. I believe that they have come to know my little caravan as we pass by them.

```
The Five Heralds
  BE the Tree
 ASK the Tree
 HEAL the Tree
 SAVE the Tree
 LOVE the Tree
```

THE FIVE HERALDS: ASK THE TREE

Dr. Jim suggests: There is a global shift in consciousness happening. We are all crossing a bridge now. We are leaving the shore of the land I'll call *domination, control, and superiority*. People who live there take plants and trees for granted. They believe that the Plant Kingdom is populated with inanimate objects that are either decoration or disposable. The new shore on the other side of the bridge is the land of *cooperation, partnership, and equality*. In order to get there, we must show respect and ASK THE TREE as if it were an equal partner.

Yes, you pose a question to the tree as if it had its own intelligence. Asking is only courteous. Before you would do something for another person, you would ask them a question like "What do you want?" A tree is a living Being and so it should be treated similarly. True, it is a different kind of living Being than a human or an animal, but it is a living Being nonetheless.

Have we become so human-centric or so arrogant that we think we don't have to ask Mother Nature? Plants are the most generous of Beings. Just by being alive, they provide oxygen, which we can conveniently breathe. And their bodies often become our food, our shelters, and other of our resources. Not only is gratitude called for, but also respect. Gratitude and respect are in the asking.

Dr. Jim gives an example: For instance, before you put a product on a tree or plant, you can connect with the plant's **biofield** in a deep feeling place: BE THE TREE. Then, you can get information about the wisdom and advisability of whatever you think should be done by asking questions. Pose a question in your heart–ASK THE TREE–and use your intuition to get an answer. It's like playing the game of 20 Questions. Ask different questions in various ways around the topic.

A professional gardener, landscaper, or arborist might think that they know what is best for a plant or tree. It's true that these professionals are usually skilled and well trained. However, they have not generally been trained to ASK THE TREE. But, they have an advantage. They can use their skills and training to ask the tree's or plant's bioenergy and innate intelligence the right questions about the usefulness, suitability, and timing of their plans.

When you play this game of 20 Questions, you must have an open mind and a deep caring for the tree or plant. Even if you think it's silly, when you ask this other living Being a question you will get a response. You may feel "yes" or "no" feelings. You might actually hear those answers in your inner hearing. Or, the answer might come as a visual image or in the form of an impression or emotion.

Dr. Jim asks: Could the plant actually tell you "no"? It could. And if it does, I would say to you, "respect that answer." Hearing a "no" answer does not have to fly in the face of your self-confidence or your agenda! The plant's "no" answer may be a guidance system leading you to a different way to accomplish what you are trying to do. Ask the plant's bioenergy field and innate Intelligence some more questions. It could mean "not now, but maybe later," or it could mean "do it another way." For example: "Don't transplant me here, put me there" or "Organic fertilizer in two weeks, not now."

Generally, the plants are willing to work with us. They are not like stubborn children. Getting a "no" answer doesn't have to mean "absolutely no!" You will probably be able to do what you want, but it may not be your way. Be open to a different way. Let the plant or tree explain it to you with this yes-or-no language or by intuitive knowing. Trust the path.

And, here's a last note on being told "no." I have found that many trees that have been under stress need to recuperate before they can tolerate a product. It's like us: If you have just had the flu, you might not want to sit down to a big steak and potatoes dinner right away.

Melanie Buzek, Cornville, Arizona, physical therapist, energy-medicine practitioner and educator: As part of my teaching duties, I show others how to hone their intuitive skills to receive "yes" and "no" answers when working with a client to determine which body areas are priorities to focus on.

Years ago in a class, a student was asking for permission to treat a fellow student, but kept getting "no" answers. A couple of us did some detective work to find out where the "no" was coming from. We determined that the student was picking up the "no" answer from a nearby plant because it needed care. After all, we are all connected! Applying the same intuitive skills and using "yes" and "no" questions, we discovered that it wanted the trash in its pot removed, to be in between two other plants its same size, and to be far enough from the heat vent. We complied with its needs. Then–and only then–did the student get a "yes" to continue with practice.

Basia teaches about "yes" and "no" responses: To ASK THE TREE a question means that you have to listen for an answer. In Chapter 4, there were techniques offered to help you become a better receiver. Chapter 5 was full of good advice from students about developing your perceptive abilities and enhancing your intuition. I would like to give you one more tool: feeling "yes" and "no" responses in your body as well as in your intuition.

We are accustomed to speaking a verbal language. However, our bodies have their own language. Science has shown that our nervous systems respond to stimuli even faster than our minds. Remember the advice you got in school for "true/false" tests? It probably was: "Always take your first answer." I believe that is because you can feel a "yes" or "no" response within your body when you make a true or false statement.

There are two parts in the following "Try This" exercise. Initially, you will be asked to make some general statements aloud. These will be statements about your name, your favorite color, your citizenship, and other simple things that should be either true or false for you. These statements are not meant to be deep psychological inquiries; they are meant to evoke simple and easy feelings of "true" or "false."

Probably, your body will have some kind of visceral or sensory response to the truth or falsehood of these simple statements.

Your responses may come as enjoyable feelings, images, colors, words, intuitions, or even smells or tastes. Each person is unique in her or his sensory capabilities, so allow yourself a rich and pleasant range of experience. I suggest that you allow your body's response to come through strongly and do your best to remember that feeling.

How do you get answers from trees or plants this way? You can use your experience as a template for receiving "yes" or "no" responses from a tree or a plant. When you are in the biofield overlap with a Green Being, your nervous system is interacting with its bioenergy field. In the second part of the "Try This" exercise, you will need to be able to touch a plant or a tree. Then, you will ask questions of that Green Being. You can get its "yes" and "no" responses or answers through your own nervous system by accessing the same "true" or "false" feelings you had in your body or intuition previously.

Try This: Receive "Yes" or "No" Responses
Read through the steps. Decide whether you feel comfortable doing this exercise. If you do not feel comfortable or have any concern whatsoever, do not do it.

For your convenience, this exercise is reproduced in your Tree Whispering: Trust the Path *notebook. Audios are also available at* www.TreeWhispering.com.

Part 1, Step 1: Be in a pleasant and private place where you won't be interrupted for about 10 minutes.

Step 2: Stand up, if convenient in your location. Take some deep breaths.

Step 3: Experience "true" or "false" responses in your body.

❑ *Read the following statements one at a time. Speak each one aloud.*

❑ *Pause between each statement and allow yourself to feel or sense your body's "true" or "false" response. Then, make the next statement.*

Note: Each statement is designed to evoke a simple "true" or "false" response, not a psychological inquiry.

❑ *I am an American.*	❑ *I am in my 60s.*
❑ *I am a Brazilian.*	❑ *I own a car.*
❑ *My favorite color is blue.*	❑ *I own a bicycle.*
❑ *My favorite color is green.*	❑ *My name is Mary.*
❑ *My favorite color is yellow.*	❑ *My name is Joe.*
❑ *I am a son.*	❑ *I live in an apartment.*
❑ *I am a daughter.*	❑ *I live in a house.*
❑ *I am in my 20s.*	❑ *I am wearing shoes right now.*
❑ *I am in my 40s.*	❑ *I am wearing clothes right now.*

Continues on next page

Step 4: Address your body with the following requests:
- ❑ *"Body, please show me a 'yes.'"*
- ❑ *"Body, please show me a 'no.'"*

Step 5: Address your body with the following requests:
- ❑ *"Body, please show me a bigger, clearer 'yes.'"*
- ❑ *"Body, please show me a bigger, clearer 'no.'"*

Step 6: Sit down, if you were standing. Jot down any notes about your "true" or "false" experience in your *Tree Whispering: Trust the Path* notebook.

Basia says: Good! Most students report feelings like upwellings of energy for "true" and a slumping feeling for "false." What feelings did you have? Be patient with yourself.

Part 2 of Receiving "Yes" or "No" Responses:

Note 1: You will need to be able to touch a plant or a tree for Part 2 of this exercise.

Note 2: Since you will be in a bioenergy overlap with the plant or tree, you can get its "yes" and "no" responses or answers through your own nervous system by accessing the same or similar "true" or "false" feelings you had in your body or intuition previously.

Step 1: You may either sit or stand.

Step 2: BE THE TREE or BE THE PLANT as you did in exercises from earlier in this book by touching the tree or plant. Create a two-way flowing Life Force and bioenergy connection with the tree or plant. You may want to review the Chapter 4 "Stepping Inside the Plant's World" exercise.

Step 3: Open yourself to a pleasurable experience of communication with this tree or plant.

Step 4: Ask permission. Say in your heart or aloud, "**I ask your permission to interact with me in this exercise.**"

- ❑ *If you feel disquiet or agitation, please stop. You do not have permission.*
- ❑ *If you feel calm or peaceful, continue here.*

Step 5: Say in your heart or aloud, "**I ask to connect with the earth, the sky, the consciousness of Nature, and this Green Being's Growth Energy. Nature Consciousness, for the highest good and in a gentle way, please assist me with a heightened intuitive, sensory, and emotional connection with this plant.**"

- ❑ *Notice that your heart's biofield and the bioenergy field of the tree or plant are overlapping.*
- ❑ *If you feel disquiet or agitation, please stop. If you feel calm or peaceful, continue here.*

Step 6: Ask the plant, "**Please show me a 'yes,'**" and feel a response.

Step 7: Ask the plant, "**Please show me a 'no,'**" and feel a response.

Note: If the plant's responses are unclear, be patient and continue here.

Step 8: Slowly and patiently, ask the plant each of the following questions. Receive its "yes" or "no" response to each question before moving on to the next question.

Note: Remember that "yes" or "no" are the only desired responses in this exercise.

1) *"Do you have sufficient water available?"*

3) *"Have you been transplanted?"*

4) *"Are you connected with the deep earth energies?"*

5) *"Are you operating at 100% functionality?"*

6) *"Would you like to receive a Healing Whisper?"*

7) *"Do you have a message for me?"*

Step 9: Ask the plant, "**Please show me a big 'yes,'**" and feel a response.

Step 10: Ask the plant, "**Please show me a big 'no,'**" and feel a response.

Step 11: Say, "**thank you**" to the plant for letting you into its world.

Step 12: Jot down any notes about your "yes" or "no" experience with the plant in your *Tree Whispering: Trust the Path* notebook.

Note: You may practice this exercise with several Green Beings.

Basia congratulates: Now you have the skills you need to have simple, easy, and practical communications with any tree or plant. You are prepared to do the next important step of the Five Heralds: ASK THE TREE. Congratulations!

TRY THIS: ASK THE TREE

Read these questions first. Before you attempt to ASK THE TREE, always take care of yourself and make sure that you feel comfortable. Don't do anything that would feel bad for you. If you have any concerns, do not do this.

Here is a list of yes/no questions that you can use when you want to get information from a tree, plant, or other Being of Nature. Use the yes/no question and answer process taught in the previous exercise as a guidance system.

Adapt this list of questions to fit your particular situation. When in doubt, or if you don't understand, continue to ask the yes/no questions until the answer is clear to you. By using this list, you are giving the tree or plant a chance to say "no." Remember, a "no" may be an indication that the plant needs you to ask other questions or different questions.

See the Holistic Chore for Transplant later in this chapter for a detailed procedure.

For your convenience, this exercise is reproduced in your Tree Whispering: Trust the Path *notebook. An audio is also available at* www.TreeWhispering.com.

Preparation: Use your *Tree Whispering: Trust the Path* notebook to take notes while you are asking these questions.

Step 1: Return to the previous section and BE THE TREE. Create a two-way flowing Life Force and bioenergy connection with the tree or plant.

Continues on next page

Step 2: Ask questions as appropriate to your situation:

❑ **"Do I have permission to ask you some questions?"**

❑ **"Do you need water?"**

    ○ *1 cup?* ○ *1 pint?* ○ *1 quart?* ○ *1 gallon?* ○ *drip hose for 2 hours?*
    ○ *more?* ○ *less?*

❑ **"Do you need a tie, band, or wire removed?"**

❑ **"Do you need compost?"**

    ○ *now?* ○ *later?* ○ *when?*
    ○ *how much of a specific compost? or what kind?*
    ○ *more?* ○ *less?*

❑ **"Do you need food?"**

    ○ *now?* ○ *later?* ○ *when?*
    ○ *how much of a specific food such as sea kelp? or what kind?*
    ○ *more?* ○ *less?*

❑ **"Do you need beneficial microorganisms?"**

    ○ *now?* ○ *later?* ○ *when?*
    ○ *how much of a specific product? or what kind?*
    ○ *more?* ○ *less?*
    ○ *on leaves?* ○ *in soil around roots?*

❑ **"Do you need a dead limb removed?"**

    ○ *now?* ○ *later?* ○ *when?*

❑ **"Do you need the soil under you loosened up?"**

    ○ *now?* ○ *later?* ○ *when?*
    ○ *how much–lightly?* ○ *how much–more vigorous?*

❑ **"Is a certain pest a problem for you?"** (Look for one you might see on or around the plant.)

    ○ *does it need to be removed?*
    ○ *now?* ○ *later?* ○ *when?*
    ○ *use a _____ product? (be specific)*
    ○ *use a different product? (ask about specific options)*
    ○ *how much? (always be within product label direction guidelines.)*

❑ **"Is this a good transplant location for you?"**

    ○ *too much sun?* ○ *not enough sun?*

❑ **"Do you need to be left alone?"**

❑ **"Do you need to be loved or appreciated?"**

Step 3: Take action in cooperation with the tree or plant.
Always ask more questions if you are unclear about any step in the process.

Step 4: Thank the tree or plant for allowing you into its world.

THE FIVE HERALDS: HEAL THE TREE

> The Five Heralds
> BE the Tree
> ASK the Tree
> **HEAL the Tree**
> SAVE the Tree
> LOVE the Tree

Dr. Jim reveals: The third Herald tells us to HEAL THE TREE so that its internal parts, systems, and functions can be fully operational. However, in modern thinking about tree and plant care, it often goes *unrecognized* that when a tree gets stressed, its **internal functionality** becomes **compromised**. If any of its many parts, processes, and systems are not operating properly or are out of sync with one another, the tree gets sick. Conventional approaches recommend applying products to the plant or the soil. Even though healthy soil is crucial, applying an amendment to the soil may or may not save the sick tree.

I say it is time to get our heads out of the soil and put them into healing the inner functionality of a sick tree first. Once the perfect timing, rhythm, and balance of bio-interactions within the whole living organism are restored, then I recommend doing the right conventional things to support the activities of new growth. Since products or invasive techniques can't restore inner operability to a tree, what can? Healing Whispers™ can.

When doing a Healing Whisper, there is a convergence between a person's healing intent and a tree's or plant's natural programming to be healthy. Interior repair or restoration of certain priority operations occur in the biofield interactions. Thus, the Healing Whispers heal sick trees and plants.

This method of healing trees is similar to bioenergy practices for people, including meditation, Reiki, or Touch for Health.® Human-oriented methodologies attempt to remove blockages and bring inner balance for cancer and heart patients. These techniques are used increasingly in forward-thinking hospitals.

TREE & PLANT WHISPERING
HEALING WHISPERS
Experiential Bioenergy Healing Techniques
Done In Partnership and Cooperation
with Trees and Plants

THE GIFT OF A HEALING WHISPER

Dr. Jim offers a gift: In Tree Whispering courses, Basia and I teach seven Healing Whispers. These are phrases or declarations to say while connected with the Life Energy of the tree or plant. This results in a re-patterning of its Life Energy or internal processes. Healing Whispers are powerful interventions. They address the puzzle-mystery I talked about in Chapter 6 by getting the priority order of functionality correct and by accounting for the circumstances of the individual Green Being.

When you use a Healing Whisper, your healing intent is directed toward helping that particular Green Being. The nonlinear part of the process allies with healing Powers to make the alignments needed by that particular tree or plant. Healing Whispers mobilize the *healing↔growth* cycle so that the Green Being can heal itself.

Basia and I would like to offer the gift of Healing Whisper Number One to you. You can use it to help trees and plants. It's something you can do anytime to help a sick tree or plant easily and quickly in your home or your own back yard. Remember, your actions spread from your backyard to the whole planet. We are all connected.

Basia teaches: Each of us knows, deep inside, the truth that Nature is much more than just trees, birds, and a walk in the woods. There is a vitality that pervades all form and, in fact, creates all form. Nature's vitality is what I mean when I use the phrase "**Nature Consciousness.**" In my model, Nature Consciousness has intelligence. It can exchange communication with humans. Nature Consciousness creates or adjusts form. When you use the Healing Whispers, you are making requests of Nature's Consciousness or Intelligence. You are offering your human intention to heal and asking for Its help on behalf of a sick or stressed tree or plant.

If you prefer to use a name or phrase other than "Nature Consciousness," you are welcome to do so.

Dr. Jim continues: Healing Whisper Number One is based on the idea that tree and plant inner operations are often blocked. Ideally, the biofield–or what we call the **Growth Energy**–of a tree or plant needs to reflect properly flowing and balanced natural functionality. In other words, the *orchestra* inside of the Green Being should be in tune and in sync.

The procedure for all seven of the Healing Whispers honors the Green Being as a life form because you will always ask it for its permission and thank it for the opportunity to enter its world.

Part of the procedure includes holding the Green Being with one hand and/or tapping on its roots or stem with the other hand. Holding it puts you in contact with it, literally. That's very intimate. That encourages expanded sensory sensitivity and emotional engagement in you. Tapping is an ancient Hindu form of healing. In the "Becoming a Better Receiver" tune-up exercises in Chapter 4, you were holding or tapping on your own body to activate body awareness and focus your attention.

This connection is good for you, too. Aside from obvious benefits–like slowing down, deep breathing, and focusing on another living Being–the HeartMath Institute suggests that allowing yourself to have caring emotions and thoughts is very healthy for your body.[1] Emotionally, it's satisfying to know that you are helping another. To me, the feeling of loving a Green Being is a deeply spiritual event. Encountering and getting to know such a different life form may bring you closer to the Divinity in all life, too.

Basia cautions everyone: Once you get to know a tree or plant, you can receive information about its health or get messages from it. You should be receiving positive information and pleasant sensations, not pain or discomfort of any kind. If you feel pain inside your body, stop the process immediately. Develop strong, healthy personal and psychological boundaries before you connect with and work with a compromised tree or plant again.

The Five Heralds
BE the Tree
ASK the Tree
HEAL the Tree
SAVE the Tree
LOVE the Tree

TRY THIS: HEAL THE TREE: PERFORM THE HEALING WHISPER

Read through the steps. Decide whether you feel comfortable doing this exercise. If you do not feel comfortable or have any concern whatsoever, do not do it.

For your convenience, this exercise is reproduced in your Tree Whispering: Trust the Path *notebook. Audios are also available at* www.TreeWhispering.com.

Review: Consider returning to Chapter 4 to review the "Stepping Inside Their World" guided meditation exercise.

Step 1: Go to the tree or plant that you think needs the Healing Whisper.

Step 2: Sit comfortably or stand with the tree or plant for 5 to 10 minutes. This process is best done with eyes closed, if you feel comfortable.

Step 3: Ask for permission to connect in the following way:

❑ *Breathe slowly and deeply. Close your eyes, if possible.*

❑ *Imagine the size and shape of your own heart's biofield.*

❑ *Imagine the tree's or plant's bioenergy field.*

❑ *Ask for permission:* "**May I connect with you**?"

If you feel peaceful or get a "yes," then you have permission.

If you get a "no" or feel disquiet or agitation, then you don't. Drink some water. Check on your own level of attentiveness. Then, try asking again.

❑ *Imagine a connection with the Green Being or experience overlapping of the two biofields.*

❑ *Allow yourself to enjoy, see, hear, smell, sense, feel, or intuit.*

❑ *Relax into coming from the Green Being's point of view. You may receive information or thoughts. You may feel sensations.*

Step 4: In your heart, ask the Green Being for permission to treat.
"I ask permission to give you a Healing Whisper."

❑ *If you feel peaceful or get a "yes," then you have permission.*

❑ *If you get a "no" or feel disquiet or agitation, then you don't. Drink some water. Check on your own level of attentiveness. Then, try asking again.*

Step 5: Hold the Green Being with one hand.
Touch or tap on the roots and/or stem with the other hand.
Repeat 4 to 8 times in your heart:
"Nature Consciousness: Please remove blockages and distribute this Green Being's Growth Energy where it is needed."

Step 6: Check in with your intuition. Find out whether the Green Being fully received the treatment. Say, "**Did you receive the Healing Whisper?**"

❑ *If you have an awareness that the Green Being did not receive the treatment or if you get a "no" answer, repeat Step 5.*

❑ *If you have an awareness that it did get the Healing Whisper or you get a "yes" answer, continue here.*

Step 7: In your Heart, ask the Green Being: **"Do you have a message for me?"**

❑ *Using a soft focus, allow words or images, sounds, or symbols to come to you.*

❑ *Accept whatever comes, even if you think it is nothing. Something will come to you.*

Step 8: Say in your Heart: **"Thank you for letting me into your world."**

❑ *Feel gratitude.*

❑ *If you are still touching the Green Being, release your hold.*

Step 9: Write notes about your experience in your *Tree Whispering: Trust the Path* notebook.

Step 10: If you received a message, take special care to jot that down.

Step 11: Find the right person with whom to share your experience and/or to share the message from the Green Being.

Debbra Gill, New York, New York, holistic nutrition and wellness director for a national children's art project: I walk regularly through Madison Park in New York City, where I live, and have a close relationship with a grandfather Elm and a grandmother Elm there. They were rotting and declining for a long time, and it broke my heart every time the park department would cut them back. After doing the workshop, I decided I would adopt the two trees. Why not? I pay taxes in New York City. I went to the park many times all summer to do the Healing Whispers and other Tree Whispering techniques with the Elms. I also scattered holy water around them and put down crystals that had been blessed.

The next spring, they started to sprout out incredible growth. They almost looked like a bush, they had pushed out so many new little branches and leaves. I hope–because they look so good now–that the city parks department won't cut them down or trim them back. I feel that the trees are grateful to me for being their partner and being respectful to them.

The Five Heralds
BE the Tree
ASK the Tree
HEAL the Tree
SAVE the Tree
LOVE the Tree

THE FIVE HERALDS: SAVE THE TREE

Dr. Jim exclaims: In the HEAL THE TREE Herald and with the Healing Whisper, the healing process begins inside of the tree. At that point, the tree wants to grow again.

Healing of internal functionality drives growth. Growth drives healing of internal functionality. Fully operational, healthy trees and plants are actively growing. When a sick tree or plant is HEALED and actively growing again, it has been SAVED from decline and death.

Healing ⇄ Growth

To complete SAVING THE TREE, you must be patient and calm. You must remain positive and connected to it. It can take more time than you think depending on how sick the tree was initially. You may have to return to do the Healing Whisper often. ASK THE TREE how often it needs the Whisper.

Please, give the tree a chance. It may take time until new, green growth appears.

TRY THIS: SAVE THE TREE OR PLANT

Read through the steps. Decide whether you feel comfortable doing this exercise.
If you do not feel comfortable or have any concern whatsoever, do not do it.

For your convenience, this exercise is reproduced in your Tree Whispering: Trust
the Path *notebook. Audios are also available at* www.TreeWhispering.com.

At all times: Be patient. Maintain a caring connection with the tree or plant.
Inspect it regularly and carefully. Take pictures. Watch for the tiniest signs
of healing or new growth. Leaking may start to dry up. Tiny, new leaves
may appear. Jot down notes about its progress in your *Tree Whispering:*
Trust the Path notebook.

Step 1: Put your hands on the Green Being and BE THE TREE.

Step 2: ASK THE TREE, "**Are you continuing to heal?**"

Step 3: ASK THE TREE, "**Do you want the Healing Whisper again?**"
  ❏ *If "yes," ask when, and do it if it says "now."*

Step 4: ASK THE TREE, "**Is there something else you need?**"
  ❏ *If "yes," go through the list in the ASK THE TREE section of this chapter.*
    Emphasize items such as adding compost or beneficial microorganisms.
  ❏ *If "no," ask if it wants to be left alone while it continues to heal.*

Step 5: ASK THE TREE for some intuitive insights about what is going on for
it. Be patient. The intuitive insight may take a while to come to you.

Note: This step will give you some clarity as to what additional questions you
might ask, or about doing the Healing Whisper, or if you should leave it alone.

Step 6: ASK THE TREE if it needs some attention other than what you are
capable of providing–including professional attention.
ASK THE TREE if you should contact Dr. Jim at
www.TheTreeWhisperer.com or a qualified local arborist.

Step 7: Thank the tree for letting you into its world.

Note: Know that by following these steps you are SAVING THE TREE.

> The Five Heralds
> BE the Tree
> ASK the Tree
> HEAL the Tree
> SAVE the Tree
> **LOVE the Tree**

THE FIVE HERALDS: LOVE THE TREE

Dr. Jim finishes the Five Heralds: The last
step across the bridge to the new land of
partnership, cooperation, and equality is
both the easiest and the hardest for some.

When a person gets in touch with the Life
Energy and bioenergy of another Being, there is a beautiful
experience of purity. At the point of connectedness, the balance
of purity flows back and forth. I call that purity flowing back and
forth LOVE. At the point of that pure connection and balanced
flow between the human bioenergy and plant bioenergy–that

loving–is where I see the opportunity for people to step onto the shore on the other side of the bridge.

TRY THIS: LOVE THE TREE–A BREATHING CONNECTION CYCLE

Read through the steps. Decide whether you feel comfortable doing this exercise. If you do not feel comfortable or have any concern whatsoever, do not do it.

Note: For your convenience, this exercise is reproduced in your Tree Whispering: Trust the Path *notebook. An audio is also available at* www.TreeWhispering.com.

Step 1: Put your hands on a tree or plant. Close eyes if comfortable doing so.

Step 2: Ask the tree or plant for permission to engage in this exercise with you. **"Do I have permission to engage with you?"**

❏ *If you feel disquiet or agitation, please stop. You do not have permission.*

❏ *If you feel calm or peaceful, continue here.*

Step 3: Imagine a stream of air coming into your heart area from the tree and going out your belly area back to the tree. This stream of air creates a connection cycle.

❏ *On the incoming stream of air, imagine the Life Force and bioenergy of the tree connecting with you.*

❏ *On the outgoing stream of air, imagine your Life Force and bioenergy connecting with the tree.*

Step 4: Continue to make the cycle of connection. Allow the tree's Life Force to come in at your heart area and allow your Life Force to go out to the tree from your belly area. Breathe in and out easily and gently. Allow yourself to enjoy this connection cycle for several minutes.

Step 5: Feel the purity of your shared connection with the tree or plant. Feel the back and forth flow of love between you and the tree or plant.

Step 6: Acknowledge that your connection is loving the tree or plant.

Step 7: Thank the tree or plant for allowing you into its world.

Step 8: Jot any notes into your *Tree Whispering: Trust the Path* notebook.

The Five Heralds
BE the Tree
ASK the Tree
HEAL the Tree
SAVE the Tree
LOVE the Tree

ALL FIVE HERALDS TOGETHER

Dr. Jim points to a transformation: By going through the five steps across the bridge to a new land–BE, ASK, HEAL, SAVE, AND LOVE–human consciousness may shift to allow new attitudes and practices of partnership, cooperation, and equality with all of Nature. That movement across the chasm is a jolt to some people. They realize that they are not just dealing with some object. Instead they feel, experience, and touch another living Being.

Dr. Jim describes his experience in the Five Heralds: When I touch a tree, I set the **intention** in my own heart and mind to BE THE TREE. When I am in the pure connection, I ask permission of the tree to interact with it. Asking permission is the right thing to do. Also, I quietly say "help me to understand what is going on for you." Then, I pose questions to the tree about its current state of health, what it needs and what is in its best interest. I ASK THE TREE a series of questions based on three things: first, my education as a plant pathologist; second, from the Green Centrics™ system that I developed; and third, from years of experience as The Tree Whisperer®

It takes time and effort to discover the inmost dysfunctions and imbalances. I keep asking and asking questions of the tree's consciousness until I have a clear idea of what is going on with it at physical and at–what you might call–spiritual levels. Then, HEALING its inner **dynamic balance** of symmetry and rhythms is a matter of using various well-known modern and ancient healing techniques. Ultimately, it is the tree that heals itself. Its life is SAVED. Meanwhile, I have enjoyed that purity of connection and flow–that LOVE–with another living Being.

GOOD PRACTICES

Dr. Jim says: When Basia and I give talks, many people have practical questions about good tree and plant care practices. In this section, I want to address some common questions because I have discovered that some people are unaware of some practices that are detrimental to the health of trees and plants.

Basia adds wistfully: There is no substitute for paying attention to practical things with trees and plants. For instance, performing the Healing Whisper won't help a tree if you don't find and remove a strangling band or tie. I'll tell a personal story about just that later in this chapter.

Dr. Jim continues: Chemical fertilizers rely on some ratio of only three constituents: nitrogen, phosphorous, and potassium. Their ratio is usually determined from the human point of view. The best way for a person to determine soil fertility is to have the soil tested by a reputable laboratory. Often, you will find that the soil is adequately fertile. For a very old tree, it's usually better not to give it any fertilizer until you know it is healthy on the inside. In human terms, that would be like giving a sexual enhancement drug to a ninety-year-old man without checking his blood pressure.

There is more to soil than fertility. The quality of the soil and its organic components matter as much to the trees as fertility. You can build up the quality of the soil and its organic components through various organic means.

Dr. Jim warns: When mulch looks like the cone of a volcano piled against a tree's trunk, that's "volcano mulching." When mulch is more than one to two inches thick, it can smother the roots of the tree or plant. Basic botany teaches: Roots need air as well as water. A little mulch keeps the roots moist but still able to breathe. Too much mulch cuts off the supply of air and favors the excessive growth of anaerobic bacteria. These bacteria rot the roots. I am not afraid to bend down and pull away excess inches of mulch from around a tree's base. However, if the tree has managed to survive and send many roots into the mulch, then I don't disturb it.

Bands and labels can kill trees. When planting, always look for any tie or rope around the trunk or stem. Remove any constricting thing immediately. Did I say that loudly enough? *Remove them immediately.* It doesn't matter if it is plastic or twine or metal. None of them decompose. All of them choke the tree's fluid flow, which is located a hair's breadth under the bark. If you need the information that is on a label, tie the label to a stick and put it nearby.

Dr. Jim advises about water: Big, old trees do need water, especially when it is hot and dry. A large Oak can transpire 110 to 200 gallons of water a day through its leaves.[2] A week without water in hot summer temperatures is a drought to any tree. I strongly suggest that you supplement its water supply, especially if the tree already shows signs of stress. Put a drip hose around it at the base and another at the drip line for a few hours during the night or very early morning. Do this as appropriate to the tree depending on heat or dry conditions.

Dr. Jim talks about pruning: Best pruning practices can usually be found by searching the Internet for "national standards for tree pruning." Best practitioners can usually be found by asking a neighbor whose trees look full and lush, balanced and beautiful. Or, ask your town's tree care division. But, remember, you can hurt a tree more by pruning it badly than not pruning it at all. Find a professional who has rapport and warmth, not only with his or her human customers but also with tree clients.

The best tree and ornamental pruning professionals listen closely to the Green Beings' preferences. They use their training in tree anatomy and physiology as well as their intuition in the process. Many of these caring and considerate pruning professionals are hesitant to admit that they have a rapport or communication with the trees. But, the results of their work usually show their commitment to their personal safety, correct practices and "in the zone" artistry.

Dr. Jim adds: As a certified organic landcare professional, I strongly recommend organic products and approaches. The tree or plant doesn't have a liver like people do. It has to work hard and use precious resources in its internal biochemical "recycling centers" to break down the cocktail of nonorganic constituents in various products. So, I believe the more that people use organic products, the better. When in doubt about the right organic product, ASK the tree or plant.

Start a compost pile. Compost or compost teas are excellent organic soil amendments for *keeping* trees and plants healthy.

Dr. Jim hopes to inspire: Most of all, trees tell me that people who pay attention to them are usually giving them good care. Sadly, the opposite holds, too; poor attention means poor care.

SIMPLE THINGS TO DO TO BE CONSIDERATE AND
TO COME FROM THE GREEN BEING'S POINT OF VIEW
- *Watch the weather for extreme conditions such as drought or ice storms. Then do the right things such as provide water or protect smaller plants.*
- *Cut off any ties, bands, or ropes.*
- *Use only one to two inches of mulch; no volcano mulching.*
- *Don't add fill.* • *Test the soil.*
- *Learn the basics of good pruning. Hire a professional, if needed.*
- *Imagine what it might be like to stand outside all day and all night for years at a time.*
- *Go out and put your hands on a tree—touch its Life Force.*
- *Thank the Green Being for its gifts.*

TREE & PLANT WHISPERING

HOLISTIC CHORES™

Practical Activities Done In
Partnership and Cooperation
with Trees and Plants

THE GIFT OF THE HOLISTIC CHORE FOR TRANSPLANTING

Dr. Jim starts: Basia and I offer a workshop called the Holistic Chores.™ These are instructions for holistic, bioenergy-based approaches to the practical activities you have to do anyway, like transplanting, weeding, applying products, harvesting, or preparing for construction.

As a gift, we offer you the Holistic Chore for Transplanting. Of course, you need to use commonly accepted good practices for transplanting your particular tree or plant and situation. We give you the gift of a holistic, bioenergy-based approach in the Holistic Chore to use in combination with good practices.

Basia teaches: In the "Stepping Inside Their World" exercise, you probably felt what it might be like to stand in one place, have roots in the soil, have leaves waving in the wind. That's called "coming from the tree's or plant's point of view." The Holistic Chores' holistic approach asks you to expand that level of awareness up to a level of empathy or deep emotional understanding of the problems and challenges that the Green Being is encountering in its life and in its environment.

The main idea behind Holistic Chores is respect. In this book, you are learning how to communicate with the intelligence in Nature. When the time comes for chores, you will want to walk the talk. Literally. The whole suite of Holistic Chores gives you methods for alerting the Green Beings to your intentions and helping them prepare themselves.

I'm not talking about some kind of diaphanous fantasy here. Your communications and actions can have a real impact in helping a plant reprioritize or redirect its bioenergy flow and avoid going into shock.

Dr. Jim tells a transplanting story with a very happy ending: I'll call this estate owner "Mrs. Jones." Her eight Blue Spruce trees were originally planted along her stone patio. Spruces get to be very big trees, and they were overgrowing that space. They were lucky. Mrs. Jones cared enough about these enormous trees to pay a lot of money to transplant them rather than just cut them down. The estate manager alerted me about her plans. He knew that I could warn the trees about being moved and prepare their interior processes for the shock of the transplant with my tree-healing system.

I had already done my Green Centrics healing techniques with those Blue Spruces earlier in the season, so they had already regained their strength. They also responded to my presence, so I was able to give them less advance notice than I would usually recommend to you.

On the day before the transplanting, I touched and communicated with each tree. I used my healing methods to tune-up their inner balance. Then, I warned them about the transplant plans by going through the steps of the Holistic Chore for Transplanting. One of the things I did was to describe what was going to happen to them: Very, very big machines with scoopers on the front would drive up to them. I told them "...when the machines arrive, pull your bioenergy and Life Force into your trunks and main roots."

I described that metal would be pushed down into the ground. Many of their roots would be cut. Many of their lower branches would be removed. They would experience being lifted out of their home and would ride in this metal monster about 100 feet to their new home. They would be dropped into a hole, and new, different soil would be put around their roots. I said that the people doing the moving would try to be careful with them, but they might still be injured. They might lose a big branch. Their trunks might be gashed.

When I finished the rest of the steps of the Holistic Chore and felt that I communicated all I could, the Blue Spruces told me that they understood and that their inner systems would be ready.

I told them that I would be back to tell them when it would be safe to release their bioenergy and Life Energy back into their whole structures. That was my agreement with them.

It is my nature to be concerned about my Green friends. So, late the next day, I called the estate manager.

"How did it go?" I asked anxiously.

"It went great!" he said. "They are all in their new places. We are watering them right now. They came out really easily. They just slipped up and out of the ground. We didn't have to struggle with them at all."

"Why is that?" I asked, feeling very pleased and relieved. There was a long silence on the other end.

"Well," he paused, "we think it's because of whatever you did."

Those Blue Spruces didn't miss a beat. When I returned the next day, I told them to release their bioenergy back into their roots and branches. Then, I checked on their condition. They were not in shock. They did have to acclimate to a new microclimate, but my methods helped them do that. They told me that the terrain and breezes in their new location were actually favorable to them. As the hot summer dragged on, the estate manager was vigilant about giving them water. They never drooped. They made a solid connection with the new soil and with Earth energies that were their new home.

Basia teaches: Advance notice is the key concept to all of the Holistic Chores. Just as Dr. Jim did with the Blue Spruces and many other transplanted trees, you want to give advance notice if you have transplant plans. A day's warning would be the minimum for a large tree or plant. We recommend five to seven days notice. For smaller plants, less time is okay. For house plants, a few hours to a day is good. That is a guideline.

But, the real rule is to ASK THE TREE OR PLANT how long it will need to prepare itself. When transplanting is done, you need to keep your agreement to tell the Green Being to release its bioenergy back into its roots and branches. Also, always thank the Green Being. You will probablly feel a deep sense of gratitude in return.

TRY THIS: PERFORM THE HOLISTIC CHORE FOR TRANSPLANTING

Read through the steps. Decide whether you feel comfortable doing this exercise. If you do not feel comfortable or have any concern whatsoever, do not do it.

For your convenience, this exercise is reproduced in your Tree Whispering: Trust the Path *notebook. Audios are also available at www.TreeWhispering.com.*

This process is done in two parts: (1) advance notice prior to transplant and (2) interactions during and after transplant.

Learn the particular good practices for transplanting the tree or plant you intend to move. Larger trees or plants should be transplanted professionally, but watch that they use good practices. You will do more harm to the tree or plant by transplanting it wrong. Poor transplanting leads to stress and decline. Maintain good practices for your particular tree or plant and its new location.

ADVANCE NOTICE OF TRANSPLANTING:

Review: Consider returning to Chapter 4 to review the "Stepping Inside Their World" guided meditation exercise.

Step 1: Go to the tree or plant that you intend to transplant. Sit comfortably or stand with the tree or plant. All steps may take 10 minutes or more.

Step 2: Ask permission to connect in the following way:

❑ *Breathe slowly and deeply. Close your eyes, if possible.*

❑ *Imagine the size and shape of your own heart's biofield.*

❑ *Imagine the tree's or plant's bioenergy field.*

❑ *Ask Permission:* "**May I connect with you?**"

If you feel peaceful or get a "yes," then you have permission.

If you get a "no" or feel disquiet or agitation, then you don't have permission. Drink some water. Check on your own level of attentiveness. Then, try asking again.

❑ *Establish your bioenergy connection with the Green Being or experience the two biofields overlapping.*

❑ *Allow yourself to enjoy, see, hear, smell, sense, feel, or intuit.*

❑ *Relax into "coming from the Green Being's point of view." You may receive information or thoughts. You may feel sensations.*

Step 3: In your heart, say to the tree or plant:

"**I want to transplant you on [day/date]** _____**because [give your reason]**_____**.**

What will happen to you is [brief description] _____**."**

❑ *For larger trees or plants, you will be giving them one to seven days notice. But ask!*

❑ *For small plants or houseplants, a few hours to a day is good. But ask!*

❑ *Explain–with compassion–why you want to transplant the tree or plant. Speak either quietly or aloud.*

❑ *Explain the steps that will happen to the tree or plant from your heart.*

Step 4: Ask the tree or plant:

"**Do I have your permission to transplant you?**"

❑ *If you feel disquiet or you get a "no" in your intuition, find out why.*

❑ *Do your best to set aside your human judgment and open yourself to come from the plant's or tree's point of view. Ask it for more insight into why it is telling you "no." Ask more questions. Trust the path.*

❑ *Reasons for a "no" might include: Another time of the season might be better for it to acclimate; it may have healthier roots on one side that it doesn't want cut; it may be under stress from recent conditions and would not survive the transplant now.*

❑ *If you feel a positive feeling or hear/see a "yes," continue on the next page.*

Step 5: Say to the tree or plant:
> **"I plan to return to transplant you on [day/date]_____. Is that enough time for you to prepare yourself for the move?"**

❏ *If you get a "no," ask incrementally about longer amounts of time: "one day?", "two days?", "another week?", "another month?", etc.*

❏ *If you feel a positive feeling or get a "yes," continue here.*

NOTE: If you have no flexibility about the timing, say instead:
> **"I plan to return to transplant you on [day/date]_____.**
> **Please prepare yourself."**

Step 6: Ask permission and give the tree or plant the Healing Whisper:
> Ask: **"Do I have your permission to give you a Healing Whisper?"**

❏ *If "no," skip to Step 7.*

❏ *If "yes," continue here:*
> • *Hold the Green Being and confirm your connection with its Life Force.*
> • *Touch the Green Being with one hand.*
> • *Touch or tap on the roots and/or stem with the other hand.*
> • *Say 4 to 8 times in your heart:*
> **"Nature Consciousness: Please remove blockages and distribute this Green Being's Growth Energy where it is needed."**

❏ *Ask: "Did you fully receive the treatment?"*

❏ *If you have an awareness that it did not receive the treatment, repeat the tapping and the Whisper.*

❏ *If you have an awareness that it did receive the treatment, continue here.*

Step 7: Be open to receive a message from the tree or plant you are planning to transplant. Also, be open to messages from surrounding trees or plants.

Step 8: Say "**thank you**" to the tree or plant and its Spirit from your Heart.

Step 9: Jot down any notes about your experience or messages in your *Tree Whispering: Trust the Path* notebook.

Step 10: You and the tree or plant have made a cooperative agreement about the time and conditions for the transplant.
Keep your word; return when you said you would.

DURING AND AFTER TRANSPLANTING:

Review: Consider returning to Chapter 4 to review the "Stepping Inside Their World" guided meditation exercise.

Step 1: Go to the tree or plant that you intend to transplant. Sit comfortably or stand with the tree or plant. All steps may take 10 minutes or more.

Step 2: Ask permission to connect in the following way:

❑ *Breathe slowly and deeply. Close your eyes, if possible.*

❑ *Imagine the size and shape of your own heart's biofield.*

❑ *Imagine the tree's or plant's bioenergy field.*

❑ *Ask permission: "***May I connect with you?***"*

If you feel peaceful or get a "yes," then you have permission.

If you get a "no," feel disquiet, or agitation, then you don't have permission. Drink water. Check on your level of attentiveness. Then, try asking again.

❑ *Establish your bioenergy connection with the Green Being or experience the two biofields overlapping.*

❑ *Allow yourself to enjoy, see, hear, smell, sense, feel, or intuit.*

❑ *Relax into "coming from the Green Being's point of view." You may receive information or thoughts. You may feel sensations.*

Step 3: Confirm the tree's or plant's preparation.

Note: Harsh weather conditions since the original advance notice could have prevented the Green Being from fully preparing itself and/or it might now be stressed.

Say in your heart: "**I asked permission to transplant you on [day/date]_____.**
You gave permission.
I asked you to prepare yourself. Are you prepared?"

❑ *If you feel disquiet or you get a "no," find out why and act accordingly.*

Do your best to set aside your human judgment and open yourself to come from the plant's or tree's point of view.

Ask the tree or plant for more insight into why it is telling you "no."

❑ *If "yes," continue here.*

Step 4: Say to the tree or plant: **"Please take your bioenergy and your Life Force into your trunk/stem and main roots.**
After you are transplanted, I will tell you to release your energy back into your whole structure and into your new location."

Step 5: Wait until you feel an inner sense of knowing that this "taking in of bioenergy" has happened.

❑ *If "no," wait and little longer. You may ask, "**Have you taken in your Life Force?**"*

❑ *If "yes," continue here.*

Step 6: Be open to receive a message from the tree or plant that you are planning to transplant. Also, be open to messages from surrounding trees or plants.

Step 7: Do the transplanting using best practices for your tree or plant and for your location. Or supervise others, such as professionals who may be doing the transplant for you. Remember to water frequently after transplanting according to the plant's needs.

Note: If you are accustomed to talking to your trees or plants as part of your usual care process, feel free to give them reassuring communications during the transplant process.

Step 8: Return as soon as possible after the transplant. Reconnect as described in Step 2 on the previous page.

Step 9: Ask permission to release the bioenergy of the plant.
Say in your heart or aloud: **"Please release your bioenergy back into your whole structure. Please release your bioenergy into your new location."**

Step 10: Wait until you feel an inner sense of knowing that this release or upwelling of bioenergy has happened.

Step 11: Ask permission and give the tree or plant the Healing Whisper.
Ask: **"Do I have your permission to give you a Healing Whisper?"**

❏ *If "yes," continue here.* ❏ *If "no," skip to Step 12.*

• *Hold the Green Being and confirm your connection with its Life Force.*
• *Touch the Green Being with one hand.*
• *Touch or tap on the roots and/or stem with the other hand.*
• *Say 4 to 8 times in your heart:*
"Nature Consciousness: Please remove blockages and distribute this Green Being's Growth Energy where it is needed."
Ask: *"Did you fully receive the treatment?"*

❏ *If you have an awareness that it did not receive the treatment, repeat the tapping and the Whisper.*

❏ *If you have an awareness that it did receive the treatment, continue here.*

Step 12: Be open to receive a message from the tree or plant that you have transplanted. Also, be open to messages from surrounding trees or plants.

Step 13: In your heart, say **"thank you"** to the tree or plant and its Spirit.

Step 14: Jot a few notes about your experience or messages you may have received from the tree or plant in your *Tree Whispering: Trust the Path* notebook.

Step 15: Water regularly! Visit the plant and check on it.
Repeat the Healing Whisper process from earlier in this chapter and do anything practical that is appropriate.
Continue with good growing practices.
If it is still not doing well, ask it if it wants professional help.

Linda Farmer, Massachusetts, herbalist, gardener, and long-time Tree Whispering student: The earth of the property where my new house was built was extremely disrupted during construction. As a result, in the last two years, I've put a lot of effort into composting, remineralizing the soil, and making new plantings. Because most of my plants are herbs, when I plant, I think ahead to harvesting time. So, I want to do the best I can for each plant right from the beginning.

Most of my plants are already started as I get them from other herbalists. My first step is to make a connection with the Life Force and Growth Energy of the plant while it is still potted.

I find that each herb has its own personality. Using the Transplant Chore technique, I ask it for information about the best location, orientation, and depth in the ground. I find that some don't care, that they just want to be in the soil. Others are more particular, asking for a certain position in the garden and certain distance from other plants. Still others want to be turned a certain way and set-in at a certain depth. Considering the intelligence of Nature within each plant makes me pay attention to the fact that all species are not alike. I pause, ask, and appreciate each one.

I feel that transplanting with attention to the plant's instructions really pays off when it comes to harvesting the herbs for eating, drying, or distilling. I know I have healthy plants. Of course, I ask them for permission and about the best time to harvest their leaves or flowers. That's when I'm reaping the benefits of having paid such close attention to transplanting them. I always remember to say "thank you" for their bounty.

BRIEF REVIEW OF YOUR ACCOMPLISHMENTS

Basia repeats: I have to say this again for your protection. Once you get to know a tree or plant, you can receive information about its health or get messages from it. You should be receiving positive information and pleasant sensations, not pain or discomfort of any kind. If you feel pain inside your body, stop the process immediately. Develop strong, healthy personal and psychological boundaries before you connect with and work with a compromised tree or plant again.

Basia recalls earlier chapters: In Chapter 3, you learned about the categories of message that can come from trees and plants. If you didn't already know that they were smart, you learned about scientific studies about **cognition** and **intelligence**. Messages were shared from various trees worldwide. You may have wondered if or how you could receive your own messages from trees and plants.

In Chapter 4, you prepared your sensitivities so that you could communicate and receive nonverbal information. You learned that plants produce biofields around their physical forms because they are alive–just like you do. You focused your attention, tapped on your own heart and head to bring their neural impulses into harmony.

When you stepped inside of the tree's or plant's world, weren't you amazed at how complex and sophisticated its life processes were? Perhaps you even felt closer to the Divinity in all life, as have many students and graduates.

Chapter 6's information about how trees and plants really operate from the inside-out gave you insight into how they get sick. Then, in Chapter 7, you learned about how Dr. Jim helps them heal their internal functionality with the Five Heralds.

Your personal paradigm shift–a transformation of your consciousness–has progressed. You are crossing the bridge into the new land of *cooperation, partnership, and equality* with Nature. And, you know you are not alone in making this crossing.

The heart of it all is that you can now help the trees you love, and feel good doing it. Feel good in body, mind, and Spirit.

This chapter's topics encouraged you to take actions. First, to validate your own inner truth. Then, to follow a regime of Being, Asking, Healing, Saving, and Loving trees and plants.

We have given you two practical gifts to use in your own backyard: the Healing Whisper and the Holistic Chore.

What is the next thing that you can do?

BE COURAGEOUS, SHARE MESSAGES, BE AN AMBASSADOR

Dr. Jim says: By this point, you probably have notes from your experiences and messages from the trees or plants written in your *Tree Whispering: Trust the Path* notebook. You can be their spokesperson, their ambassador. Who else do they have to spread their stories and their wisdom? You may even ask the tree or plant you are healing what messages it would like you to share with others.

Basia talks about courageous action: You can be courageous and talk with other people about your experiences and about the messages that you get from members of the Plant Kingdom and from Mother Nature. And, it takes courage. I know.

In the early years of teaching Tree Whispering, I bought a small house plant at my favorite garden center–a plant that I had never seen before. I was so excited. This plant had multiple canes braided and growing together. I talked with it, and it flourished. Well, it flourished for a while.

Suddenly, it dropped all its leaves. While checking it closely for the possibility of insect damage, my jaw dropped. There, at the top of the interlaced canes was the tiniest, green twist-tie holding them together. I was shocked because I knew that I checked the plant for just such a thing when I bought it. I know how dangerous ties and bands can be for plants. I removed it immediately. I provided all seven Healing Whispers and other Tree Whispering healing techniques to the plant. I felt relieved and lucky that it survived, and eventually thrived.

Basia continues: Soon afterward, I returned to the garden center while doing regular errands. I found a shelf of these braided plants ready for sale. I looked closely. Sure enough! All of them had the same tiny green twist-tie on them. Surreptitiously, I started to remove the ties. Then, I stopped. I realized that I had to walk the talk. Just removing the ties might help these few stragglers but it wasn't going to change the practices of the garden center business.

Many excuses went through my head: "I'm late for my next meeting. Maybe the manager isn't here. What if she would hate me? Oh, it wasn't that important."

"Oh, yes, it is that important!" I reminded myself.

I retwisted the ties I had taken off and then marched right to the office.

"Excuse me. I'd like to tell you about a plant I bought here about four months ago." I assured her that I wasn't looking for my money back, and I told her what happened.

"Now, can I show you what I found in your greenhouse?" I took her to the shelf of plants. She and I pushed leaves away and found the twist-ties.

She shook her head, frowned, and said: "Yup. These darn things are gonna kill these plants. Then, you're right. People won't know what happened and are gonna bring them back and want their money back."

Together, we removed every twist-tie. She told me that she would check all the plants for ties or ropes that were in the store now. And, she would tell her staff to be on the lookout when replacement orders would come in. She would make it a policy of the garden center to warn their customers about ties, bands, and ropes on house plants and landscape plants and trees.

Whew! Not only was she not angry with me, but my courage inspired her to educate people and to save plants and trees.

Have you had a similar moment? Did you find the courage to talk with someone who could do something about a problem?

Basia has a few other suggestions: Ask the server for a pitcher of water in a restaurant where you find a dry plant. Water it. Talk to the manager and kindly request that they put their plants on the same kind of watering schedule as when they rotate their food reserves. Suggest to them that it looks bad for their business to be feeding and watering people but to forget about the plants in their establishment. Gently remind them that there are a lot of people like you who come in to have a meal but who might be upset by their lack of care for their plants.

How about the plant that you find in a dark corner of a store or inside of a company's bathroom? I am pretty brash, so I usually just drag it out into the light somewhere. Then, I talk with the manager or owner. You might want to reverse that order of things to be polite. A kind word about the beauty of the plant and its light requirements might educate that person. Attention to detail means survival for businesses. Attention to their plants should be part of their business's success.

Communing with Nature and telling people about what you learned may even turn out to be a valuable survival skill if moving to the countryside or going "back to the land" becomes a choice or a necessity for you.

> **COURAGE. Noun.** *The quality of mind or Spirit that enables a person to face difficulty, danger, pain, etc., without fear.*
>
> *Synonyms: audacity, bravery, backbone, daring, determination, dauntless, fearlessness, fortitude, gallantry, gameness, guts, heart, heroism, intrepidity, lion-heartedness, mettle, nerve, pluck, Spirit, stoutheartedness, temerity, tenacity, undaunted, valiance, valor.*[3]
>
> *Roget's II: The New Thesaurus and Dictionary.com*

TRY THIS: MUSTER COURAGE TO BECOME AN AMBASSADOR FOR TREES AND PLANTS
Read through the steps. Decide whether you feel comfortable doing this exercise. If you do not feel comfortable or have any concern whatsoever, do not do it.

For your convenience, this exercise is reproduced in your Tree Whispering: Trust the Path *notebook. An audio is also available at www.TreeWhispering.com.*

Step 1: Think about the range of people who you know.

- *Family*
- *Friends*
- *Neighbors*
- *Children*
- *Clubs you belong to*
- *Other parents*

- *Business associates or coworkers*
- *People at your place of worship*
- *People who do services*
- *Garden center manager*

- *Town officials*
- *Alumni or current classmates*
- *Newspaper editor*
- *Online groups*
- *[other]_____*

Step 2: In your *Tree Whispering: Trust the Path* notebook, make two lists of people using the categories below.

- *Title the first list: "People with whom I can share trees' and plants' messages as they truely came to me."*
- *Title the second list: "People for whom I must adjust the wording of the message so that it seems more neutral."*

Step 3: Write down the actual names of people in your life on these lists.

Step 4: Think about the kind of courage it will take to share messages. Will you have to find the right moment? Will you have to explain something first–such as explaining that you are doing an exercise from a book you are reading?

Step 5: Designate yourself the trees' or plants' ambassador. What messages did a specific tree or plant want you to share on its behalf?

Here are some suggestions for sharing their messages.

❏ *Talk directly about your personal experience with someone of your choosing. Begin by sharing something from your personal point of view, then share the communication you received from the specific tree or plant.*

❏ *Talk about the messages the tree or plant wanted you to share on its behalf.*

❏ *Talk about the needs or health requirements of the tree or plant to someone who can do something about them.*

❏ *Write a note, article, or letter to someone. You may also post it online.*

❏ *Post the message you got at* www.TreeWhispering.com.

❏ *Do something creative: tell a story, paint, draw, compose music, do a play, etc.*

❏ *Lead others–especially children–to do something meaningful and/or creative.*

❏ *Bring people back to the tree so they can experience something themselves.*

❏ *[Add your own]_____.*

Step 5: Jot a few notes about your experience into your *Tree Whispering: Trust the Path* notebook.

Step 6: You may go back to the Green Being. Tell it from your heart what happened when you shared its messages. Then, go out and share that message or experience. You are the trees' and plants' ambassador.

Dr. Jim praises tree and plant ambassadors: If you get a message or experience from one or more trees or plants, it is a gift. Like any gift, you may want to go out and share it. Then, you become an ambassador for Green Beings. By being their ambassador, you are one with all. We are all connected. Bless you for your courageous work.

Mary Cypress, Racine, Wisconsin, sTREEt artist: I was terribly upset at the Racine Parks Department for aggressively cutting down so many beautiful trees in the city's parkway.

Due to a recent storm, many branches came down. I feel that the city used that storm as an excuse to cut down trees. Homeowners no longer had the choice to either spare or cut down the trees.

As I lay in bed at night, angered by this tree slaughtering, I sensed the trees whispering to me, "Do not be angry. Your anger doesn't do us any good. What is to be will be. Would you take that anger and turn it into something positive that would benefit and bless us?"

In the morning, I had an idea. With *magical* markers in hand, I set out to find a certain young tree that had been cut down only a few blocks from my home. I knelt down by the stump, took out my colored markers, and began drawing and writing words such as "I love you" and "Thank you for growing." I thanked it for its young life, and all of its gifts, then blessed it.

As I got ready to leave, I heard children's voices chattering behind me. I turned to see little faces peering down at me. A woman–their teacher from the daycare center–was commenting on my drawing. I asked the children if they would like to send the tree some love and sign their names. I handed each of them a marker. They wrote their names and drew hearts. My Spirit was encouraged—my sadness was turned into joy.

Even as I write this, I hear the distant buzz-saw ending another tree's life. Yesterday, I found the stump from a tree that was more than one hundred years old; it was recently cut down in the parkway. It had outgrown its small space and heaved a sidewalk slab. The tree spoke a beautiful message to me of gratitude for living and growing in the neighborhood.

I have since *drawn images and written on* five more trees. These artistic forays have reduced the sting of seeing a tree stump. I now travel equipped with my emergency tree-stump art-bag, filled with healing, blessings, and love.

Leo G. Kelly, West Haven, Connecticut, arborist and master gardener: What I learned in class was in line with what I thought and felt about trees all my life. That was so reassuring. I was trained as an arborist in a forestry school about thirty years ago but ended up working as a fireman and a paramedic. I just retired from that work when I took the class. It really changed my life. Dr. Jim suggested to the students that we get involved with the trees in our towns. So, I did! I brushed up my arborist's license and jumped in. I became the Tree Commissioner.

Sally Malanga, West Orange, New Jersey, business owner and tree protector: My husband and I just spent four years of our lives and a major financial investment to fight a misguided interest in my town that wants to cut down a thousand trees in one of the few remaining historic, old-growth forests in New Jersey. I don't believe that providing sports for young people is more important than preserving a forest. Instead, the forest could be a prized resource for education in environmental studies.

I am passionate about saving trees. I feel that as living Beings they deserve to live and have a right to stay in their place and grow. Also, they provide housing and food for many other creatures. The kind of future that I want to see is where people wake up to the benefits that trees provide and, so, would give the trees equal protection.

Basia adds encouragingly: Whether you simply share a personal experience with a friend, get involved with your town like Leo did, or go all the way into the kind of courageous activism that Sally spearheaded, I believe that sharing will feel good to you. It's not that scary, really, once you do it.

Other people will appreciate your candor and courage. Each of us who steps out and talks about love of trees, experience healing trees' inner health, and trees' wise messages will contribute to the shift in consciousness budding and growing on our dear planet now.

A Vision: From Your Yard to the Whole Planet

Basia looks ahead: Dr. Jim and I have a very positive and expanding vision for the work of Tree Whispering and for the expansion of consciousness on Earth. We have a lot of faith in people's compassion and resourcefulness. We observe positive changes in people's awareness all around us. We want to address the expansion that you can directly and positively influence.

Whether you realize it or not, advances in quantum mechanics and experiments led by the Global Coherence Initiative show that each and every one of us is connected to everything and everyone.*4*

Explanations of this connectedness by the Global Coherence Initiative implies that every individual who has a heart-based intention–whether acting alone or in coordination with others–can have a profound impact on the health and well-being of the entire human population and global environmental circumstances.

The Global Coherence Initiative was launched by the Institute of HeartMath. The Global Coherence Initiative's mission is

> **The Global Coherence Initiative is a science-based, co-creative project to unite people in heart-focused care and intention, to facilitate the shift in global consciousness from instability and discord to balance, cooperation and enduring peace....**
>
> **The Global Coherence Initiative is designed to help individuals and groups work together, synchronistically and strategically to increase the impact of their efforts to create positive global change....**
>
> **The Global Coherence Initiative will include an important scientific measurement component. Advanced sensing technology, now being developed at the Institute of HeartMath, will allow us to observe changes in the earth's magnetic field and test the hypothesis that the earth's field is affected by mass human emotion, positive or negative....**
>
> **Our long-term goal is to correlate the following: coherence-level data collected from the GCI community with changes in the earth's magnetic field, along with changes in various social, environmental and health outcomes....[4]**
>
> WWW.GLCOHERENCE.ORG/ABOUT-US/ABOUT.HTML

Basia encourages: In day-to-day living, most people make use of an invisible web of interconnection—called the Internet or World Wide Web—all the time to get information and to communicate with other people. And, we humans live in another invisible web, too. It is the web of bioenergy interconnections and sacred oneness that is a mystery. This web of connection and sacred oneness is like water to the fish. All of us live in it, but we just don't see it.

Even if we can't perceive the strands that link us, we are able to know that the latticework is there. I believe that all of us can access it as easily as we close our eyes, breathe, and imagine going beyond our physical limits.

Dr. Jim makes use of this multidimensional grid of connection and interconnection in his healing work.

Dr. Jim explains how: Trees operate in community. It's not just that their roots overlap or grow together. Even trees of different species operate at a level of community. Their biofields overlap. In that overlapping, they communicate with each other and strengthen each other. What most people call a forest is actually one really, really big tree, even if there are different species. All the trees, plants, animals and other organisms all act together in a self-reinforcing, self-creating system.

Basia finishes: Let me ask you this: What if you were part of that self-reinforcing, self-creating system?

Just because you have legs and arms and they have roots and branches doesn't mean that both of you are so different. The ideas Dr. Jim and I have presented show that there is a fundamental similarity or affinity between you and plants as living Beings.

What if your communications and healing efforts with the tree in your backyard were actually overheard, multiplied, and magnified around the neighborhood or even around the world in a mysterious, web-like network of energy and consciousness?

That would be a remarkable opportunity for the well-being of the Plant Kingdom and the health of the whole planet. What I am trying to say is this: Whatever you do to commune with and to heal a single tree can reverberate locally and even globally. Dr. Jim and I believe that it is possible.

So, he and I have the vision we call "from your backyard to the whole planet." And we mean it. The trees and plants that you heal become stronger and healthier. Their greater vigor improves that of their neighbors near and far.

Your actions to heal the trees may also heal yourself in body, mind, and Spirit. Your new thinking, ideas, and practices of communicating with tree and plant consciousness or Spirit ripples out to other people, and they become more respectful. Throughout the invisible tapestry of life's essence, news of your choices and actions as an individual spreads and touches all others. And, news of all others returns to you through the invisible web of life and bioenergy as well.

That's a long way of saying: What you do and–more importantly–who you are matters to yourself, to all people, and to all Green Beings on the planet.

Chapter 9: The Tree Whisperer's Insights

Insight 1: Trees and plants don't get over stress factors easily and must manage their inner resources.

*Insight 2: Stress is additive. The effects of three or more stress factors can lead to **decline**.*

Insight 3: It is possible to save a tree or plant in decline.

Insight 4: Trees and plants are *their goals.*

Insight 5: Trees and plants operate in community.

Insight 6: Plants and trees signal for help–which attracts pests.

Insight 7: We are all connected.

Insight 8: To solve any situation, come from the tree's or plant's point of view.

Insight 9: Plants and trees tell the truth.

*Insight 10: Assumptions put us out of balance with **Nature**.*

Dr. Jim Conroy, The Tree Whisperer,® explains: The discoveries I have made depart from the conventional, linear interpretation of trees and plants as mechanisms. My insights have not been proven by the scientific method; rather they are discoveries that come through other valid ways of knowing. I make observations of Nature. Then, accepting that trees are alive allows me to incorporate empathy for them based on my own life's experiences. In all the years I've **communicated** with them, I've got a lot of practical knowledge of their ways. I've come to trust the consistency of it. It's true that my intuition plays a role in generating these insights. Intuition uses the right-brain functions of nonlinearity and wholeness. So, I feel that my intuition is a powerful ally. And, you might say that my working conditions are conducive to visionary experiences. Standing quietly with my hands on a tree's bark, feeling its **biofield**, is a meditative and revelatory experience. So, I come to know about trees' lives directly from their Source.

Trees and plants have shared much with me about their inner physical workings as well as their more mysterious ways. Knowing about their workings through these insights will help to expand your relationship with them and will provide guidance in your healing efforts with them.

Ms. Basia Alexander, The Chief Listener, adds something about ways of knowing: Dr. Edmund Bourne, in his book *Global Shift—How a New Worldview is Transforming Humanity,1* talks about the coming expansion of people's attitudes about what are valid ways of knowing. Ancient and indigenous ways of knowing the world through experience, empathy, intuition, or even mystical perceptions suffered near extinction as a result of the rise of the scientific method over the last more than 400 years. Now, he says, those ways of knowing are on the comeback.

Dr. Jim and I believe that our work is on the leading edge in the new, burgeoning field of "participatory and subjective" methodologies for acquiring valid knowledge. We strongly believe that personal engagement and experience with a life form supplements and reinforces objective, repeatable science.

INSIGHT 1: TREES AND PLANTS DON'T GET OVER STRESS FACTORS EASILY AND MUST MANAGE THEIR INNER RESOURCES.

Dr. Jim says: People think that just because it rains after a drought, a tree is over the drought stress. Wrong. From our discussion of how a tree goes into decline from Chapter 6, it's easy to see that a stress factor, such as drought, would compromise the **internal functionality** of the tree. A human example might be prolonged lack of sleep. One good night's sleep helps, but it does not return your body to full functionality. The sleep deprivation may have taken a toll on your body, which you don't get over easily.

Once compromised, a tree cannot easily repair or restore its own health. It has dedicated resources to compensating for the stress factor. For example, its circulation system has slowed and there are blocks in its xylem and phloem in various places. This is sometimes why you will see sap oozing out of the lower trunk of a tree. Another example: Some of a tree's cells–such as the cells in the growing points–may have lost the ability to divide. That's why you might see exceptionally small leaf buds at the base of existing leaves or at the tip-ends of branchlettes in late summer or late autumn. Or, you might see very few leaf buds at all. This is very dangerous for the tree because it will need new leaves in order to produce food for itself in the next season.

1–MANAGING THEIR RESOURCES: AN ALL OR NOTHING BID

Dr. Jim tells this story: It was late August in Connecticut and my customer's Hickory tree had a few very small leaves on it. It was probably suffering from two major stress factors but was not quite in full decline. However, it was headed into decline because it could not produce much food with few, small leaves.

Dr. Jim mentions feedback loops: Trees and plants operate in beneficial feedback loops. All related organisms such as insects and diseases also operate in beneficial feedback loops with the plant. Once you understand this, then it is clear that disturbing any single part of these beneficial loops, disturbs the whole looping system. This causes imbalances in Nature.

The Hickory's healing session consisted of a patchwork of network patterns cobbled together, which I didn't understand at the time.

This might sound mysterious or cryptic, but I'll briefly relay the topics from my treatment notes: Getting growth processes

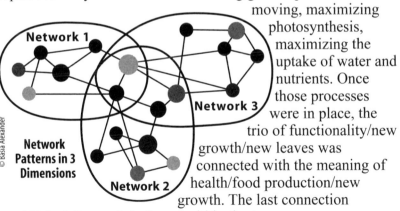

moving, maximizing photosynthesis, maximizing the uptake of water and nutrients. Once those processes were in place, the trio of functionality/new growth/new leaves was connected with the meaning of health/food production/new growth. The last connection established **dynamic balance** within the tree as repair/health/new growth with filling out and being beautiful.

I didn't understand it at the time, but I accepted that the tree's innate **intelligence** knew what it wanted so I left it at that. I trusted the path upon which I was being guided by Nature's consciousness.

At the end of the session, the Hickory told me: "*Now, I will HEAL.*" Normally, I would expect the results of an August healing treatment to show up the following spring.

Two weeks later I saw that the tree put on abundant new leaves. I was shocked! In that very short period of time in "tree-time"and even though it was late in the season, the Hickory used its remaining resources to push out new leaves immediately. By committing all of its resources–in an all or nothing bid–it was now able to bring itself back to health, produce more food to survive the winter, and push out new leaves the next spring.

HICKORY TREE

I will use up my energy now to make more food for myself. I will risk this: I will not conserve that energy to try to live through the winter and try to make leaves in spring. I want to get healthy, put on new growth, fill out, and be beautiful.

Dr. Jim recounts: I was concerned about its ability to push out new leaves the next spring since it seemed to have used up its buds. But, leafing out there and then in late summer, made sense in order for it to produce more food and set up its own growing↔healing cycle. That way it was also preparing for the coming spring. It may have conserved a few buds and it was also able to set new buds. Setting new buds means that a plant or tree creates specific new tissues that will become leaves. In a subsequent, short healing session late that Autumn, I helped it to increase its circulation of fluids to the leaf buds, replacing unhealthy cells with healthy cells.

The Hickory had undergone unknown stress factors before I originally arrived. Then, my biofield healing treatment gave it the boost it needed to manage its remaining resources and do the right things to heal itself. Sure enough, the next spring it was on-the-spot with abundant, large, new leaves. It grew with lush, beautiful growth and regained its health throughout the rest of that year.

1–MANAGING THEIR RESOURCES: AN EXISTENTIAL DILEMMA

Dr. Jim remembers: I do my research and development on annuals and crops at an organic community-supported garden in northern New Jersey. One year, the "Davis" variety green bean seedlings grew as far as their second bract of leaves when there was a cold snap–no sun, lots of rain–that lasted over two weeks. The small seedlings had a life-or-death dilemma: Should they let their roots drown or should they let their stem and leaf tissues become waterlogged? With so little sunlight for transpiration and photosynthesis, do they pull as much water as they can up from their roots taking the risk of imbalancing the water/sugar/nutrient ratio in their tissues, or do they let some precious roots drown?

With my Green Centrics™ System, I was able to help them bring their inner physiologies into a more balanced state. The bean seedlings were able to hold themselves in that balanced state for a few days so that they could tolerate the extreme environmental factors. The rain stopped and the sun came out soon enough.

INSIGHT 2: STRESS IS ADDITIVE. THE EFFECTS OF THREE OR MORE STRESSORS CAN LEAD TO DECLINE

Dr. Jim says: Let's say, in your life, you add some lack of sleep to deadlines at work. Then, an emergency occurs within your family. Sound familiar? If you were healthy, you could probably handle one of the stress conditions at a time without ill effects. But, put one stress on top of another and another, then your own health is compromised.

It's the same with trees. Not only don't they recover from stress factors easily, but, those stresses add up. Take the stress factors very seriously that we talked about in Chapter 6. Trees may not be as resilient as you think. Sometimes the trees look healthy to a casual observer, but their inner functionality is compromised. Once compromised, they don't get over the effects of multiple stress factors and can go into the "pulling in" pattern of decline.

INSIGHT 3: IT IS POSSIBLE TO SAVE TREES OR PLANTS IN DECLINE.

Dr. Jim warns: I want to highlight why it is possible to save a tree in decline with my **holistic**, hands-on, biofield-healing, no-product, green-friendly, and sustainable approach. First, I am not adding stress to the tree since I don't add products or do invasive techniques. Therefore, it doesn't need to use up precious resources to break down the components of those products. Second, my focus is on restoring the dynamic balance within the tree's internal constitution–its state of health–through the use of biofield healing techniques. The techniques are similar to those that work for people in hospitals that include complementary or integrative holistic techniques in their programs. Third, most importantly, I usually discover that the tree wants to live, because I ask it. So, healing techniques serve to set up the conditions within its **bioenergy** field so that it can heal itself.

The healing techniques give the tree or plant a chance to turn around its flow of **Life Force** from a declining or pulling-in pattern to a growing or pushing-out pattern. Decline can be reversed.

Declining trees and plants that I have treated are here to tell the tale.

3–DECLINING TREES CAN BE SAVED: COPPER BEECH TREE IN PARK

Dr. Jim tells the story: In a lovely Long Island, New York, town, the curators of a park asked me to save a Copper Beech tree that was already ribboned for removal. The tree was very sick but they were truly tree lovers and tree protectors. They would not allow it to be taken down, if it had a chance to live. When they found me, it was already December, so the tree had already lost the few leaves they told me it had that year.

Normally, if I were to treat a tree in December, my work would "wake it up" from dormancy. So I usually don't treat trees at that time. However, this particular tree was fighting to regain its health rather than "going to sleep" as it should have. It would not have survived the winter. So, I was still able to interact with it and heal it.

The tree's circulation was stuck. The tree could not go into dormancy; it was fighting to live. In order for me to help unblock its circulation system, which is the flow of fluids in the xylem and phloem, I had to get the circulation moving again and get the plant "chemistry" to clear up. I accomplished this "clearing" of the "chemistry" in the bioenergy field of the tree but not by physically doing anything to the tree.

I have to interact with the tree's bioenergy field in such a way that I rearrange its allocation of energies so that there is a little "extra" available to it. Then, it can drive its circulation and its own process of clearing the plant chemistry. Once the circulation was cleared, the tree would go into dormancy by itself. It would contain within its design intelligence and formation dynamics the "knowledge" or "memory" that it had some renewed circulation with which to drive its inmost processes the next spring. It could now go to sleep for the winter.

Dr. Jim reports: The Copper Beech tree did survive the winter and started to recover the next spring! I checked on it often, giving it tune-ups. By August, nine months after my first healing treatment, it showed good foliage on the limbs that were still alive. Of course, dead limbs will not grow new leaves. The curators told me that its leaves were a bit bigger and more plentiful. They agreed to postpone any pruning so no more stress would be put on the tree. I gave it another healing treatment in autumn so that it would go into dormancy properly again and to prepare it for the extremes of winter.

Sixteen months after the original treatment, the tree was flourishing. Leaves were even bigger and more abundant. After the dead wood was pruned out by a professional tree service, the curators enthusiastically agreed that it looked a lot healthier.

In later years, since its recovery, it has shed older branches on its own and pushed out new branches close to its trunk. The tree's growth pattern wants to take the path of least resistance. The Beech has told me that it is literally becoming a new tree.

COPPER BEECH EXPLAINS

I use less energy growing new branches. I'll get rid of these old, useless branches and just grow new ones.

Dr. Jim explains what the tree said: The tree can push out new growth more easily on younger tissue than it can add new growth onto older, compromised limbs. The bigger limbs that are further up in the structure have too much unusable tissue. The tree looks much smaller than it did, but it is still old and wise.

3–DECLINING TREES CAN BE SAVED: "WE WERE GOING TO CUT IT DOWN NEXT WEEK"

Another story from Dr. Jim: One of the board members of a house of worship in a New Jersey town is a deeply committed environmentalist, organic gardener, and tree lover. It troubled her that the majority on the board decided to take down the declining Native Dogwood tree in front of their building. She found me, The Tree Whisperer, just in time and called saying, "They want to cut it down next week! They think it's too old. I would hate to have someone tell me that I'm too old and I should be taken down."

Basia and I agree with her wholeheartedly! Trees do decline, but they rarely get "too old." "Too old" is often an excuse that people will use to cut down a tree that they don't like. "Too old" is an excuse overused by some tree care professionals, too. Don't accept it as an excuse! Don't give up on a sick tree, unless it is a hazard to people or a building. A tree in decline can be saved, if you can communicate with it and understand its inner workings.

I asked the board members of the house of worship to give my services a try and to give the tree a chance. They did, on both counts. The tree recovered beautifully. It grew robustly for the remainder of the season. Years later, it is still gracing their building's entrance.

3–DECLINING TREES CAN BE SAVED: TOO MUCH SALT

Dr. Jim frowns: At a Greenwich, Connecticut, property, the snowplow truck broadcast salt crystals right into a mature, hundred-yard-long Hemlock tree hedge and burned the needles right off. Salt that fell to the ground went into solution and was taken up by the roots. By spring, every tree in the hedge was browning, especially at about six feet high where it was hit directly by the salt. The hedge was in decline, looking terrible. I did a biofield healing treatment. At the end of my treatment, I always check with plants if they need any conventional-type of care.

Part of the communication from the hedge was that it would accept the addition of some organic compost to its soil to build up the microbial activity that had been destroyed by the salt. But, it didn't want that right away. As a community, the trees of the hedge specified a wait-time of exactly five weeks before adding the compost. I told the homeowner "June 1st and not before!" It also wanted some natural fertilizer three weeks after the addition of the compost. Compost and fertilizer may be sensible treatments to support a tree or plant *after* it has gone through some of its inner healing process. But, always ask the **Green Being** first.

At that five-week point after my treatment, the very happy homeowner called me to tell me how good the Hemlock hedge already looked. It had put on new growth and was beginning to fill in. She also mentioned that a local landscaper stopped her while she was walking her dog. The landscaper wanted to know what she did to the hedge. He saw it when it was all brown and was stunned at its recovery. She told him about my treatment.

3–Declining Plants Can Be Saved: Corn Rebounds in Iowa

Dr. Jim smiles: Crop fields aren't flat, even in Iowa, which is pretty flat. Most acreage rolls gently. Corn in low-lying areas can suffer decline after heavy rains because it stands in water for extended periods of time. That corn becomes stunted. The stunting shows that it is in decline. Generally, waterlogged corn never fully recovers. Even after the water dries up and the corn resumes growing, the corn doesn't catch up in size or in yield to the high-ground corn. It's a financial loss for the grower.

I was called out to look at a four-acre area of organic corn that was stunted due to extended waterlogged conditions. After my bioenergy treatment, this corn rebounded. Its decline was reversed.

The grower was thrilled! He said, "I never saw corn do this. The corn came back extremely fast, caught up in size, and yielded as well as the rest."

Insight 4: Trees and Plants *Are* Their Goals

Dr. Jim explains: Trees and plants are their goals. Sometimes their goals are related to their own health, such as to be healthy or to be strong. Sometimes their goals are related to their Life Force, such as to grow vigorously or to put on more leaves.

Their goals could be to enhance their own situation, such as to be the centerpiece of the yard. Or, their goals could be to correct a human error, such as to overcome severe or improper pruning. Trees and plants don't have goals or think goals. They *are* their goals. What people would call trees' or plants' "goals" are multidimensional energies infused within their current Life Energy and infrastructure.

Many people hold the belief that a goal is something to strive for. In some cases, this is correct. But, what if the goal existed in the same time and same space dimension as our current situation? Suppose that all we had to do was to emotionally and energetically connect to the goal that already was in the same timeframe as our current situation?

For trees, their current situation always lives inside their goal. And conversely, at the same time, the goal lives inside their current situation. It's a fluid situation; it's nonlinear. Therefore, the two-way connection of the current situation and the future is made. It is in two directions. As the goal becomes a physical reality, the relationship of the goal and current situation does not change. If people did that, we wouldn't be striving toward our goals; we would be allowing the goals to occur. It would be a two-way connection between the current situation and the future, bringing those two pieces together. Within the current situation exists the future, and within the future exists the current situation.

Dr. Jim chuckles: If you don't understand this, go ask a tree. However, you might have to stand there a couple of days with it.

4–GOALS: THE BLUE BLUE SPRUCE IN RUMSON, NEW JERSEY

Dr. Jim remembers: In September, I was called to a property in Rumson, New Jersey, by an arborist concerned about the health of a Blue Spruce on a small estate. It was about 25 feet tall and probably 18 to 20 years old. The arborist had been trying for years to turn its health around since the tree held a key position in the yard. By September–very late in the growing season–the Blue Spruce was looking very brown, not blue at all. By that time, it would be hard to see improvement in a tree since it is usually preparing to go into dormancy. I faced a quadruple problem with the owner: He was unsatisfied with the arborist's work, still had a sick tree in a key position, didn't want to wait until the next spring to see results, and didn't believe in my work.

I proceeded with my Green Centrics treatment, after the arborist's prompting. In the network patterns of the tree's bioenergy field, I perceived that its "plant chemistry"–its biochemical processes and enzymatic reactions as well as the ratio of water, nutrients, and sugars flowing in its fluids–was not organized, coordinated, or synchronized. I also perceived that the vascular system, which carries the fluids, showed many blockages of tissue. Imagine if ketchup were mixed with crystalized honey and white school glue. Yuck. Then imagine trying to squeeze that mixture through a bent straw. Impossible. That was the situation the Blue Spruce faced.

In order to clear this situation–to reestablish the proper flow of the biochemical processes, to correct the ratio of fluid constituents, and to break up the blockages–I use only my conscious **intention**, focused attention, and established healing techniques. I do not apply products.

Dr. Jim specifies: In the language of my treatment notes and records, I "cleared" the plant chemistry's thickness; got the xylem and phloem "opened up," "increased circulation," and adjusted other activities necessary for the synergy of functionality.

I was fortunate to be there when the tree's declining bioenergy flow shifted upward. I felt the "fireworks" and had a strong feeling in my body that it would have new growth in a matter of time. In fact, later that afternoon, I commented to the estate manager, "Doesn't the tree look better?" He looked at it with a smiling glimmer. Then, he called over one of the workers and said, "Take a look at this tree." The estate worker said, "Yeah! I think he fixed it!"

In the process of performing my Green Centrics healing system with the tree, I discovered its goals. Its first goal was to put on new branches and new growth at the tips of existing branches. The second goal was to "fill in"–in other words–to have that new growth fill existing blank spots in its physique. Those goals seemed logical to me. The third goal made me smile. It wanted to be a fully grown *Blue* Blue Spruce. This goal seemed to come from the very *heart* of the tree. The goal sounds to me like a desire to fully express exactly what it is–as a living Being. Those three goals are mutually supportive and can co-exist. Within those goals are included its current situation: very brown in September. The tree made the two-way connection between its current situation and its goals.

Basia interjects: Let me try to say this goal idea in another way. As a human being, I can understand that I must acknowledge my own current reality in order to move toward something I desire. For example: It would be impossible for me to travel to the store if I did not acknowledge or realize that I was at home, or vice versa. In treating this tree, Dr. Jim realizes that–in its own way–the tree held within its unique tree consciousness a knowledge about its own situation and a understanding of its desired state of health all at the same time.

Dr. Jim finishes the story: In treating this tree, I learned something about how I approach my goals. Then, I incorporated this insight into the Green Centrics System in my quest to constantly improve it.

The following May, I visited the *Blue* Blue Spruce. Its goals were a visible current reality. It put on substantial new growth despite a cold winter. The new growth was filling in the blank spots and, of course, it was very deep blue. The tree was expressing itself as a fully grown *Blue* Blue Spruce.

4–GOALS: SMART CABBAGE HEADS AT THE FARM

Dr. Jim reminds: It sounds a bit strange but remember that trees and plants *are* their goals. They don't have goals. The difference in those statements comes from a different relationship with time. They are *being* themselves fully in the moment so both their current circumstances and their goals live together in that space.

Such was the case with the cabbages at an organic farm. This was to be a fall cabbage crop. When I first saw them in September, they were quite small in size, considering that the people intended to harvest them before winter set in. Temperatures in September were already getting cooler and days shorter, which does not favor quick growth.

The innovation for me was that I could perceive the small physical cabbage head inside of the larger biofield of the cabbage head. The small physical head just had to "fill in" in order to fully occupy the space that the big biofield head already formed. The goal of the Cabbage was already there within the biofield level.

More than that, the small physical head and the big biofield head were connected. In the process of growing, the small physical cabbage was already *being* the big cabbage head. The passage of time within the human dimension would help it to "fill in" within the energetic aspect of the biofield. Since plants don't recognize time and since they *are* their goals, they just grow to fill in the physical level until the physical reality occupies the energetic level of reality. You could say that when they first started to sprout, that *is and was* their goal.

Someone might say that the goals are all in the genetics. I say that the genes help support the energetic biofield level already formed. Genetics supports moving into the energetic or biofield reality. The whole plant at every level holds connections between the physical reality and the energetic reality.

At the farm, those big cabbage heads fully expressed themselves and were harvested in early December. Their goal was physically reached.

INSIGHT 5: TREES AND PLANTS OPERATE "IN" COMMUNITY

Dr. Jim draws a distinction: Trees and plants operate in community, but this is not just because their roots touch. Trees may operate in community while they are not near enough to each other to have touching roots. Trees and plants of the same species or of similar, nearby species may operate in various layers of community. It may be Oak with other Oaks, Beech with Beeches, Oaks with Beeches, etc. What makes the community? It is the sharing of signals among individuals. What is this signal that keeps trees and plants operating in community?

Scientists say that it is chemical or hormonal molecules traveling on the wind or in the underground rhizosphere. It is true that plants send out such molecules.[2, 3]

But that is not the community I am talking about. I believe that community is formed among trees and plants through their bioenergy field vibrations or *song*. One member of the community sings to others in the community. It is the same song for similar species. That song is also compatible or in harmony with related species of a larger community. Native Americans have told me that they hear and dance in rhythm to the trees' songs during their ceremonies.

Dr. Jim continues talking about community: Have you heard the expression "can't see the forest for the trees"? Well, people usually can't see the community for the trees. In other words, our idea of what a tree is has been shaped by the cultural notion that this thing with a trunk and branches is the tree. When I say the word "community," you probably think of all these individual things we call "trees" teaming up to work in a group.

I ask you to expand your thinking. Community–the synergy of all those individual trunks with branches and leaves–really acts  as the whole tree. Perceiving individual trunks would be like looking at your fingers and thinking that each of them is a separate individual—not seeing your whole hand. Your fingers operate in community *as* your hand. It is much the same with trees.

Community among trees and plants is like a group consciousness such as a flock of birds or school of fish. All of the members operate as one. It is the community that is the *whole* tree or plant. Each member of the community sends out a signal or a *song* to the other members. This is how each member stays healthy and continues to *actively* grow. Each member of the community helps other members using the various levels of community. If any member becomes sick, it falls out of community. Why? To protect the health of the overall group.

Here's an example. When you transplant several trees or plants of the same type, one or two of them might die. Why did the rest survive? Those that died may have been weak or sick, so they fell out of community in order to protect the others. All trees or plants operate for the good of the community. Other layers of community cross a wide variety of trees and plants on both a physical and biofield level.

Dr. Jim adds: The last question you might have is "How big is the community?" It varies. I believe that communities are like overlapping rings. One community is connected to another, connected to another. You might think of the symbol of the Olympic rings and how they overlap. I do not know how far communities of trees really go. Like a tsunami wave that touches every shore–communities of trees and plants are potentially enormous. A community may not be infinite, but I believe that, ultimately, all trees form a global community.

After all, we are all connected.

5–COMMUNITY: THE OLD BEECH AND THE YOUNGSTERS, LONG ISLAND, NEW YORK

Dr. Jim's example of how trees' community works: In this chapter, I already told you about how well the Old Beech tree in the park on Long Island, New York, was recovering. During my many visits, I explained the idea of trees operating in community to the curators. There was an open field around the senior Beech where they wanted to plant more trees.

They asked, "Would the Beech tree like buddies?"

I said, "Yes, of course!"

Their park contained acres of wooded land. The three of us walked into the forest to find small Beech trees that could be transplanted. The curators asked me to prepare three young trees with a healing session before the move so that they wouldn't go into shock. Then, afterward, I did another session to balance them to their much smaller root system. It's hard to get a good root ball when removing trees from a forest.

I discovered that the senior Beech and these three youngsters already started the process of forming a community for themselves. However, the community could not be fully formed because the individuals were still not healthy enough. After additional healing treatments, which restored dynamic natural balance to all, I could feel the community forming. Through their stronger songs, I could sense the support that each tree was giving the others. The senior Beech was giving the three youngsters a sense of groundedness. Since their root systems were so small, the groundedness would help them have a closer connection to Earth, and to put down new roots into the new soil in which they were planted. They could put on new roots faster. Meanwhile, the three youngsters had that boundless, youthful buoyancy that you see when human children are running around in play. The tree youngsters gave the senior Beech the resilient, full-of-life pep it needed to fuel its own inner healing process.

This is only one example of how community works among trees. Through their sharing of Life Force–their song–every healthy tree or plant bonds in some way with the others nearby. Each supports all the others' growth and well-being.

5–COMMUNITY: YES, THE ORANGE IS HERE SOMEWHERE

Dr. Jim recalls: In a lovely Florida backyard, the homeowner showed me her prize Orange tree. It was looking poorly. I set out to do my healing services. At a certain point, the prize Orange asked to be reconnected to another Orange tree. When it got sick, it fell out of contact with the other. I didn't have to see the other tree in order to make the connection between the two biofields. I had a general sense of it being "over there somewhere." The two Orange trees would form an Orange community. One would help the other stay healthy.

When my healing services were done, I told the woman what happened in the treatment. She declared: "There is no other Orange tree around here! None of my neighbors have Orange trees!" I was confused. The trees are usually right. In her protest, she spoke quite loudly and that must have roused her husband from his slumber in the house. He came outside and walked us to the fence at the far corner. He pointed beyond the immediate neighbors and on the other side of the fence. Yes, there it was–the other Orange tree.

5–COMMUNITY: THE HOTEL LOBBY GANG

Basia adds her story: This was one of those spacious, two-story hotel lobbies. While waiting for Dr. Jim to check out of the hotel on one of our many speaking engagements, I thought I'd have a "little chat" with a beautiful potted tree. It was not as cordial as I expected. Gruffly, it communicated to me that "they" didn't really care about humans because "they" had their own association, right there in the lobby, without anyone really knowing about it. When I looked around, I saw dozens and dozens of philodendrons hanging from above the registration desk, a clutch of potted palms on the other side of the door, and many other plants scattered throughout the area. I laughed! There they were—like Martians in our midst—having tea parties, and the people didn't have a clue.

5–Community: Knitting the Greens

Dr. Jim describes: I was working on a golf course in the Northeast United States that had trouble in the heat and humidity of summer. Some of the grass on the golf course greens died. Some grass remained, but it was spotty. The superintendent roughed up the soil and planted new grass seeds in the dead spots. As the new seeds began to germinate and send their new, green sprouts through the soil, I was amazed at how quickly the older, established grass wanted to connect with the sprouting seeds, and vice versa. There were two purposes here. First, the established grass could help the younger seedlings continue to sprout and become established. Second–most importantly–all of the grass could cover the ground, conserve moisture, and shade each other's roots and blades for optimal growth conditions. I felt their urgency to knit together and form a community. That made me believe that all their lives depended on their bonding together and knitting together quickly.

Insight 6: Plants and Trees Signal for Help–Which Attracts Pests

Dr. Jim talks about signaling: When a tree or plant is sick and falls out of community, it sends out a signal for help. That call for help also attracts insects and disease organisms.

What comes first? The so-called "pest" or the weakened tree?

Weakness in the tree or plant comes first. It is the associated biofield messages that the Green Being broadcasts about its weakness that attracts most insects and diseases. I believe it is the song they sing and the scents they emit that are the attractants. Only the most aggressive or nonnative insects and diseases will go to healthy trees.

When I use the Green Centrics System, I plug the sick tree's biofield into its community. When it is restored to the shared biofield of the community, the other trees can help the healing process so that the sick tree can become fully operational. In another sense, the whole community gets the treatment.

Dr. Jim asks: What about when a tree or plant has had an insecticide, fungicide, or other chemical put on it to knock back a pest? I have found that just killing the pests will not stop the tree's call for help. It was the tree's or plant's signal requesting help that attracted the pest in the first place. Healing the internal operations and reconnecting the tree into its community will stop that message from being broadcast and stop more pests from being attracted.

Without healing the internal operations, the vicious cycle continues. People are tempted to spray again, not knowing that the tree or plant is still sending out the plea for help, which attracts more pests. It is only by restoring the inner constitution–the health of the tree–and rejoining it into its community that the vicious cycle can be broken and the tree be brought back into full health.

6–Signaling: The Wrong Plant in the Wrong Place

Dr. Jim describes: On the South Fork of Long Island, New York, people build large homes at the edge of the beach so that they can see the Atlantic Ocean. But, these homeowners don't want people on the beach or on the roads to see into their homes, so they put in privacy hedges. This particular property used Privet for their hedge—a small-leafed plant with dense, criss-crossing branches. Privet is usually a vigorously growing plant, but the community of shrubs at this house was just too close to the salt water, salt air, sandy soil, and weather extremes of the beach. Its downward spiral of weakness over several years attracted insects, called Scale, which further defoliated it by crawling along stems and congregating at the base of leaves. When I arrived one spring, I could see right through the hedge in many places.

The plants could not get up and move. The homeowner didn't want to replace them. The only holistic solution was to help the hedge regain its inherent health so that it would naturally resist the Scale. Healthy plants naturally resist diseases and insects. Any university extension agent or landscape professional will tell you that.

I did my bioenergy field treatment. I did not use any products whatsoever, nor did the homeowner. When I returned several weeks later, delightful little oval leaves were filling in the bare spots. New, light-green growth was everywhere. What about the Scale? I examined the new leaves and did not see any sign of the insects. The hedge grew strongly for the remainder of the season. But, the plant was still in the wrong place. Stress from the weather, the ocean, and the poor soil would add up again. The hedge would need lots of attention with–preferably–organic products and periodic inner strengthening with my bioenergy treatments in order to stay healthy.

INSIGHT 7: WE ARE ALL CONNECTED

Dr. Jim talks about community and connection: We are all fundamentally forms of energy, say the quantum physicists. Therefore, we are all connected in at least that way, if not in a more vast, spiritual way. I see the truth of this connection through my work with the Life Energy and biofields of trees. And, that is a very spiritual experience for me. In working with the Life Force of trees, I get to see what a fine-tuned instrument they are. My Life Force being connected with the trees' Life Force helps me to see that we humans are also fine-tuned instruments. So how could it be a surprise that two such amazing instruments are connected?

I could talk to you about quantum physics, or show you the billions-of-years-old family tree of organisms on Earth, or mention the teachings of various spiritual systems, but I cannot convince you that we are all connected. You either know this is true in your own experience of life, or you do not agree. And that is okay.

Tree Whispering® workshops are designed to be experiential. We lead people through guided visualization experiences. We ask people to go outside and touch the trees, feeling their Life Energy and their majesty. People who learn our tree healing techniques report a profound experience of kinship with the trees and plants that they touch. They tell us that they know "we are all connected."

7–WE ARE ALL CONNECTED: NEW HOPE AFTER A TERRIBLE MISTAKE BY A WASHINGTON STATE APPLE GROWER

Dr. Jim relates a happy ending: On a tour of Northwest Pacific fruit growers, one owner approached me with a gloomy look and a desperate request–would I please come to his orchard as soon as possible? The previous year, he accidently sprayed the trees in one field with a popular total vegetation control chemical. Intending to use a fungicide, he simply picked up the wrong tank without looking and started spraying. The chemical completely defoliated the trees. Anguish was plaguing him. His trees did not bloom and were very thin and weak. This was not just an income for him. He loved his trees. He was worried about losing many years of production and even losing the trees entirely. He knew he made a mistake that hurt the trees.

First, I interfaced with the trees. Yes, they were sick, but not fatally. My work boosted their ability to process out the foreign chemical and to generate more leaves that season so that they could feed themselves. This would put them well on the way to healing themselves. It was not hopeless, but the grower was in such deep pain over his mistake that he felt hopeless. That was the real problem. He kneeled down next to me while I was treating the trees. I explained how I was restoring the trees' interior workings and told him about the steps involved. That was intriguing for him because he didn't know such a thing was possible.

Then, I asked him to put his hands on the tree, close his eyes, and allow himself to receive a sensation or a feeling. Meanwhile, with my hands on the same tree, I communicated to it that the owner was there, too. I told the tree that the owner wanted all the trees to survive and thrive. In a few minutes, we both felt the tree's Life Force. We felt positive activity in the trees. Most of all, by connecting with the trees, the owner felt his hope for their well-being return. He was joyous! He grinned from there to the Mississippi. He was reconnected to the trees emotionally. His hope for the survival of the orchard was restored.

After fearing a loss of years of production because the trees would either limp along or have to be replaced, all turned out well. The following year, there were enough apples for limited production. The year after that, the trees were back in full production and he was a wiser and grateful man. Trees, people, and everything—we are all connected.

7–WE ARE ALL CONNECTED: FINANCIAL TROUBLES? JUST ASK THE CORN

Dr. Jim recalls his innovative approach: In the early years of system development, I did a trial on a corn field belonging to a conventional grower, Bill, in New Jersey. He was agreeable to have any bit of help he could get for his corn. As I did my healing treatments, I had a clear impression that Bill was having some kind of money problems. But, Bill was not the kind of guy I could walk up to and say, "Your corn told me that you are having financial difficulties." That just wouldn't fly. So I decided to try another approach.

I knew from my years in the agricultural chemical business that good farmers take the time to walk through their fields. They look for signs of diseases and insects. They look at the rate of growth. They think about the crop and how they want to market it. I suggested that Bill walk his fields. His reaction was a shock.

"Listen, young man! The price of corn is going down this year. The price of fuel is skyrocketing! I have a stack of bills this high for this corn already." He held his hands two feet apart. "I don't know whether I can afford to harvest it! So you are telling me that I should go out and walk these fields?"

Without a moment's hesitation, I said, "Yes! Listen, just walk a few rows. Look at the corn. Think about it. It's really a good crop. You never know what kind of idea you might come up with to market your harvest."

And so he did. Not only did he walk the fields, but he also had an excellent harvest. The best result was his new idea. Instead of taking his corn to traditional markets for pennies, he decided he would shuck and bag the corn for wild animal feed. The following year, he bought a bagging machine because he was doing so well.

INSIGHT 8: TO SOLVE ANY SITUATION, COME FROM THE TREE'S OR PLANT'S POINT OF VIEW

Basia illuminates: What do Dr. Jim and I mean when we say, "come from the tree's point of view?"

Let me ask you, what does it mean to come from anyone's point of view? Perhaps your spouse, child, friend, or a coworker has said, "Gee, if you could see it through my eyes, then you would understand." That's what we mean. But, trees don't have eyes, they have roots. You have to feel as if you are standing in their roots, trunk, and branches, looking out at the scene from one place.

> *I think that I shall never see a poem as lovely as a tree.*
>
> *A tree whose hungry mouth is pressed against the earth's sweet flowing breast.*
>
> *A tree that looks at God all day and lifts her leafy arms to pray.*
>
> *A tree that may in summer wear a nest of Robins in her hair, upon whose bosom snow has lain, who intimately lives with rain.*
>
> *Poems are made by fools like me but only God can make a tree.*
>
> TREES, BY *ALFRED JOYCE KILMER (1913)*

Maybe now this old poem will take on a new life for you. Mr. Kilmer stepped into the tree's world and felt what its life must be like. He told us that he understood its Divinity and appreciated it in the only way he knew how: iambic tetrameter and rhyming couplets.*4*

8–TREE'S POINT OF VIEW: FLY UP TO GET THE BIRD'S EYE VIEW

Basia shares one of her secrets: I like to visit notable and large trees. Before I go–or before Dr. Jim makes a house call to a large property–the Internet is my first stop. I plug the address into one of the mapping sites then zooooom way in on the satellite view. Check out a few trees just for fun. Search on *Santa Barbara, California, Moreton Bay Fig Tree,* or *Tane Mahuta, Waipoua Forest, Waipoua Kauri Forest, Northland, New Zealand,* or *Fortingall Yew tree, Fortingall Church, Perthshire, Scotland,* and go to the satellite view. Just look at how big they are from the bird's eye view. To come from the trees' perspective, I ignore the roads and the buildings. That lets me see how they interrelate in community and with the land. For me, that's a good first step in "coming from the plant's point of view."

8–Tree's Point of View: The Yoyo of Not Enough then Too Much Water

Dr. Jim describes the situation: On the East End of Long Island, New York, a developer transplanted 27 Linden trees, all in a row. By the time I was asked to work at the property, they were in their location for about two years. I could tell that they were not healthy trees when they were originally transplanted. I got there in the heat of summer with temps in the upper 90s and low 100s Fahrenheit. At first, the Lindens were dry and showed signs of wilting. Then the watering system was turned on. The soil got too wet and Phytophthora set in.

Linden Trees at Development Site, Long Island

We are weak! We are trying to get water into the leaves. Our leaves wilt because they don't get enough water. Then, too much water at our roots! Our roots are sitting in water! The disease in the soil comes alive and colonizes our roots. Now we have bleeding spots on our trunks. Do not put chemicals on us. We would have to diffuse them and that would take our precious energy. We are not sure if we have enough strength to do that. How will we survive?

Dr. Jim explains what the Lindens were saying: The Lindens were not healthy to begin with. Excess heat and no rain caused their inner **feedback** cycles to slow down. Circulation had nearly shut down and photosynthesis was inhibited. So, what little food the trees were producing was not moving to create new growth.

It was already late August when I started to heal these trees. I'll give a few of the treatment details in case you're curious. The plant chemistry needed clearing. Then, it was important to get the little food that the trees were able to produce moving around in the tree, again. By that food moving around and breaking down, fuel would be produced for the trees' operations, such as circulation. Having circulation moving would, in turn, connect the feedback loop to get food moving around and breaking down to create even more energy for the trees. With a return to healthy operations, the trees could naturally resist the effects of the disease organism.

See how everything is connected when you come from the tree's point of view? More energy and especially increased circulation would help drive photosynthesis. Therefore, maximizing the photosynthesis processes became a priority. I had to connect to the feedback loop to make more food. More food would increase energy production and, thus, more energy production would increase circulation. Everything needed to be operating in sequence and then simultaneously. Go ahead and try to visualize this in three dimensions because a tree is a multidimensional Being. By late September, the Lindens were regaining their health and the canker spots were beginning to clear.

8–TREE'S POINT OF VIEW:
EFFECTS OF DROUGHT WHILE WATER IS EVERYWHERE

Dr. Jim talks about dehydration: At the same developer's Long Island property, seven Holly trees were transplanted the previous year. With the onset of summer, they weren't getting enough water. Their roots hadn't had a chance to grow outside of their burlap-covered root balls when the extreme temperatures hit. They went into "shut down," like you might say of a person in cardiac arrest. Leaf buds dried out on larger branches. Smaller branches were also drying up. There was no new leaf development and they were looking very thin.

Of course, the developer–a tree-loving man–had the watering system going but the trees weren't getting enough. Just like any tree after a drought, their exquisitely designed inner operations shut down. When a tissue of any kind–plant or human–is hydrated, that means that the water can easily transfer across the cell wall and operate in balance with all the interior structures. When a cell becomes dehydrated, its wall is no longer as permeable, and the inner structures shrink. My first bioenergy healing priority was rehydrating the xylem and phloem–the "tubes" themselves. Sadly, we can't just hook up an intravenous solution in the tree's "arm" like we can with people. These inner "pipes" are fragile tissues, only a few cells across. They are as delicate as a china cup. You can't hit them with a metaphorical sledge hammer. As I stood with my hands on a larger branch of one of the Hollies, I noted that the tone of its communication to me was fragile-sounding. What was the Holly's point of view?

HOLLY TREES AT DEVELOPMENT SITE, LONG ISLAND

Ask my friend Water to visit me. But ask that he come like breath, as a vapor. He will come as a thief in the night. He will slip into my cells quietly and slowly. Ask the earthen hardness of my cells to soften and give way. The walls will yield if you will surround them with a softening Light. Then, ask my friend Air to step aside so that Water might take its place inside my tubes. This will be a relief to me. Then, I can drink, but only a little. Slowly. Slowly.

Allow my friend Water to do his job as a bearer. Ask him to carry food and deliver himself into my arms and to my good children at the ends of my arms. My buds are dried up and I cannot cry for them. But the Fire in the Water will revive them. Ask my friend Fire to move quickly into new leaves. Ask Air to join Fire in my leaves. They will work together. Then, Water will carry. More children will grow.

Thank you for your help.

Dr. Jim interprets what the Hollies were saying: In their symbolic but very moving communication, the Hollies were telling me how to get their circulation systems going from their point of view. Using my knowledge of the Four Classical Elements—Air, Fire, Earth, Water—the metaphors were the trees' way of telling me to use what I would call "hydrating" bioenergies. In this way, they told me to first hydrate the cells of the xylem and phloem "tubes" from the tips of the roots to the ends of the branches. Then, fluids, which could be drawn up from the roots, could move as streams all the way to the buds at the ends of the branches. Whatever food they could make inside of their existing leaves could then be transported–especially to leaf buds–in order to get cells dividing again. Any leaf buds that could be re-hydrated would provide even more food-energy to support the establishment of a new growing↔healing cycle. Then, I asked the developer to turn up the watering system.

Later, the Hollies told me that the soil they were living in wasn't acidic enough and asked me to lower the pH. That confirmed soil testing that was done earlier without my knowledge. The Hollies added that the developer should not attempt to lower the pH for another three to four weeks, until they had healed. At first, when the water was turned up, their exquisitely designed natural operations could not gear-up to take advantage of the presence of water. It's like leading a horse to water, but he won't drink. In this case, the Hollies *couldn't* drink right away. As they began to incorporate the healing treatment, their ability to assimilate and use the water increased.

After about three weeks, tiny new leaves appeared at the ends of branches. Then, they told me they were ready for the soil around them to be more acidic. The timing of the soil amendment was crucial so that it didn't put stress onto the Hollies' healing process. By about six weeks after my healing session, the ends of live branches were filling out. Two more weeks—mid October—and the Hollies had abundant leaves.

I stepped into the Hollies' world. I allowed myself to listen at a deep place to their assessment of their condition and of what would solve their problems. It's the kind of thing you can do, too. Just try it!

8–TREE'S POINT OF VIEW: A MYSTERY SOLVED

Dr. Jim visits the countryside: A big old Catalpa was lagging behind others in leafing out during spring. It showed other signs of being stressed, including small leaves and dead branches. I used my Green Centrics System to get its inmost parts and functions operating in harmony and in sync.

At one point, I had to balance the whole tree's physiology to a foreign substance inside the tree. The substance–over the years–had caused the tree to weaken. The tree was continuously fighting it. During the later steps of the system, the old tree told me–from its point of view–that the foreign substance was metal. I looked around the tree and did see old, rusty metal signs nailed into its trunk. But, the tree clearly indicated that the nails and signs were not the source of the metal problem. Metal came from another source.

I finished my treatment without knowing the source of the metal. A few weeks later, I happened to be telling someone from a nearby town the story of the metal in that tree. They said, "Oh! That tree is due east from where a coal-burning powerplant is located." I later asked the tree, and it confirmed that it accumulated an airborne source of metal in its structure— mystery solved! Just by looking at the tree, no one could know that accumulated metals were the cause of the weakness, unless they came from the tree's point of view.

Just by looking at an old tree, we might forget that it was once young and living under different circumstances. The Catalpa was younger when the coal-burning power plant was venting heavy metals into the air. The west winds carried the metal toward the tree. As the tree aged, it gradually took more and more of the metals inside of its physiology. After many years, the accumulated metals along with other additive environmental stress factors weakened the tree's inner physiology to the point where it showed stress and decline.

There is nothing that anybody can do to get metals out of a tree's tissues. However, my treatment can balance the tree's bioenergy to the presence of metal in its physiology. The tree did recover and lived to be a healthy tree.

8–TREE ROOTS' POINT OF VIEW: POT-BOUND TREES

Dr. Jim tells: My customer's home was on a hillside. The Beech tree she asked me to treat was looking stressed. I did my normal Green Centrics treatment. At one point, I had to balance the tree to where it lived. I quickly understood–coming from the root's point of view–that there was some constriction in the growth of the roots and that the roots could not grow any deeper.

As I explained this insight to the caretaker, she nodded in understanding. She said that not very far underneath the soil surface was a layer of shale rock. This would explain why the roots could not grow deeper. After treatment, I gave the caretaker, some practical tips such as watering on the upside in the heat of summer. The Beech recovered.

Similarly, an Oak tree was growing between another customer's garage and the neighbor's house. Coming from the Oak's point of view, the roots were pot bound and the tree was showing signs of stress. When the tree was small, it thrived there. As it became larger, the space was too small. I told the tree it could send out roots in the direction of the neighbor's open yard. At the same time, I told the customer to warn the neighbor not to disrupt their yard because that would hurt the tree. The Oak fully recovered.

8–Tree Canopy's Point of View: Growing Up into Salty Breezes

Dr. Jim recalls: The Maple trees were living near a river bank, not far from the river's outlet to the ocean. They were showing signs of environmental stress. I sought the cause of the stress by asking the trees. Coming from the trees' point of view, they told me that when they were young, their leafy crown was protected from the salt breezes. This made sense to me because they could be protected by nearby houses and other trees. They added that as they grew older, their leafy canopy grew above the houses and taller than other trees. The salt breezes from the ocean were now beginning to cause stress.

The breezes can't be stopped, but the trees's physiology can be healed. The treatment would keep the trees healthy in spite of salt breezes blowing on them.

Insight 9: Trees and Plants Tell the Truth

Dr. Jim tells the truth about people's lies: On many, many occasions when treating trees and plants on people's properties, I have had to balance the Green Being's natural functionality to the presence of some product that was applied to it.

See, they use precious resources to clear foreign substances out of their systems in much the same way that our livers purify our blood. In all cases, I ask the property owner or manager what he or she has put on the tree or plant. Sometimes the people are straightforward and tell me what was done. Sometimes, I get an evasive answer: "Oh, nothing." I continue to ask until they admit that they used something or other on the tree or plant.

The Green Beings tell me the truth.

9–TELLING THE TRUTH: CHEEKY SOYBEANS

Years ago, I was working with an organic soybean grower. In one field, the crop showed a thin stand, weak and unhealthy. After my third attempt to get the truth from him, I politely told him that I had to perform a balance between the soybeans and something that was applied to the field. He finally conceded that he used some kind of soil augmentation product bought from a catalog that sold primarily human-based health products. The soybeans told the truth!

9–TELLING THE TRUTH: WILLOWS WITH ALIEN DNA

There was a couple who asked me to check their stand of Willow trees at an old farm. They failed to tell me that the trees had been genetically modified. I started to work on the trees. I felt a sense of dark presence in the area. Initially, I had to balance the trees to the presence of a foreign material inside them.

It was then that the phrase "genetically modified" came to me. So I asked the trees. They told me that they were fighting the foreign genes in their DNA. The trees knew they were changed and they didn't like it.

I have a passionate distaste and loathing for the practice of genetic modification with trees and plants. It is putting an entirely alien force into the genetic structure, bioenergy, and the biofield of a Green Being. It **compromises** their natural processes and inner functionality, and risks the entire species.

The Willows at the farm preferred to subsist on their own. They did not want me to bring them into a higher state of health. I left there very sad that humans would tinker with such arrogance and disrespect for **Mother Nature's** creations.

9–TELLING THE TRUTH: BAD DIGESTION FOR THIS HONEY LOCUST

The assistant superintendent of a well-known golf course in the Northeast United States brought me in to do healing treatments on a few key trees. The president of the course, who can play on the days that the course is closed, asked what I was doing. The assistant explained. The golf course president understood and said, "Take a look at the tree in front of my house."

After I had my hands on the Thornless Honey Locust in front of his house, it was clear to me that something had been sprayed on it that did not agree with it.

I asked the assistant, "What was sprayed on the tree?"

He said, "Nothing. If anything had been applied to the tree, I would have been told about it."

I asked him to double-check. A few days later, he called with the news. Without his knowledge or approval, an outside contractor had applied an insecticide to the tree. Trees always tell the truth!

9–TELLING THE TRUTH: SOMETIMES ONLY THE TREE KNOWS

Dr. Jim smiles and recalls the scene: Sometimes people don't know what the truth is, but the trees do know.

In a coastal California town, an enormous and historic tree was mysteriously ailing. The past town arborist really loved this tree and asked me to help it. He told Basia and me that he cared for this tree so much he would check on it after a storm before he did anything else.

On the day Basia and I arrived, three arborists–including our host–and three contractors greeted us. We found the tree in a very small, triangular town park, bordered by a large highway, a road, and a parking lot on the third side.

Everyone had their theory about what was going on with the tree. Some thought it was too close to the main highway and the problem was pollution. Others felt that carvings into the trunk were a problem. Still others blamed compaction of the soil. Someone even mentioned that homeless people liked to visit the tree and may have used it as a bathroom. These theories were all logical and sensible best guesses from their human point of view.

Then, I put my hands on the tree. I assumed its point of view. The first thing I felt from the tree was the sensation that it wanted to move toward the main highway. In fact, I felt that if the tree could have stood up and walked over to the highway, it would have done it. That's how strong the feeling was. This phenomenon gave me a clue that perhaps the tree wanted to move away from something on the opposite side.

The parking lot was on the opposite side. My heart posed the question to the tree, "Is there something in the parking lot that is hurting you?" The tree replied, "Yes."

Through a series of questions, I found out that a problem happened in the parking lot about 80 years before, that was affecting the tree now.

I paused my treatment to talk to the group. I suggested, "If you tell me what happened in that parking lot eighty years ago, I will tell you what is going on for that tree."

They put their heads together in conference while I went back to the tree to continue my healing treatment.

I repaired the internal functionality including circulation and photosynthesis. After the tree told me that healthy patterns were now reestablished, one additional problem came up. It said that its roots were being "stung" whenever heavy rains occurred. So, I gave some additional attention to the functionality of the roots to help strengthen them. This whole process took about an hour and a half.

I returned to the group to discover that they had solved the mystery. About eighty years before, the town experienced an earthquake. Much debris from the earthquake was dumped into the area that is now under that parking lot. This information completed the puzzle.

During that eighty-year period, the canopy of the tree grew much larger. Correspondingly, the roots extended their growth toward the parking lot. Now, when it rained, some of the run-off from any remaining debris was adversely affecting the tree. The tree had to continuously tolerate this stinging effect when it rained. Over time, the tree's inner operations were weakened.

My treatment repaired the tree's internal functionality. It also helped to strengthen the roots to resist the effects of the run-off.

As a practical solution, the contractors discussed the possibility of installing a dam in the earth between the parking lot and the tree's roots, thinking that might help.

In any case, the tree went on to be healthy and continued to grow. All along, the tree knew the truth of what was wrong. All I had to do was come from the tree's point of view and ask it.

INSIGHT #10: ASSUMPTIONS PUT US OUT OF BALANCE WITH NATURE

Basia offers some views on balance: Have you ever stood on a rock with a rippling stream flowing all around you? Were you steady on your feet? Was the rock buried deep enough in the stream-bed to be steady or did it teeter-totter on another rock? Did you *almost* fall in—but saved yourself by stretching your arms, bending your legs, or shifting your torso? Our ability to balance our bodies depends on inputs from our senses about body position while our muscles make fast adjustments. Stability results—or not. Maybe you shifted and swayed but fell in the stream anyway.

I will talk about what balance means in a larger context later, but, first, Dr. Jim tells two important stories about how trees physically balance themselves.

10–OUT OF BALANCE: OAK ON THE EDGE

Dr. Jim says: I worked on a seventy-five-year-old Oak that was living on the edge of a sheer twenty-foot cliff. During my treatment, the tree told me it was well-balanced on the edge. I noticed a dead limb on the tree that had grown in the opposite direction of the drop-off.

I asked the tree, "Should the dead limb be cut off?"

OAK LIVING ON EDGE OF CLIFF

Oh, no! Please don't cut off that limb. I use it to stay balanced on the cliff, especially in storms or high winds. Please allow me the chance to fill in and to grow new branches in the direction of the dead limb before you cut it off. This way, I can maintain my balance.

Dr. Jim continues: Trees understand balance. Living on the edge of a drop-off, this Oak had roots growing in only one direction, so natural limb placement and root growth had to compensate to create balance.

What about people who don't communicate with a tree; who don't ask it about pruning? They might see that dead limb and cut it off. We say that ASKING THE TREE, the second of the Five Heralds, allows the *person* to be in balance with Nature.

10–OUT OF BALANCE: OAK ON THE 18TH HOLE

Dr. Jim says: An Oak tree was a key feature on the 18th hole at a well-known golf course. It lived on the edge of a steep drop-off to a sandpit. I was called in because it was ailing. Before I arrived, someone removed a living limb that was opposite the drop-off. This limb was keeping the tree balanced. One of the early parts of my treatment was to work with the growth of the tree to set down more roots in the direction where the large limb was cut from. This would help the tree balance itself and stop it from toppling over the drop-off on the opposite side. The Oak recovered its health after my treatment and it stayed upright.

Basia continues with some views on balance: All of the creatures of Nature engage in their own unique balancing acts–not only as individuals maintaining upright stature but also as groups acting in ecosystems. The balance of Nature refers to the idea that ecosystems usually seek dynamic balance–called "stable equilibrium." In other words, predator and prey species or herbivores and their food sources live within balanced relationships so that both can continue to exist.

Continued existence–surviving and thriving–currently seems to be a critical question for each of us in our relationship with Earth as a whole as well as with the ecosystems that are close to home.

From our point of view as spokespersons for the Plant Kingdom and as guardians of our work, Dr. Jim and I suggest that many people are relying on assumptions about Nature that result in their being out of balance with Nature and result in Nature going out of dynamic equilibrium and into extreme fluctuations.

The very nature of assumptions is that they are unquestioned. We ask you to question the truth of these ideas.

ASSUMPTIONS

Assumption 1: Killing pests will solve a tree's or plant's problems.

Assumption 2: People can dominate and control the Plant Kingdom, the Insect Kingdom, and the world of microorganisms.

Assumption 3: Science and technologies have made people superior to Nature, therefore people don't have to ask other living Beings for their input in order to solve human problems.

Assumption 4: Humans play a win-lose game with the Beings of Nature.

Dr. Jim describes common but often invisible assumptions:
What about when a tree or plant has an insecticide, fungicide, or
other chemical put on it? Let's talk about the assumptions that
underlie the use of these kinds of products on trees and plants.

Generally, the first assumption is that a person can control the
pest by killing it, so that the tree's or plant's problems will be
solved and it can grow again. False! You have learned that pests
are not generally the cause of a tree's or plant's weakness.

The second assumption is that people can dominate the insect
world and the world of microorganisms. Even when insects and
microorganisms develop what we call "resistance" to products,
people think that if they just create stronger or better products
then people can dominate again. This is folly. The thinking that
supports this assumption is flawed. Microorganisms and insects
will always and ultimately evolve to win that war.

Dr. Jim suggests an alternative: But, we can declare peace.
How about learning to co-exist and cooperate with insects and
microorganisms? They have their place and their purpose in
Nature. A shift in human consciousness–yes, personally in your
consciousness as well as in that of others'–is needed to wage
peace and to co-exist with the rest of Nature. Co-existence
means learning to live in dynamic balance with other life forms.

Basia highlights two more assumptions: The third assumption
is about arrogance: people thinking that they know best and
assuming that science and technology make people superior.
While it's true that the advances and conveniences that science
and technology have brought do not have to be surrendered, the
illusion of superiority, which they give us, needs to be examined.

Lastly, we assume we are in competition; the very idea requires
winners and losers. Assuming competition, people approach the
Beings of Nature as if playing a win-lose game; people may win
a few skirmishes to dominate various Beings of Nature, but I say
that humanity will ultimately lose that war.

Basia suggests an alternative: You have learned how to ask
questions to trees, plants, and all of Nature's Beings so you
already recognize them as partners. You know that they have
valuable input. They can help us to solve our problems–personal
and global. I suggest changing to a cooperative approach. Such a

shift in our own consciousness does not have to mean relinquishing the quality of life that so many in the West have come to enjoy. Dr. Jim and I think that the consciousness and practices associated with cooperation, partnership, and equality with Nature can result in the creation of a sustainable way of life and earth-friendly, harmonious practices and perhaps even a higher quality of life than we enjoy currently.

Basia gives an example: In my investigations for this book, I uncovered lots of scientific research that seeks to make crops produce greater yields or seeks to make plants more effective in repelling insects. As I read the scientific papers, I was struck by the scientists' assumptions underneath their intent.

If scientists assume that Nature can be controlled, dominated, and has no intelligence of its own, then those scientists may form and test hypotheses without considering the plant's point of view or long-term consequences. They may even go forward with their research without regard to far-reaching ramifications for the whole planet's delicate ecosystems, such as development of genetically modified organisms. GMO seemed like a good idea to some people, and because they *could* do it, they *did*. No one really knows how this grand experiment will turn out for humanity and for the whole planet. Such scientists are working in the vacuum of their own assumptions. I say that they are out of balance within themselves and with Nature.

However, imagine that the same scientists could shift their own consciousness, recognize the intelligence in Nature, and be willing to be humble enough to ask Nature for information in an attitude of cooperation, partnership, and equality. The human desire to make plants become more productive could take on a whole new dimension. No longer would scientists be working in a human-centric system to that end. Instead, scientists *and* Nature's Consciousness would be equal partners in the quest to create a new form. The newly **co-created** form would meet *both human specifications as well as satisfy the wisdom, balance, sustainability, harmony, and vitality of Nature's intelligence.* In this way, the scientific process would be done co-creatively, in partnership, and with wisdom and respect.

In Chapter 10, you will see that cooperation, partnership, and equality with Nature are ideas whose time have come.

❧ Chapter 10: An Idea Whose Time Has Come

We cannot solve our problems with the same thinking we used when we created them.

ATTRIBUTED TO ALBERT EINSTEIN
GERMAN-AMERICAN PHYSICIST, 1879–1955

In order to change an existing paradigm, you do not struggle to try and change the problematic model. You create a new model and make the old one obsolete.

BUCKMINSTER FULLER
AMERICAN INVENTOR, 1895–1983

All the forces in the world are not so powerful as an idea whose time has come.

VICTOR HUGO
FRENCH NOVELIST AND STATESMAN, 1802–1885

You must be the change you want to see in the world.

ATTRIBUTED TO MAHATMA GANDHI
INDIAN POLITICAL AND SPIRITUAL LEADER, 1869–1948

A DIORAMA WALK THROUGH THE PAST TO NOW

Ms. Basia Alexander, The Chief Listener, explains: Your personal relationship with trees, plants, and all of **Nature** isn't as personal as you think. It is contained within a 2.6 million-year history that you inherited by being alive now.

For some perspective on the present time, and in order to understand the *idea whose time has come*, let's take a quick look at the development of people's relationship with Nature as if we were walking past museum exhibitions.

As we tour, we will gain insights into the ebb and flow of harmony and balance in humanity's relationship with its world. The scenes we view will focus on three specific points: (1) how people feed themselves, (2) how they organize themselves into groups, and (3) how they perceive or interact with the Divine.*1*

Keyworks used below correspond to the three criteria above.

The PALEOLITHIC Age: 2.6 million BCE until around 12,000 BCE. This represents about 99% of human history.
Keywords: (1) To Know. (2) Co-Exist. Equality. (3) Reverence. Inseparable.

For at least 2.6 million years, hunter gatherer societies obtained their food and resources directly from the environment through which they moved. Typically nomadic, small groups of humans relied on their intimate knowledge of animals and plants to survive. They respected their place in the natural environment, even if they feared the power of the elements. They lived in an egalitarian condition of relatively harmonious co-existence within their small groups–mostly matriarchal, some patriarchal. Inseparable from the ecosystem, their reverence for other life resulted in personal relationships with animal and plant deities and deference to the unseen.

The NEOLITHIC Age: *approximately 12,000 BCE to 3,000 BCE.*
Keywords: (1) Grow and Tend. (2) Rule. (3) Entreat.

Early agrarian peoples discovered that they could grow and tend animals (herding) and plants (farming) to eat and live locally. As populations increased with better food productivity, people gathered in settlements. Ruling families arose. Entreaties made to human-faced gods and goddesses appealed for bounty in the harvest.

BRONZE, IRON, and MIDDLE AGES: *3,000 BCE to 1500s AD in Europe and Middle East. (Different elsewhere in the world.)*
Keywords: (1) Manipulate through Technology. (2) Govern in Hierarchal Patriarchies. Writing. (3) Worship of Abstract Deities.

Later agrarian societies developed advanced technologies, such as irrigation systems and plows pulled by beasts of burden, to manipulate their agricultural ecosystems more efficiently. Greater yields supported growth of cities. Larger populations were governed in hierarchal systems. The invention of writing accelerated the rate of technological development. Any deity the agrarian peoples worshiped had neither a human nor animal face but was non-material, abstract, or separated from Nature. Familiar religions arose in this time. [1, 2]

RENAISSANCE, INDUSTRIAL, and the MODERN Ages:
1,500s AD to about 2,000 AD (Varies in different parts of the world.)
Keywords: (1) Control. Domination. Superiority. (2) Freedom. Bureaucracy. (3) Organized Religion.

The Renaissance of the 1500s eventually produced an industrial society in which people considered themselves superior to all else. Methods of producing food were based on controlling plants (large-scale farming, hybridizing or bio-engineering), animals (factory farming, animal testing), and extracting Earth's resources–ultimately–beyond the capacity of the local ecosystem to sustain. Human populations boomed.

*People fought for the freedom to choose. They made use of hierarchal bureaucracies to administer daily life. The philosophies of both the Renaissance's **Cartesian** sciences and agrarian-based organized*

*religions resulted in the development of a mindset that Nature could be
overpowered and should be dominated, consumed and used for
whatever was perceived as the human good.*

*People had the means to build technologies (i.e., cities, computers,
etc.), which ended up distancing people from the source of their food
and enhancing people's experience of alienation from the natural
environment, from each other, and from the world.3*

A Shift in Thinking: Old and New Paradigms

Basia points to the old paradigm: In the last 400 years, the
reductionist and mechanistic ideas born of the Renaissance and
Enlightenment periods fundamentally shifted the relationship
between people and Nature. Humanity's mechanistic types of
approaches to the environment have already cost humanity a
measure of its Soul.4 People in the West came to believe that
they could *control* Nature, that they should *dominate* Nature,
and that science and technology make them *superior* to Nature.
These four assumptions pit humanity against Nature in a one-
sided war, which–we fear–humanity will lose.

*Detailed at the end of Chapter 9, these are assumptions about Nature
that result in people being out of balance with Nature and result in
Nature going out of dynamic equilibrium and into extreme fluctuations.*

Assumption 1: Killing pests will solve a tree's or plant's problems.

*Assumption 2: People can dominate and control the Plant Kingdom,
the Insect Kingdom, and the world of microorganisms.*

*Assumption 3: Science and technologies have made people superior
to Nature, therefore people don't have to ask other living Beings for
their input in order to solve human problems.*

*Assumption 4: Humans play a win-lose game with the Beings of
Nature.*

Basia continues: Ideas and practices involving control,
domination, and superiority are now so ingrained in the culture
as to be invisible to most people. Dr. Jim and I see these *control-
domination-superiority* habits of thinking when we appear at
public events. Many homeowners tell us about their trees,
gardens, and landscape, wanting to know what to do about this
vexing problem or that troublesome insect. We don't blame them
for asking us because asking an expert is what they have been
taught to do. These well-meaning people assume that someone

knows best and that scientific advances or technologies will somehow solve all the problems. They think that the invasive–or unwanted–plants, insects, or animals are the "bad guys" and should be killed. Such homeowners, and others like them, are unaware of their own comfortable human arrogance. Right in their own backyards, the Beings of Nature are in a state of lopsided struggle–in other words–in profound imbalance.

How has more than 400 years of *control-domination-superiority* thinking turned out for the planet? Not very well, I believe. The opportunity of the twenty-first century is to move away from those destructive and unsustainable attitudes, practices, and beliefs. How could people do that? People might have to let go of arrogant assumptions like "I always know best," or "science and technology have all the answers," or "I don't have to ask, I can just do it my way."

Basia explains the relevance of the quotes on the first page of this chapter: I don't have to provide a laundry list of all the environmental problems threatening human life on Earth. Dr. Jim and I acknowledge that advances have been made to rectify such problems. But, even while well-meaning people act to "save" Nature, they attempt to exert their control, domination, and superiority. They assume they know the best solutions to bring balance back to Nature. Insanity–doing the same thing over and over, expecting a different result–still runs rampant.[5]

Albert Einstein is said to have pointed out that solutions don't come from the same thinking or mindset from which the problems came. The same old, tired thinking that created our problems has not yet been fully perceived as the real problem itself. In other words, it's not pollution, global warming, deforestation, or genetic modification of organisms that are the real threats to humanity's earthly environment. The real problem is the human mindset or Western framework for thinking— domination, control, and superiority—that allows deforestation or the other things to happen.

Buckminster Fuller recommended that humanity not bother with the struggle to change the old; "...create a new model and make the old one obsolete," he said.[6] For example, people tried to build a better horse and buggy. Then, the automobile was invented. That made the horse and buggy antiquated.

Basia declares a new paradigm: Dr. Jim and I are inspired to establish the new model–the new paradigm–that we call *cooperation, partnership, and equality within the Plant Kingdom, among the Beings of Nature, and between people and Nature*, and we are dedicated to making the old paradigm of *domination-control-superiority* obsolete.

The idea of *cooperation-partnership-equality* envisions mutual **communication** and respectful co-existence between members of humanity and members of the Plant Kingdom along with all their related organisms, including insects and diseases. All have their place in purpose.

A shift in human consciousness and changes in attitudes and practices are needed to establish peaceful co-existence with the rest of Nature, since humanity is not and has never been separate. Co-existence means learning to live in dynamic balance with other life forms. A cooperative approach to real partnership with our partners on the planet can help to solve our shared problems. This shift in consciousness and practices may ask of humanity that it return to a deeper spirituality in its relationship with other life forms such as trees and plants.

At the same time, in making such a leap, I believe that humanity does not have to leave behind its scientific or technological advances. Rather, a blending of the best of both worlds is not only possible, but could bring about superior results while using respectful and **co-creative** approaches.

Dr. Jim interjects: This reminds me of the sculptured plants in a botanical garden. The plants told me that if the people would ask them how to do the pruning, they–the plants–would be far more beautiful than the humans could ever imagine.

In our vision, everybody wins. We foresee robustly healthy trees and plants in full expression of their natural potential and interacting healthily with other organisms, as well as foreseeing people who are healthy in body, mind, and Spirit.

Basia says that now is the time: The idea of *cooperation-partnership-equality* within Nature and with Nature is so powerful that all the existing forces in the world are becoming obsolete in favor of it. We believe it is–as *Victor Hugo* described–an idea whose time has come. When an idea's time has come, its implementation cannot be stopped; existing forces and institutions align with it as a matter of course.[7, 8]

Actualizing this new framework within Western culture would be analogous to constructing a new building with never-before-seen architecture and using innovative substances. The architect, Frank Lloyd Wright, is famous for his revolutionary designs, which filtered into common usage. Similarly, we believe that bringing a new paradigm into existence can be done.

Basia continues: Our main reason for writing this book is because of our commitment to spreading the ideas of *cooperation-partnership-equality with Nature* and promoting the practices of touching, healing, and communicating with trees, plants, and all of Nature. Together, you and Dr. Jim and I have the opportunity to make the approach of *control-domination-superiority* to trees, plants, and all of Nature obsolete. Otherwise, Dr. Jim and I fear that the old paradigm might make humanity obsolete.

On the bright side, Dr. Jim and I believe that this shift in worldview is happening *now* all over the world. We believe that transformation is happening within each of us on the planet.

As a result of the experiences you have had in this book–such as the "Stepping Inside of a Tree's or Plant's World" exercise in Chapter 4–your own individual sensibilities may be forever expanded and enlightened. We hope your viewpoint of trees and plants will never be the same as it was, even if you loved trees and plants already. After BEING THE TREE, you can "be the change"–as *Mahatma Gandhi* said–that you want to create for yourself, for your trees, for your plants, and in your world.

WALKING INTO THE FUTURE

Basia asks: What's next for you? How you feel and what you think about trees and plants is not unchangeable. Your relationship with Nature may be in for an upgrade. You may feel a new bond with trees and plants.

I felt like I was part of the current wave of transformation when I read Dr. Edmund Bourne's book *Global Shift-How a New Worldview is Transforming Humanity.* In succinct chapters, he painted a picture of ten trends that have been washing ashore since at least the 1940s. In reflecting on my own life, I related to the trends he outlined. Perhaps you do, too.

1) The popularity of Eastern philosophies and doing Yoga exercises.

2) The Environmental movement.

3) Quantum Physics's core idea that everything is energy vibrations.

4) The idea that Earth is Herself a living organism: "Gaia."

5) Appreciation for indigenous cultures.

6) Acceptance of paranormal events.

7) The rise of metaphysical topics and beliefs.

8) Emergence of alternative or complementary health practices.

9) Women's rights, with a return to the spirituality of the "Mother."

10) A largely transparent but worldwide charitable and nonprofit-based do-gooding movement.9, 10

Basia continues: I believe that these ten trends combine–like wind, rain, and waves–to make a perfect storm. Do you think that you are in a storm now? You may, if you are feeling buffeted around in the ship of your life. But, what comes after the storm? We subscribe to a positive vision for the future. Please let me describe the world that we foresee on the horizon.

THE TRANSFORMATION AGE: *From about 2,000 AD and beyond.*

Keyworks correspond to three criteria representing the ebb and flow of harmony and balance in humanity's relationship with Nature: (1) how people feed themselves, (2) how they organize themselves into groups, and (3) how they perceive or interact with the Divine.

Keywords: (1) Respect. Local. Sustainable. Holistic. Balanced.
(2) Equality. Partnership. Cooperation. Network. Local and Global.
(3) Experience of Connection. Gratitude. Reverence.

People know where their food comes from; they can shake their farmer's hand. Urbanites are also growing their own food. Local, organic, or Cooperative BioBalance-type farming practices abound. People make food choices based on seasonal, regional, and carbon-footprint sustainable criteria. Hunger is eradicated through mutually cooperative social, educational, and political solutions. Plants and trees receive respect and gratitude for their usefulness to humanity. Holistic, **bioenergy***-based approaches such as Tree Whispering® and Green Centrics™ are used to return plants and trees to health, then enlightened conventional means are used to keep them healthy.*

*Populations without borders are technologically networked and move
their agendas forward through equal and mutually cooperative
partnerships such as "friends" or "fans." People have an expanding
awareness of the interconnection and fragile state of the earth's
ecosystems. They cooperate with each other to heal whole ecosystems.
Cooperation transcends conflict. Local, bioregional, global, and human
ecosystems are respected as intradependent and interdependent webs of
life that need to be treasured, protected, and upgraded.*

*The validity of personal experience trumps fundamentalism or
pedagogy. Insight and intuition—as sources of information—gain new
respect as being valid. Science and spirituality call a truce, finding
common elements and common purposes.*

*People express gratitude to trees and plants for their gifts. Partnerships
between people and the Beings of the natural world transcend perceived
obstacles. People experience connection with all life forms. The
experience of connection expands into reverence for the Spirit within all
living systems and Beings. People form cooperative partnerships with
trees, plants, related diseases and insects as well as all of Nature as if
Nature were Itself a whole living Being on a grand scale: "Gaia."*

*People understand the complex levels of dimensionality and
interrelatedness of all of Nature's components. Beings of the Plant
Kingdom and all related organisms–including people–form cooperative
relationships and partnerships among themselves. Harmony and a true
balance within Nature exists.*

Basia looks ahead: I believe that humanity is on the way to
making the shift to a more sustainable model in which to survive
and thrive together on Earth. How? By recognizing that Nature
has its own kind of **intelligence** and has answers about how to
live in balance. By accepting that people and Nature can
communicate and cooperate with one another.

Do you feel that you are ready to move into this kind of future?
How can you best prepare yourself for this future–or help it to
come true in the world?

New Paradigm: The Idea Whose Time Has Come

Dr. Jim Conroy, The Tree Whisperer,®️ talks about the shift:
The establishment of the new *cooperation-partnership-
equality* model has already begun. Basia and I already see
people making a transformational shift to balance with Nature.

One minute, people are in the old paradigm. They think that they know what a tree or plant needs because of what they learned from science, from school, or from a product label. The next minute, in the new paradigm, people are having an insight or an understanding about the true, inner qualities–or the Spirit–of the **Green Being** from their own experiences of it. That dynamic shift represents a person's relationship with the Plant Kingdom coming back into balance.

In this book, Basia and I have given you information about trees and plants; for example, about how they operate internally and that they can be healed from the inside-out. But, none of that is as important as the few minutes you spent with a Green Being, feeling its Life Force, or appreciating it is a living Being.

After spending those moments, a new relationship of *cooperation-partnership-equality* began in your heart and in your personal experience by touching the Life Force, and being touched by the Life Force of a tree or plant.

Dr. Jim asks: What does it mean for you to cooperate with trees? to become a plant's partner? to feel equality between yourself and Nature?

How does Tree Whispering help you shift your relationship with Nature?

I tell my students this: "Come from the tree's point of view." I find that when people forget any limiting ideas for a while–when they can be open-minded and adventurous–they find out that a tree does have its own perspective and that its life is as real as their own.

You can get to know trees–even as individuals. It means asking the tree what is going on for it and asking the plant what is best for it. They contain that information in their bioenergy fields and will share that insight with you. "Coming from the tree's or plant's point of view" means taking their perspective. If you can imagine or experience yourself within a tree's setting, in a tree's roots or in a tree's leaves, something amazing happens. You begin to experience understanding. There is a kind of rapport or compassion that develops for the other Being. It's totally experiential. It's like looking out of a tree's eyes. It's like walking a mile in another's shoes.

Dr. Jim talks about holism: Tree Whispering is a **holistic** approach at several levels. I begin by assuming that the tree or plant is a whole Being; it's a living system composed of complex systems. We, as human Beings, are whole systems doing this Tree Whispering work. Other organisms are also whole Beings. The result of wholes interrelating with other wholes is greater than the sum of its parts. Like a caterpillar becoming a butterfly, a transformation takes place.

Basia interjects: Practicing Tree Whispering expands the mind and consciousness because it involves healing trees by using both the left and right sides of the brain. The left-brain—or linear and logical side—is engaged to deal with practical information, such as how the tree looks on the outside. The right-brain—the intuitive and holistic side—is accessed for insight about the *whole* tree's inner parts and functions operating as an integrated living system. Then, the power of the loving heart is added into the mix. People have been taught that the mind resides in the brain so they assume that thoughts are powerful. And thoughts *are* powerful. However, thoughts are but a shadow compared to the power of the loving heart.

In order to Tree Whisper, Dr. Jim and I suggest that you to set aside your own ideas about what is supposed to be right for the health of trees and plants. Dr. Jim and I teach people to actually ask the tree or plant questions. Use your knowledge to ask the right questions. You don't speak into a plant's ears. Plants don't have ears. But trees and plants are part of the web of life; they are creative in living and surviving in their environments. And, it is possible to have an exchange of information between your **biofield** and theirs.

Dr. Jim adds: Having an exchange of information with a tree is what is so different about Tree Whispering from conventional tree care. Allowing yourself to engage intuitively in order to feel something with a tree is also very different. Having an exchange of information and an emotional engagement with a tree or plant is what will shift and expand your relationship with all of Nature. BE the tree, get to know it well, and it follows that LOVE grows for it. Remember the Five Heralds from Chapter 8.

From that simple yet fundamental personal experience of contact with another life form, a shift in thinking and changes in behavior can grow. For you, results of shifting your thinking and making changes in actions can mean a personal expansion of well-being and even a reconnection to the sacredness of Life. For trees, plants, and Nature, results can mean vigorous growth and co-existence with diseases and insects. For Earth, it can mean a reconstitution of dynamic balance on a large scale.

Basia heralds the new: Our world is transforming, but it's hard to see. Think of time-lapse photography. A photographer takes a picture of a flower unfolding once a minute then plays that back at regular speed. The bud seems to burst open. And so it is with both personal and global transformations.

The new worldview or framework for living, thinking, and acting can be described in a practical way as this idea whose time has come: *cooperation, partnership, and equality within the Plant Kingdom, among the Beings of Nature, and between people and Nature.*

People are, of course, part of Nature. There is no separation. All of us can cultivate our own relationships with the members of the Plant Kingdom based on beliefs of equality, attitudes for cooperation, and actions done in partnership. All of us can be Nature's partners.

And, Nature wants to be our partner. That is what the trees and plants tell Dr. Jim and me. They tell anyone who asks.

Actual partnership with trees and plants is what Dr. Jim and I believe is called for at this crucial time on our planet. People like you—who believe that they and their Green Being partners can relate cooperatively and as equals—are the individuals and the teams we think can solve global problems at a higher level than when humanity created those problems.

Operating in a context of cooperation means that you will find your place as an equal and as a co-creator with Nature. To live in the transformed global framework of cooperation, partnership, and equality, people–like you–will tune up abilities to communicate. That means to ask questions, to listen, and to interact as partners with Green Beings.

How will this future come to be? It is *the goal of Dr. Jim's and my work* that the future unfolds, like a flower, through the principles and practices of Cooperative BioBalance.™

Chapter 11: Futuristic Vision in Practice Now: Cooperative BioBalance™

DYNAMIC BALANCE AND PEACEFUL CO-EXISTENCE

Dr. Jim Conroy, The Tree Whisperer,® poses the challenge:
Earlier in human history, before humans could impact a local environment on a large scale, the teeter-tottering between species was not a problem; **Mother Nature** always seeks and establishes **dynamic balance**. However, in the last 100 years or so, humans have intervened with mechanized practices and strong products as if humanity were smart enough to take over this balancing act for Mother Nature. Some people have had temporary successes, but humanity is not, by itself, that smart.

The idea whose time has come is *cooperation, partnership, and equality within the Plant Kingdom, among the Beings of Nature, and between people and Nature.* How can this ideal state of peaceful co-existence and dynamic balance be achieved within the Plant Kingdom on a planet where we humans are having such a great environmental impact?

People could show some humility. On their own, people do not know how to devise a plan or set conditions to re-establish dynamic balance in Nature. But, Nature knows. All we have to do is ask Nature.

People can make peace with the Plant Kingdom.

The Plant Kingdom is already at peace with humanity. The plants and trees tell me that they want to be healthy from the inside-out, express their full potential, and live in dynamic balance with other organisms, including people.

Dr. Jim inspires: The potential for partnership, cooperation, peace, and balanced co-existence as a new global paradigm is possible in three ways.

First, by establishing dynamic balance *within* the inner functionality of individual members of Plant Kingdom, between plant and plant, and within their related communities, as Tree Whispering® and Green Centrics™ does.

Second, by establishing dynamic balance and a peace treaty *among* plants and their related organisms, including diseases and insects, as done through Co-Existence Technologies™.

Third, by implementing changes in practices *between* people, the Plant Kingdom, and all Beings of Nature, as done through Tree Whispering. And, by inspiring people to recognize the possibility of such peaceful co-existence as suggested in Cooperative BioBalance™.

Dr. Jim gives perspective: This book—up until this chapter—has been about the first possibility: establishing dynamic balance within individual members of the Plant Kingdom, between plant and plant, and within their related communities.

The remaining two possibilities follow this way. If the plants are healthy and their related organisms are healthy, then each can interact in a healthy manner with each other. The possibility then exists for each to live in harmony with the other.

Each organism has a will to live. Thus, the tree can *be* the tree, and the insect can *be* the insect, and a disease organism can *be* itself—all living in state of dynamic balance. But when the plants are unhealthy internally–perhaps due to a variety of abiotic stress factors–other life forms continue their biological activities until they destroy their host. Insects or disease organisms may or may not be out of balance at that point.

If members of the Plant Kingdom are internally healthy and expressing their full potential, then they are *being* themselves. In doing so, other organisms that live in ecological relationship with them–*being* themselves at the same time–all have the opportunity to express their full potential and exist in balance.

When you touch and are touched by the Life Force of a tree or plant, you can see that its **internal functionality** is a fine-tuned instrument. When I am in the purity of the connected balance and flow between the bioenergy of trees and plants, I am reminded that their health is a mirror for my own health. I see that my own body is a fine-tuned instrument as well.

All of us on this planet are connected. By healing and saving the trees and plants, you heal and save yourself. Peace between all living Beings is the result of moving away from the unworkable, unsustainable state of domination, control, and superiority and moving to the new land of cooperation, partnership, and equality. All of us can help to light that path. All of us can deeply know and acknowledge that our lives depend on healthy plants and trees. All of us can express our gratitude for the oxygen, food, beauty, and other resources for which we use the Plant Kingdom. All of us can love the trees and plants.

The trees and plants love all of us, too. They have told me so.

COOPERATIVE BIOBALANCE STORIES: "THAT WEEDY FIELD"

Basia tells a story from the early days: Dr. Jim had a test trial on a soybean field in central New Jersey. This was an organic grower's field so he used no herbicides. During late spring, it rained a lot so the grower could not use his cultivator equipment to get the weeds out from between the rows of soybeans. Dr. Jim used his Green Centrics System on the soybeans. The soybeans said, "We could mature into a good crop if we didn't have to compete with these other plants." Then, Dr. Jim asked the other plants what they wanted. The other plants said, "We just want to survive, mature, and go to seed."

Dr. Jim tried a new procedure. In an innovative treatment, he asked the soybeans and the other plants to work together rather than compete. The new allies told Dr. Jim that they would cooperate. This way, both the other plants and the soybeans could survive and mature.

By late in the season, the weeds matured, turned brown, went to seed, and fell over earlier than expected. They were no longer shading the soybeans from the sun. The soybeans–still green–could now soak in all the sunlight. Later, the soybeans matured and produced an excellent crop for the grower.

Serendipitously, Dr. Jim and I met neighbors of the grower's. They described driving past the field and thinking that the grower never planted it because it was so weedy. They told us that later–after the other plants browned and fell over–they were shocked to discover soybeans in what they called "that weedy field." They were amazed to see the good crop of soybeans even though the field had been heavily infested with unwanted plants.

Basia says: Subsequently, Dr. Jim repeated his innovation on organic soybeans on Iowa farms. The new procedure Dr. Jim created to use in the relationship between the soybeans and the other plants is called Co-Existence Technologies. By asking the crop and the other plants to work together, both were able to survive, mature, and reach their full potential. Co-Existence Technologies has become a set of techniques, procedures, and ways to implement the principles of Cooperative BioBalance.

WHAT IS COOPERATIVE BIOBALANCE?

Dr. Jim describes a new field of study and inquiry: The principles, practices, and soft technologies of Cooperative BioBalance offer alternative choices to well-meaning environmental stewards who may unconsciously use outmoded methods that include controlling or dominating Nature. Such people may assume they know the best solutions. Do they stop to ask the trees or plants? With Cooperative BioBalance, they would learn to do so.

The fundamental principle of Cooperative BioBalance is "live and let live" because all life forms want to live. Cooperative BioBalance is a new field of inquiry and practical techniques in which people form equal and cooperative partnerships with trees, plants, forests, crops, and their related insect and disease organisms. Partnerships are forged for multilateral and multidirectional balancing and healing. Cooperative BioBalance represents the peace treaty among trees, plants, crops, forests, and their related organisms that Nature lovers have been waiting for. It means no products, no chemicals, no killing.

By allowing sensory awareness and **communicating** through expanded consciousness, people "ask and listen" to the innate **intelligence** in trees, plants, and Nature. Partnerships they form demonstrate the shift to a new **paradigm** in action: equality and cooperation among all life forms. Use of innovative and proven **bioenergy** healing techniques leads to peaceful co-existence and dynamic balance within the parts, systems, and functions of Nature's Beings and between people and Nature's Beings. Effects are local and ripple out globally. We are all connected.

Dr. Jim points forward: Cooperative BioBalance is the direction for the future. It offers the opportunity for people to adopt a new way of thinking, which they can apply to their current practices to transform those practices. Its principles are both revolutionary and ancient.

> ### *FUNDAMENTAL PRINCIPLES OF COOPERATIVE BIOBALANCE*
>
> - *Live and let live. All living Beings want to live.*
> - *Trees and plants are alive and have their own intelligence.*
> - *All living Beings produce bioenergy fields, which overlap, interact, and can be healed through conscious communication.*
> - *Communication is possible and valid among species and through the consciousness of Nature.*
> - *The intelligence within Nature can be asked questions co-creatively. People ask for advice and guidance; they don't assume that they know the way. Enlightened and aligned actions follow.*
> - *Personal beliefs and day-to-day practices can be transformed to show partnership, cooperation, and equality.*
> - *Trees and plants have interior parts, functions, and systems that need to be healed "from their points of view" when stressed or in decline.*
> - *Each organism's needs and goals can be determined and met. "Gettin' 'em all to play nice together" (Green Beings and related organisms such as insects and diseases) is the cooperative methodology.*
> - *The total ecosystem–all component parts–must be brought back to health for any part to be healthy.*
> - *Cooperative BioBalance addresses the main issues about Nature operating out of balance; it is not a bandage for a local problem.*
> - *Green Beings, other organisms, (including diseases and insects) and the total ecosystem operate in multilevel, multidimensional feedback-loop relationships.*
> - *By working in multidimensional relationships–including all organisms–people bring balance into the physical level. In some level of the multidimensional, all of the various organisms (including their feedback loops) are healed and are in balance already. Through understanding, intentionality, and focused concentration, people bring this whole balance forward into the physical. Then, what shows up in the physical is trees, plants, insects, diseases, ecosystems, and all of Nature living in balance and harmony.*
> - *We are all connected. People's efforts in their backyards ripple out to the whole world.*

Dr. Jim comments on the fundamental principles: My way of saying all this is "gettin' 'em all to play nice together." I know that doesn't sound very technical or sophisticated, but it is the truth. It's just like children who need to be peaceful and cooperative in play so they don't harm each other. Trees, plants, and their related organisms all need to survive and live to their full potential. They all need to co-exist without hurting each other or each other's potential.

Dr. Jim adds: I find that parts of an ecosystem—even someone's backyard is an ecosystem—cannot be healed or brought into balance without addressing and healing the whole ecosystem. Since Cooperative BioBalance addresses the main issues about Nature being out of balance, it is not a bandage for a local problem such as invasive weeds in a local forest. By bringing the ecosystem into balance, the invasives don't take over; they live in balance and harmony with the healthy forest.

RECOMMENDED PRACTICES OF COOPERATIVE BIOBALANCE
- *Respecting trees and plants as life forms.*
- *Giving thanks and having gratitude.*
- *Having experiential partnership with trees, plants, and all of Nature.*
- *Using the tools of "asking and listening" to be in cooperative partnership with trees, plants and other Beings of Nature.*
- *Using Tree Whispering® Holistic Chores,™ Healing Whispers,™ and all the experiences and techniques in this book.*

RESULTS OF COOPERATIVE BIOBALANCE
- *Dynamic balance and peace within the Plant Kingdom itself, among plants and their related organisms, including diseases and insects, and between people and the Plant Kingdom.*
- *Sustainability on a healthy planet.*
- *Peace. People know themselves as part of Nature's balance. Cooperation flourishes. Health in body, mind, and Spirit prevails.*

Ms. Basia Alexander, the Chief Listener, smiles: By using a co-creative approach, anyone can purposefully engage with Nature's Consciousness. The game of 20 Questions done cooperatively with the intelligence of Nature, as we suggested in Chapter 8, can be a jumping-off place for amazing innovation. Scientists, managers, technologists, growers, tree lovers, or anyone may approach any project or challenge through the principles and practices of Cooperative BioBalance. Such people would no longer be attempting to fulfill some goal using their own personal–and I might say "limited"–resources. Rather, they would have the unlimited wisdom, balance, sustainability, harmony, and vitality of Nature's intelligence serving as their partner in discovering and achieving their goal.

In fact, Dr. Jim and I would like to point out that learning the principles and practices of Cooperative BioBalance can be a useful prequel—a first study—before engaging other studies such as arboriculture, farming, horticulture, environmental studies, Permaculture®, BioMimicry®, or BioDynamics®. By first learning to touch, heal, and communicate with the Beings of Nature through expanded perceptual abilities, by overlapping bioenergy fields, and with specific Tree Whispering techniques, the practice of those other disciplines may be more effective.

WHAT IS THE STRUCTURE?
THE SCOPE OF TREE WHISPERING® AND COOPERATIVE BIOBALANCE

Tree Whispering experiences begin as profound personal perceptions of overlapping one's Life Force with the Growth Energy of trees and plants.	Tree Whispering techniques and practices such as Holistic Chores™ and Healing Whispers™ are specific ways to interact with trees and plants for their healing and balancing.	Tree Whispering results in a more respectful approach to trees and plants. Partnership begins here. New attitudes and practices go into use. People feel good in body, mind, and Spirit.	Cooperative BioBalance establishes the new paradigm: Cooperation, Partnership, and Equality among all the Beings of Nature. People embrace other organisms and work in multiple dimensions.	Cooperative BioBalance results in balance and peace among all the Beings of Nature, and fosters sustainability. People know themselves as part of Nature's balance, so cooperation flourishes.

Tree Whispering gives people the tools to form cooperative partnerships with trees, plants, forests, and crops so that people can balance and heal those living Beings, and also feel good in body, mind, and Spirit.

Tree Whispering is the prerequisite to Cooperative BioBalance and is the initial step to balancing and healing activities that occur:
• *within the Plant Kingdom itself,*
• *among plants and related organisms, including diseases and insects,*
• *and between people and the Plant Kingdom.*

The scope of Tree Whispering begins very personally and has a global reach through the principles and practices of Cooperative BioBalance.

First, Tree Whispering begins as a personal experience of tree and plant **bioenergy***. This experience is how people learn to come from the plant's point of view. When people and other living Beings* **communicate***, a new relationship arises based on cooperation and equality. One could say that a friendship develops. Tree Whispering gives people a way of thinking that is holistic and respectful. People can apply this holistic, respectful thinking to transform their current practices. It is also healthy for people in body, mind, and Spirit.*

Second, Tree Whispering is a set of hands-on bioenergy healing techniques for restoring functionality to the parts, systems, and **inner functions** *of trees, plants, crops, and forests for their own sustainable balance. Through Tree Whispering techniques, trees and plants are strengthened, and* **decline** *can be reversed. It is done in an environmentally sound way and without the use of products or invasive techniques. Since all Beings are connected in the vast web of life, this strengthening spreads from people's yards out to the whole planet.*

*Cooperative BioBalance offers a new model/mindset/***paradigm** *for attitudes and practices that uses Tree Whispering and other techniques, and is based on principles of partnership, cooperation, and equality with Nature. People realize that countless organisms are involved within the balance of all of Nature. People learn that their cooperative work with trees and plants extends to partnerships with other organisms–such as diseases and insects–in multidimensional* **feedback loop** *relationships. By working in these multidimensional relationships–including all organisms–people bring balance of Nature into the physical level.*

Soft Technologies Used in Cooperative BioBalance

TREE WHISPERING *techniques are the initial steps into* Cooperative BioBalance. *Usually, people first learn the* Holistic Chores *and* Healing Whispers. *Partnership begins here. New attitudes and practices are put to use.*

Green Centrics™ *is the professional-level system that Dr. Jim Conroy created and uses to connect feedback loops of specific parts, functions, and systems in plants and trees through his hands-on holistic, bioenergy-healing, green, and* sustainable methods.

Co-Existence Technologies™ *are advanced professional techniques used to bring dynamic balance to trees, plants, and their related organisms. It is also used to bring the multilevel and multidimensional framework of all of Nature's organisms in an ecosystem into balance.*

Principles and practices of Cooperative BioBalance *shift the paradigm so that people see the possiblility of bringing Nature back into balance.*

CREATION OF

Learning Opportunities

The Institute for Cooperative BioBalance offers learning opportunities. Workshops and classes are offered in various physical locations, including The Omega Institute, Rhinebeck, New York.[1] Online offerings are forthcoming.

Students can enroll in workshops and classes such as Trees Are Your Healers*. Various offerings involve hands-on guided visualization experiences, practicing specific healing techniques and learning holistic approaches that people can use in their backyards—the effects of which ripple out to the world. Additional courses are being developed.*

Institute's Initiatives Being Created:

• Strengthen Forests™ *is about strengthening sick trees–while bringing insects and diseases into balance–and healing forests on a large scale.* www.StrengthenForests.com.

• Botany in Balance™ *is outreach to the tree and plant care industry.*

• Have You Thanked™a Plant or Tree Today? *engages children's creativity and parents' appreciation.*

• Tree Protectors™ *provides solid information and networking opportunities for people acting to protect heritage or important trees, open land or forests.*

• Leave Leaves™ *re-educates people to shred, mulch, and compost with their own leaves as part of cooperating with Nature.*

MULTILEVEL, MULTIDIMENSIONAL SYSTEMS

Dr. Jim explains: Cooperative BioBalance is a fully **holistic** approach. Cooperative BioBalance includes not only working with plants and related organisms but also working with the multilevel, multidimensional system that includes all organisms.

Trees and plants operate in beneficial feedback loops. Refer to the illustration on this page. Think of plant internal systems such as circulation, cell division, and photosynthesis each operating within itself, as represented by each numbered network pattern. Then think of them all operating together as shown by all the overlapping patterns.

All related organisms, such as insects and diseases, also operate in beneficial feedback loops with the plant. For example, when nonliving (abiotic) stress factors affect a tree's circulation system, the circulation becomes clogged. The tree compensates; it diverts functionality to alternate routes. The more inner detours it must create, the weaker it gets. As it loses vitality, it sends out a message to its nearby community for energetic support. Insects–attuned to that message or vibrational song–are attracted to the sick tree. Disease organisms–also attuned–are able to increase their numbers. When people perceive how the patterns overlap, it becomes clear that imbalances in Nature can be corrected in all of the looping systems by restoring the integrity of any of the parts, then by restoring their relationships.

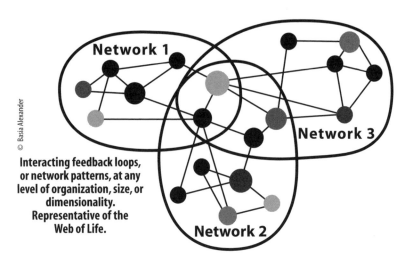

© Basia Alexander

Interacting feedback loops, or network patterns, at any level of organization, size, or dimensionality. Representative of the Web of Life.

Read through the steps. Decide whether you feel comfortable doing this exercise. If you do not feel comfortable or have any concern whatsoever, do not do it.

It may be easier to download the audio from www.TreeWhispering.com *so that you can listen to the instructions as you do the exercise.*

Step 1: Look at the diagram as a static, two-dimensional image.

Step 2: Notice that there are little black dots as well as dots in shades of grey. Look at the diagram with a soft focus.
Now, it may appear to have depth.

Step 3: Imagine that **Network 1** represents a plant. Each dot represents an aspect of its complex interrelated inner functionality such as circulation or photosynthesis. Imagine that the oval border represents not only its physical properties but also its bioenergy field. Playfully, or with a soft focus, experience Network 1 coming to life, appearing to have depth.

Step 4: Imagine that **Network 2** represents insects. Insects have complex inner functionality, each producing a tiny bioenergy field, and all living as a complex society among individuals. Playfully, or with a soft focus, experience Network 2 coming to life, appearing to have depth.

Step 5: Imagine that **Network 3** represents microorganisms. Microorganisms also having complex inner functionality, each producing a minute bioenergy field, and all living as a complex society. Playfully, or with a soft focus, experience Network 3 coming to life, appearing to have depth.

Step 6: Notice the area of **overlap** between **Network 1** (the plant) and **Network 2** (the insect). Imagine what functions or communications the plant and the insect might share. Playfully, or with a soft focus, experience the **overlap** of of Networks 1 and 2 coming to life, having depth.

Step 7: Notice the area of overlap between **Network 1** (the plant) and **Network 3** (the microorganism). Imagine what functions or communications the plant and the microorganism might share. Playfully, or with a soft focus, experience that **overlapping area** coming to life, appearing to have depth.

Step 8: Notice the area of overlap between **Network 2** (the insect) and **Network 3** (the microorganism). Imagine what communications the insect and the microorganism might share. Playfully, or with a soft focus, experience that **overlapping area** coming to life, appearing to have depth.

Step 9: Notice the **area of overlap among all three networks**. Imagine what functions or communications all might share. Playfully, or with a soft focus, experience that **overlapping area** coming to life, having depth.

Step 10: Return to **Network 1** (the plant.) Imagine that the **Large Light Grey Dot within Network 1** represents the plant's circulation system. Playfully, or with a soft focus, imagine that the Large Light Grey Dot–the circulation system–glows or becoming stronger.

Step 11: Playfully, or with a soft focus, imagine how the change in that Light Grey Dot affects or interacts with the rest of **Network 1** (the plant).

Step 12: Playfully, or with a soft focus, imagine how the change in that Light Grey Dot affects or interacts with **Networks 2 & 3** (insects & microorganisms).

Step 13: Playfully, or with a soft focus, perceive **all 3 Network Patterns** (plant, insects, microorganisms) interacting. Notice any shifting, rearranging or balancing. Take your time with this. What happens?

Step 14: If you can, try to imagine more network patterns being added to and overlapping in this diagram. What happens?

Step 15: If you can, imagine that each network pattern has another level or exists at another dimension. What happens?

Step 16: Write any notes or reflections in your *Tree Whispering: Trust the Path* notebook.

Dr. Jim comments on multilevel, multidimensional systems:
By now, I'm sure you see that doing one thing interacts with everything else. Feedback loops are present in both the physical as well as nonlinear and multidimensional levels. If people interact with trees, plants, and Nature only at the physical level–which is what most conventional tree and plant care does– such an incomplete interaction throws the multidimensional system out of balance. Then, everything shows up out-of-balance in the physical.

In other words, doing something in the physical that is not in cooperation with the plant or does not account for nonlinear or multidimensional interactive levels, serves to negatively impact the multidimensional levels. Multidimensional levels become out of balance. Then, the out-of-balance condition shows up in the physical *as* trees, plants, insects, and diseases fighting each other and not living in harmony.

Dr. Jim reminds: Remember, all the loops that show up in the physical are nonlinear and multidimensional. People cannot solve the puzzle of dimensionality by only looking at or working at the physical level. People need to perceive the total, multidimensional, interrelated aspect of all the many levels of **tree↔plant↔bee↔insect↔disease↔organism↔ecosystem↔ earth↔air↔fire↔water** beneficial feedback loops.

So, you and I can work with trees, plants, and organisms where they live–to heal them or to do practical activities such as pruning. Working multidimensionally, you and I *trust that whatever healing or work that is done shows up as a physical plant and its related organisms all in dynamic balance.* If we are tuned into this, then no matter what we do–healing techniques or practical activities–we can trust that all Beings will show up in balance in the physical level.

In some level of the multidimensional, all of the various organisms' feedback loops are healed and are in balance already. With understanding, intention, and focusing concentration, people can bring these healed feedback loops forward. Then, the living Beings show up in the physical level or dimension as balanced. The trees, plants, bees, insects, diseases, organisms, and all of Nature are living in dynamic balance and harmony.

COOPERATIVE BIOBALANCE STORIES: ALGAE AND WATER COOPERATE

Dr. Jim describes: I started looking for other ways to apply the innovative techniques of Co-Existence Technologies. A client in coastal New Jersey asked me whether I could do anything to solve the problem of algae blooms in a pond between her property and several neighbors. The pond was fed by a stream that entered and exited along her property line.

Sitting under a Willow, I touched the water of the pond to connect with the algae which, as you know, is a plant.

I asked the algae what it wanted.

The algae replied, "We just want to survive."

I asked the water what was happening for it.

The water said, "We are being depleted of oxygen."

I asked the algae further, "Do you understand that by spreading out over the whole pond, you are depleting the water of oxygen and thus, harming plants and fish in the water?"

Algae said, "We do not know that. In fact, we are being heavily fed by food dripping down from the grass hills surrounding this pond. So, we think that we are supposed to grow."

Dr. Jim explains: The food that the algae is referring to is the phosphorous in the lawn fertilizer. It was running off into the water and causing the algae to grow into mats that covered the water's surface. I asked the water and the algae to cooperate.

I came back a few weeks later. The algae receded so that there was both algae and clear water in the pond.

I returned again in mid summer. I found the algae had, once again, grown into mats and covered the pond.

I asked, "Algae! What happened?"

Algae said, "We were heavily fed again so we thought we were supposed to grow again."

In other words, people spread more fertilizer on their lawns and it ran off into the water. Once again, I asked the water and the algae to cooperate.

Several weeks later, the algae receded and there was clear water. The property owner told me, "The only reason that there is clear water in this pond at this time of year is because of your work! I wish it could always stay like this."

COOPERATIVE BIOBALANCE STORIES: TRIALS ON LODGEPOLE PINES IN WINTER PARK AND VAIL, COLORADO

Entire mountainsides of Lodgepole Pine Trees have died in Colorado. The conventional interpretation of this blames the Pine Bark Beetle. While expanding beetle populations due to warmer winters were the immediate agents of death, Dr. Conroy says that they were not the authentic cause. Forests suffered a human policy of fire suppression and at least nine years of extreme drought following snow-melt. Drought weakened the trees making them more susceptible to the increased beetle populations.

A perfect storm of conditions existed for Lodgepole Pine decline as seen as large brown area on the mountainsides.

When he first contacted the innate intelligence of the Lodgepole Pine trees in autumn of 2007, Dr. Conroy discovered severe weaknesses within all intrinsic parts, functions, and systems such as circulation of water/nutrients/sugars, cellular repair and growth, food production with photosynthesis, and others. Heavily infested trees would not survive. But, health and dynamic balance within functionality were bioenergetically restored to most pines. Through Dr. Conroy's conscious healing interactions, the result was less burrowing beetles and robust new growth in the then-recovering treated trees. By spring of 2008, Lodgepole Pine trees on eleven private properties showed high survival rates and good growth. After four years of trials, trees still showed excellent growth with little new incidence of tree decline.

Through the techniques of Co-Existence Technologies, Dr. Conroy also connected with the Life Force of the Pine Bark Beetles. He reports that the insect intelligence said that the insects would simply go to trees that were weak. Strong, healthy, fully functional trees naturally tolerate a few Beetle "hits," while the weak trees attract beetles in large numbers, and then they succumb.

Dr. Jim tells the whole Colorado Lodgepole Pine story: Go to the Colorado Rocky Mountains, west of Denver, Colorado. There, you will see many mountainsides covered with dying reddish-brown or dead silver Lodgepole Pine trees. It's shocking! What happened to those trees? Conventional wisdom about the death of the Lodgepole Pines is that–due to warmer winters–higher populations of the Pine Bark Beetle survive and attack the Lodgepole Pines. Some people also call this the natural reforestation cycle: Older trees die and new growth regenerates the forest.

Between 2007 and 2011, I had the opportunity to develop my Co-Existence Technologies methods on many private homeowner's tracts of land ranging from two acres to more than fifty acres. This was a real adventure since it turned out to be a true example of Cooperative BioBalance.

What was really going on for the Lodgepole Pines?

Homeowners told us that for about nine years before we arrived to do trials, the snow pack would melt and there would be a drought each year. After multiple years of drought, trees became more and more stressed–thus weaker and weaker each year.

What was really going on for the Pine Bark Beetle?

From communicating with them, I realized that the beetles were attracted to weak trees. They declared "Lunch time!" meaning that they had plenty of food all of the time. Perhaps populations had increased because of warmer winters, but the important point is this: Weak trees were attracting the beetles. In some cases, beetles carried a virus that infected and was lethal to the trees. But, the real problems were, first, the weakness in the tree's inner health and, second, beetles being attracted to the sick trees.

Proof of this idea was that trees near a water source–such as a stream–were green and not attacked as much by the beetles. Those trees were less stressed because of their access to water during drought. Trees just slightly uphill and away from the water were stressed and subject to beetle attack.

Initial healing work with the Pines on the test properties meant getting all of their internal parts and processes operating individually and then operating in sync. It was clear to me that living trees with beetle "hits" possessed severely **compromised** circulation systems.

Initial work with insects was much different. I did not have to heal the beetles. They said "Oh! These healed trees are strong. We will go and find weak trees and use them for our needs."

Dr. Jim speaks of results: The results of the work were nothing short of incredible. The trees that were heavily infested or dying when we arrived in 2007, did die. After those died, most remaining trees survived. As the years progressed, some treated trees were infested by beetles but the trees continued to survive. Other trees showed Pine Bark Beetle pitch–and sometimes the

beetles themselves–draining from entry holes.

Why do I consider this work to be Cooperative BioBalance? It is because the Pine Bark Beetles want to survive and the Lodgepole Pine trees want to survive. The healthy trees can survive easily, even with some attack from the beetles. The beetles are happy since they

On the left, "Champion" was strengthened by treatment and attracted very few hits. It survived. "Fallen Hero" on the right, was weaker prior to treatment and attracted many insects (seen as leaking pitch holes).

All photos this page © Basia Alexander

can go through their natural life cycle. It is a win-win-win situation: healthy trees, healthy Pine Bark Beetles, and a healthy environment. It's wonderful to see green trees populating my test site mountainsides.

Dr. Jim mentions community: I treated nine different locations: north, south, east, and west across one of the test site towns. Since trees operate in community, I connected the communities so that a more extensive area was covered and healed.

Basia and I started to call these connected communities the "Peace Pipe Global Network Pattern," first because the area was originally Native American land and, second because of the way the various test sites interconnected in overlapping, networklike patterns. The overlapping patterns reminded us of linked Internet sites or dual doppler radar systems, as shown on television, that display weather systems passing over land and towns.

Dr. Jim addresses common questions about these tests: Is this natural reforestation? My Green Centrics System is permission based. If I were disturbing a natural process, I would not have been able to treat the trees. They would have said "no" in answer to my question, "Permission to treat?"

Oh, yes! One more point about the Pine Bark Beetles and natural reforestation. In some cases, on the test properties, I found that younger trees were under attack. Why? I say it is because they are weak internally as well, and thus subject to attack from the beetles. In a natural reforestation situation, the younger trees would not generally be attacked since they are usually vigorous. The younger trees are there to reforest the area. If the younger trees are infested, they are not able to repopulate the area.

I believe this issue circles back to the messages from the trees in Chapter 3. The trees said, "We are weak and thus susceptible to damage from insects and diseases." Why are so many tree species weak? I believe that they have all been subjected to major stress factors including drought, global climate change, pollution, and any number of other local stress factors.

Along those lines, I ask that you look at the appearance of the Pine Bark Beetles on Lodgepole Pines in the big picture. At the same time that Colorado is having trouble, various parts of the United States are having similar problems: Emerald Ash Borer is attacking Ash trees, Bronze Birch Borer is threatening Birches, Oak Wilt is hurting Oaks, Sudden Oak Death is devastating both the Live and Coastal Oaks in California, Aspen Decline is happening in Colorado, and bleeding canker is showing up on Beech trees everywhere.

Is this all natural? I doubt it! Trees are weakening everywhere.

In Charles Little's 1995, factual and disturbing book *The Dying of the Trees*, he reports his findings and illustrates that tree species after tree species and global ecosystem after global ecosystem have already suffered massive environmental degradation and tree death. He describes the non-natural causes in vivid and sickening detail.[2]

Dr. Jim emphasizes: He is not very hopeful, but I am.

I believe that Tree Whispering and the principles, practices, and technologies of Cooperative BioBalance, along with caring Nature lovers like you, can reverse the global and local trends toward tree weakening and return health to Earth's standing but endangered forests.

COOPERATIVE BIOBALANCE STORIES:
COPPER BEECH TREE WITH BLEEDING
CANKER

Majestic–over four stories tall–this Copper Beech in New Jersey, appeared healthy. But, it showed the bleeding canker of Phytophthora. The disease normally lives in the soil and is not aggressive, but it can kill a weak tree.

The owner did not allow chemicals on her estate–another solution was needed. Dr. Conroy would not try to kill the disease organism. Instead, treatment based on the concepts of Cooperative BioBalance would first strengthen the inner health of the tree itself. Then–as if he were a mediator–Dr. Conroy provided a bridge of communication to both tree and disease organisms so that they could both survive. The tree regained active growth so the canker cleared on the tree and the organism continued to live in the soil.

 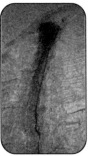  

All Beech photos © Basia Alexander

| October 8th | December 3rd | The following March 25th | July 3rd |

COPPER BEECH SAYS: *I am the perfect example of Cooperative BioBalance. My circulation was restored and my chemistry was returned to balance. After that, I was able to heal myself. I was able to cooperate with the organism so that I could live and it could live. The organism will live in the soil near me. People will know that if they see a bleeding canker on me, it is a sign to all that I am weakening again. So, the organism and I live together in peace, supporting each other.*

COOPERATIVE BIOBALANCE STORIES: FIELD TRIALS ON FLEA BEETLES AND CROPS

© Jim Conroy

Flea Beetles are aggressive insects, usually found in vegetable gardens. With healthy plants, there is an opportunity for both to co-exist. Since plants can withstand a certain amount of Flea Beetles, "to get 'em to play nice together" is a real possibility.

Dr. Conroy initially returns the plants to a healthy state of inner functionality, then he works with the insects and the crop so that they can co-exist. This affords the opportunity for the crop to be fully productive and for the insects to survive.

BEING FUTURISTIC GOALS NOW: COOPERATIVE BIOBALANCE FOR DYNAMIC BALANCE IN NATURE

Dr. Jim illustrates: Cooperative BioBalance may sound futuristic but it already exists in a multidimensional space. Cooperative BioBalance for dynamic balance in Nature exists now! This seems paradoxical. Why do I say that?

Let me remind you about the cabbages and their goals from Chapter 9. I explained that plants are *being their goals* rather than striving for them. When I talked with the cabbages during that healing session, the little heads were *being* their goal as big cabbage heads. The small physical heads that I saw in the soil in front of me just had to "fill in" in order to fully occupy the space that the big **biofield** heads had already formed. The goal of the cabbages was already within the biofield level. The big cabbage heads already existed in that dimension and simply had to fill in.

© Basia Alexander

Big Cabbage Heads

Small Cabbage Heads

The current situation in the physical dimension is "Small Cabbage Heads." This will become the old or obsolete current situation.

Small and big cabbage heads exist together in the "now" moment. For the cabbage plant, both situations exist simultaneously in a multilevel, multidimensional space.

"Big Cabbage Heads" becomes the new current situation in the physical dimension.

I use the words "fill in" to indicate a nonlinear, multidimensional, and outside-of-time occurrence. For the cabbages, all situations exist at the same time. That may seem paradoxical to you. I am talking about multidimensional and multilevel spaces which cannot be easily understood by the linear mind. Even though the flat illustration here cannot show multidimensional levels of processes, reviewing it periodically may help you to retain moments of clarity about this nonlinear explanation.

Dr. Jim applies *being* the goal to Cooperative BioBalance for dynamic balance in Nature: Similarly, the *ideas* of "live and let live," cooperation, partnership, and equality exist–now–at the same time as the ideas and realities of domination, control, and superiority exist. Dynamic balance in Nature also exists–now– at the same time that disrupted balance in Nature exists.

Basia's and my stand is to bring forth Cooperative BioBalance for dynamic balance in Nature, and so to make a new current situation in the physical. In other words, the new paradigm of "live and let live," equality, cooperation, and partnership just has to fill in to fully occupy the multidimensional space called "dynamic balance in Nature." Then, dynamic balance in Nature will show up in the physical dimension. At the same time, the old paradigm of control and domination becomes the old current situation, and therefore obsolete. Anyone participating in the principles and practices of Cooperative BioBalance *is and would be* working in the new paradigm called Cooperative BioBalance for dynamic balance in Nature. This is *being* the futuristic goal *now*.

THE BALANCE IN NATURE: THE PENDULUM SWINGING

Dr. Jim explains what happens inside of a tree or a plant:
Nature acts in perfect dynamic balance, much like a pendulum swinging to the right and left of the center.

An individual tree or plant is normally healthy and growing. It is going about its life healthily and happily. A few insects or disease organisms come along. Humans become alarmed and say, "Oh! We have to spray the tree or plant and kill the enemy!"

Nobody asks the plant, "Are these diseases or insects a problem for you?"

So, the person sprays or uses a product on the tree or plant.

Now, imagine that the pendulum–balance in Nature–swings far to the left. The plant needs to biologically break down the product. Then, the pendulum–balance in Nature–swings far to the right. The plant must compensate for the damage done. Actually, it overcompensates to the extreme right to gradually bring the balance back to center from the left-sided damage done by using the product. This overcompensation to the right is meant to restore a series of factors, such as normal flow of operations inside the plant, balance of microorganisms, and balance of plant chemistry.

At the same time, either the insect or the disease goes out of balance as well. It goes into survival mode.

Remaining on its own, the plant that was sprayed can bring back its own balance. Its interior functions that moved to the extreme right to compensate–acting like a pendulum– gradually move back to center for a dynamically balanced condition.

Is this a likely scenario? No.

What is a very likely scenario? Another, more aggressive insect or disease organism may come along. During the time that the "pendulum" in the plant is either to the extreme right or to the extreme left–which is not normal–the plant is weakened and thus more susceptible to the insects and disease organisms. This could cause the plant to get sick or to die. Or, someone comes along–not asking the plant what is going on for it–and applies a product to the plant again. So, the out-of-balance cycle continues or starts all over again. The pendulum moves to the extreme left to biologically break down the product and then to the extreme right again to compensate.

Some people may say, "I use organic products, so they are less toxic to the plant and this balance of Nature." To some degree, this is true, but it depends on the organic product. Even the right product applied at the wrong time can still be dangerous to the plant or can put the **tree↔plant↔bee↔insect↔disease↔ organism↔ecosystem↔earth↔air↔fire↔water** ratios out of balance. Even with organic products, ask the plant.

Dr. Jim emphasizes: How does a person determine what's best for the plant? Ask the plant! A person can use his or her basic knowledge of plants to ask the right questions.

How does this illustrate Cooperative BioBalance? Cooperative BioBalance is about interacting with the consciousness of the plant—communicating with its innate intelligence—and determining its relationship with the disease organism and/or the insects to keep the "pendulum" in the middle so the balance of Nature prevails. And, it is about similarly communicating with the consciousness of the disease organisms and the insects to discover their relationship with the plant.

Dr. Jim continues: A potential "peace treaty" among the plants, insects, and disease organisms is then possible. This keeps the pendulum in the middle so the dynamic balance of Nature prevails. Cooperative BioBalance is about working with the tree or plant and the insect or disease organisms to always have their needs in mind and to come from their points of view.

Where do human needs fit in? Humans have needs, too, like wanting healthy trees or plants or wanting to grow a healthy crop. Humans need these plants to be healthy in order to receive gifts like oxygen and food.

The trees, plants, insects, disease organisms, and people all want the same thing!! All want to live, grow, and be healthy. With Cooperative BioBalance, it is possible for all to live cooperatively within the balance of Nature. And, people can receive what they need, too, by asking and partnering with Nature—not manipulating Nature.

To go a step deeper in explaining Cooperative BioBalance, the balance between trees, plants, insects, and disease organisms already exists in another dimension beyond human comprehension. People can, however, be aware that it exists. Cooperative BioBalance is about bringing the balance of Nature back into the physical dimension.

Please remember that what you do in your backyard reverberates throughout the whole Plant Kingdom. Am I saying that trees and plants gossip? Not in so many words, but they do share their bioenergy fields when they live in community. When they receive respect, or get a healing treatment from a person, or when love is offered, that vibration rings in the tree or plant where it is given and then echos throughout the rest of the Plant Kingdom. In other words, offering healing to them, and feeling good about what you can do in your own backyard, ultimately affects the whole ecosystem.

Do not underestimate the profound meaning of balancing your relationship with Nature. Do not underestimate the immense power of bringing dynamic balance to even a single tree or plant.

Top Ten Reasons For Nature Lovers' Interest in Cooperative BioBalance

10. *Nature lovers can live comfortably and safely on the leading edge of global transformations occurring in human consciousness.*
9. *Cooperative BioBalance is totally sustainable. No products are used for healing.*
8. *Most Nature lovers want to live in balance and want balance in Nature; it is an ancient idea whose time has come—again.*

7. *Cooperative BioBalance is a learnable philosophy and set of skills. It is easy to learn and quick to use.*

6. *This is the enlightened kind of guardianship Nature lovers would want for their own land and for the whole planet. It addresses the main issues about Nature operating out of balance; it is not a local bandage.*

5. *The planet doesn't have to lose its stressed and weakening standing forests.*

4. *Cooperative BioBalance is likely to be consistent with Nature lovers' spiritual beliefs.*

3. *Through Cooperative BioBalance, the individual is reconnected to the web of life in co-creative, cooperative, and effective ways.*

2. *Gardeners, growers, and scientists have the prospect of food safety.*

1. *Health, balance and vitality are the result for all organisms– including people–and the planet as a whole. The total ecosystem is brought into healthy balance, multidimensionally.*

Basia explains reason number ten: Global shifts in both technology and philosophical perspectives are happening at a furious pace. Many people are looking for a reliable compass and sails that can give them stability, safety, and security as they navigate the unfamiliar waters of these times. The best compass points to the true north of one's own life values. Since Nature lovers cherish the land and likely favor cooperative approaches, the principles and practices of Cooperative BioBalance provide a comfortable yet powerful path through some of the chaos into a positive future.

Many Nature lovers like to be on the forefront of changes. Global shifts in human consciousness occurring now on Earth involve making the old **Cartesian** paradigm of domination, control, and superiority obsolete. The shift invites Nature lovers toward partnering with Nature equally and for multilateral good.

Dr. Jim explains reason 9: Cooperative BioBalance is based on the no-product, hands-on, bioenergy healing, and totally sustainable methods of Tree Whispering, Green Centrics, and Co-Existence Technologies. These bioenergy field-based healing approaches work effectively with all life forms–such as trees, insects, and diseases–so that all may co-exist in a cooperative way. Once a Green Being and its related organisms are healed, then organic products and approaches can be effectively used to keep them healthy.

Most Nature lovers appreciate sustainable approaches; they care about avoiding use of unsustainable methods. Since the soft technologies re-establish the health of trees, plants, and related organisms through bioenergy healing no products are used.

Basia explains reason 8: What is living in balance? Dr. Jim and I suggest that a life lived in dynamic balance is one that is true to inner values and does harm to none. Nature lovers probably agree with the principle "live and let live"; they feel that all of Nature's Beings want to live, including insects and disease organisms. One of the tenants of Cooperative BioBalance is that the so-called "pests" want to live, too, and can be brought into a balanced relationship with their hosts. The circle of life and Nature's balance is an ancient idea that we are sure Nature lovers recognize instinctively. The idea's time has returned!

Dr. Jim explains reasons 7 and 6: Cooperative BioBalance, as a new field of inquiry, involves the study of co-creative practices and dynamically balanced relationships among all living Beings. It's a new scholarly discipline for anyone to embrace.

Most Nature lovers want to learn Tree Whispering techniques and Cooperative BioBalance principles so that they can help and heal all the Beings of Nature that are under their guardianship. These practical, bioenergy field-based healing techniques were inspired by healing methods that some Nature lovers may already employ in their own health regimens–or may practice as healing professionals.

Dr. Jim explains reason 5: Nature lovers' tree and forest replanting efforts will be beneficial in time. However, the act of strengthening forests that are standing *now* will have dramatic short-term effects such as contributing to a positive spiral of reversing climate change or global warming. Most Nature lovers want to save forests from the negative effects of climate change. They know that forests are weak due to pollution, changes in global weather patterns, and other stress factors, and so are more susceptible to the vicious cycle of decline. Standing forests can be strengthened now with Tree Whispering, Green Centrics, and Co-Existence Technologies.

Basia explains reasons number 4 and 3: Appreciating balance in Nature and honoring the web of life are spiritually important and fulfilling experiences for many Nature lovers. Cooperative BioBalance is recognized by many as tying into both ancient and modern spirituality as well as indigenous wisdom. Even though each human Being is an individual, most understand that everything and everyone are connected. Cooperative BioBalance incorporates individuals into the global scope of connection within Nature in a practical ways that are good for the individual in body, mind, Spirit.

Nature lovers may also be excited to know their bioenergetic tree and plant healing treatments ripple out from their backyards to the whole planet. The principles and practices of Cooperative BioBalance mean that Nature lovers co-create with all of the Beings of Nature in cooperation, partnership, and equality. This leads to peaceful co-existence on the planet within all the Beings of Nature and between Nature and people.

Dr. Jim explains reasons 2 and 1: People who grow food while using the principles and practices of Cooperative BioBalance can reasonably anticipate abundant and safe harvests. Scientists who approach their research through the wisdom of Nature, as well as while using the cooperative and co-creative approaches of Cooperative BioBalance, can reasonably anticipate satisfaction of their goals, no harm done to the environment, and results that may even seem miraculous.

Most Nature lovers know that healthy trees, plants, crops, forests, and healthy related organisms are a win-win-win situation. Health is needed in the Plant Kingdom and its related organisms. Health is desirable in people. Health is sustainable for the entire earth. Because the principles, practices, and soft technologies focus on balanced relationships among all living Beings, health, vitality, co-existence, harmony, and peace result in Nature and on Earth.

The total ecosystem is brought into healthy balance. Nature lovers are already asking the plant for information and partnership and are attuned to multidimensional relationships of all organisms–not just the physical level. Then, no matter whether they do healing techniques or practical activities, they can trust that all Beings will show up in balance in the physical level.

Basia makes the list personal to you: Finally, I believe that you–as a Nature lover–want hope, options, and information about new, sustainable trends and technologies. You want to see tomorrow's results today! You want a philosophy you can stand behind because your heart resonates with it.

Exploring the ideas, practices, and technologies of Cooperative BioBalance will give you satisfaction and skills to improve the health of trees, plants, and forests in the new paradigm of cooperation, partnership, and equality with Nature.

WHAT'S NEXT?

Basia points to the future: Dr. Jim and I are creating the Institute for Cooperative BioBalance. It will be both an educational organization as well as a foundation for social and philanthropic initiatives.

Dr. Jim says: The Institute for Cooperative BioBalance will develop outlets for activism consistent with its principles.

And, there are things you can do now.

Begin with personal sharing, then see where your heart leads you. Be connected with Nature.

Learn to ask the tree or plant about its life.

Stand up and protect that tree, the open land, or your forest.

By changing and implementing respectful attitudes and practices, you can bring balance to your backyard, which ripples out to the ecosystem and the whole planet.

At the end of the day, it's your heart connection–and humanity's heart's connection–to trees and plants that will make the difference as all of us walk the path of Nature in Balance into the future.

Afterword: Change and Celebrate

When we try to pick out anything by itself, we find it hitched to everything else in the universe.

JOHN MUIR
AMERICAN NATURALIST, EXPLORER, AND WRITER, 1838-1914

OLD MODEL: NATURE OUT OF BALANCE

Dr. Jim explains: People are so accustomed to taking actions inside of the model "**Nature** Out of Balance" that they think their actions are normal or even beneficial. Unconscious practices of domination, control, and superiority perpetuate the "Nature Out of Balance" model. The uncomfortable truth is that every time—every single time—a person does anything with a tree or plant, a bug or microorganism, without **communicating** with it, the model "Nature Out of Balance" is perpetuated. These actions include using products–even organic products–without asking the plant first. People who take such human-centric actions cannot expect ecologically balanced results—it is insanity to act this way.

The alarming truth is that the planet's ecosystems, which have supported human life up until now, are drastically changing. Whether you *believe* that people have had anything to do with ecosystem changes is *irrelevant*. Whether people have actually had anything to do with changes in ecosystems is *unimportant*. Nature is out of balance now.

Every day, in my work, I see ecosystems changing. I also follow reports of new insects, new diseases, and new unwanted plants that are continuously appearing. Stable equilibrium is a thing of the past. **Mother Nature** shows signs of extreme fluctuations in local and global areas. As you know from hearing a loud screech when a microphone is put too close to a speaker–fluctuations in **feedback loops** expand on themselves to the extreme.

You may wonder, "Can we survive as fluctuations in ecosystems become more extreme?" Mother Nature is powerful; just ask anyone who has been through a tornado. But, we are not helpless in the face of Her power. We are not victims. We do not have to be at the effect of forces we think are beyond our control.

Mother Nature is also a potential partner. Trees, plants, organisms, and living Beings want to return to sustainable equilibrium. They have told me so.

So, the better question is this: For bringing balance back into Nature now—what are we going to do, each of us and all of us?

This book suggests that what we–each of us and all of us–can do is to form a partnership-of-equals with Nature and to communicate and cooperate with each of Her Beings. You've read the whole book now and have an understanding of how Tree Whispering and Cooperative BioBalance works. The solutions for bringing balance back into Nature are now in your heart, in your willingness to listen to Nature's Beings, and in your hands.

New Model: Nature In Balance

Basia interjects: The models that we live in–that represent our guidelines for thinking and acting–are the true powers behind human interactions with trees, plants, or with any living Beings.

Dr. Jim declares: It's time to shift the model. And in doing so, you will also have to change your practices! Going forward into the future, what do you do while living inside the model called "Nature In Balance"?

First and foremost, remember the major principle of Cooperative BioBalance: live and let live. The plants, insects, and diseases all want to live. They all have a purpose in the balance of Nature. In reality, the plants, insects, and diseases can live cooperatively. A tree can live to its full potential with insects and diseases, when they live in balance. In fact, a balanced presence of insects might actually stimulate a tree or plant. A balanced presence of disease organisms or insects should be an indication to people that the plant or crop is in balance.

Where can you start? Start in your own backyard.

How can you start? Start by changing the way you relate to trees and plants: Have more respect. Start by implementing new practices such as being, asking, healing, saving, and loving the trees and plants as taught in this book. In those ways, you can bring balance to your backyard that ripples out to the ecosystem and the whole planet.

Basia adds: When you realize that you are operating inside of a model, you have true power; you can make new choices. You can change the model by examining what you believe and by changing what you do. That is the secret methodology for accomplishing a personal **paradigm shift**.

Taking bold actions, such as the ones suggested in this book as well as other actions you may be inspired to take, will require confidence and leadership on your part. Why? Because the experiences and insights you garnered from reading this book are not shared by most people—yet. You may be up against harsh realities, but now you know differently. You know that there is a better way.

Dr. Jim points to results: Basia and I have prepared you. You can follow these guidelines: Move to attitudes and practices of cooperation, partnership, and equality with all living Beings; come from the plant's or the tree's point of view; heal the **internal functionality** of trees and plants, and their related organisms; be aware of the multidimensional relationships among trees, plants, ecosystems, and their various related organisms, including bees, other insects and diseases.

Then all the healthy Beings of Nature strengthen and heal the ecosystem—as interlocking network patterns—and the ecosystem strengthens, heals, and supports all the Beings of Nature *in balance*.

I believe that each and all of us have an obligation—a sacred duty—to change the model to "Nature In Balance."

The results that will show up in the physical for you and for trees, plants, and ecosystems are true possibilities. First, mutual cooperation can exist within the Plant Kingdom. Second, a truce can be attained between plants and their related organisms. Third, peace can prevail between people and all of the Beings of Nature. And, last but not least, harmony can grow during your next quiet walk in the woods!

On that walk, you may hear the same quiet as before, but from reading this book, the possibility of quiet *underneath* the quiet exists. The possibility of harmony exists among all of Nature's Beings. Now you know that your quiet walk in the woods can truly be quiet on the inside of all Beings in Nature, including you. This is real peace in Nature. This is cause for true celebration!

Both Dr. Jim and Basia cheer: The celebration begins! Communicating with and being in **co-creative** relationships with trees and plants and all of Nature is a joyous accomplishment for humanity.

By understanding that other life forms have the ability and desire to communicate and cooperate–peacefully–among themselves and with people, is cause for a huge celebration.

This celebration resonates throughout humanity, the Plant Kingdom, other living Beings, Earth, and the universe beyond.

It's an honor to serve you.

We thank you for reading this book.

The trees and plants thank you for reading this book.

The trees and plants wait for you to communicate with them.

Appendix: The Philosophy and Relevant Sciences

THE PHILOSOPHY:
SIX BASIC PREMISES OF TREE WHISPERING®, GREEN CENTRICS™,
COOPERATIVE BIOBALANCE,™ AND CO-EXISTENCE TECHNOLOGIES™

Premise 1: All trees and plants are alive; they are living Beings.

Premise 2: Stress compromises internal functionality.

*Internal functionality can be thought of as all of the interacting and interdependent **feedback loops** operating inside of an organism. Functionality operates like an orchestra. When an orchestra is playing harmoniously, all the instruments are in tune, on beat, and playing the same music. If not, there is discord. Similarly with a tree, all aspects of inner functionality must be coordinated and working properly in relation to all other aspects of inner physiology for the tree to be healthy.*

*For example, just because it rains, it doesn't mean that a tree is no longer affected by the drought stress. **Compromises** in its hydration system can persist well beyond the next five or fifty rains.*

*Examples of **internal functionality** for a tree or plant include:*
- *Circulation of fluids*
- *Photosynthesis*
- *Uptake of water and nutrients*
- *Movement of water and nutrients in the xylem and phloem to the growing point*
- *Cell division*

Premise 3: Three or more stress factors lead to decline in trees. *Insects and disease organisms rarely are the cause of stress but rather are drawn to already stressed trees, thereby deepening the tree's stress.*

Stress factors are additive as shown in this example. A summer drought that compromises the circulation system may be followed by an excessively wet autumn. That further taxes the system and may open the door to fungal diseases. Then, abnormal warmth may persist into winter followed by a drop to extreme cold. This can freeze buds that were beginning to swell in the abnormal warmth. Frozen buds may die. New buds will have to be regenerated, using precious food stores. The expected food supply from the original leaf generation is postponed, so availability of food in spring is either late or stores of food must come up from the roots. Spring may be dry so rains do not activate the microbial life in the soil to interact with the roots. Insufficient water uptake imbalances the ratio of sugars to water to nutrients. *Meanwhile, the tree's water and fluid transportation systems are still not operating at full capacity, so the food that is produced may not travel to the growing points to make more leaves.*

Then, a long cloudy and cold snap in spring may shut down further photosynthesis. This may open the door to an insect attack on the ailing and too-small leaves, further reducing photosynthesis. And the downward cycle may continue. Then, there may be a hot spell in summer. Other challenges may arise: Construction on the site may compact the soil or cut roots, well-meaning landscapers may pile mulch higher than recommended, thereby rotting the roots, tree-loving homeowners may fertilize, ignorant of the fact that a stressed tree will be overtaxed by too much nitrogen.

Premise 4: Decline can be reversed even after conventional tree-care approaches are exhausted.

*Decline can be reversed by reestablishing functionality and **dynamic balance** inside of the tree; in other words, by healing the tree's inner operations. Conventional tree-care techniques are primarily applied outside of the tree, with the hope that the tree can heal itself on the inside. Decline can be reversed—not by adding additional stressors such as fertilizers or doing invasive techniques—but by **communicating** in partnership with the powerful bio-electromagnetic **Growth Energy** of the tree itself and by working with the tree's physiology and **bioenergy** field. The downward spiral of decline can be reversed. An upward spiral of growth results with bioenergetic and **energy medicine** based techniques. Products such as fertilizers or biological additives and techniques like root aeration may then be effective to keep the tree healthy.*

Premise 5: "Coming from their point of view" represents a new kind of bioenergetic partnership with Nature and is respectful to it. The potential for peaceful and balanced co-existence is possible in three ways: within the Plant Kingdom itself, among plants and related organisms including diseases and insects, and between people, the Plant Kingdom and all Beings of Nature.

*"Coming from the tree's point of view" is possible using proven "new science" findings, **intentional** thinking, heart-based sensitivity, and intuitive approaches. Modern humans assume—as a result of 400 years of **Cartesian** scientific methodology—that people are objective. However, recent findings in quantum physics and other new sciences have proven that everything is related and there is no such thing as objectivity. Ancient peoples knew this and current indigenous peoples survive based on this truth.*

*Therefore, Dr. Jim Conroy developed the Green Centrics™ System—a system that respects the **Life Force** or Growth Energy of trees and plants. In this system, the practitioner separates the human or self-focus and "comes* *from the tree's point of view" in order to assist it in bio-energetically healing itself.*

Cooperative BioBalance and Co-Existence Technologies take the partnership a step further to include all living Beings in harmonious balance and peaceful co-existence.

Premise 6: Hands-on techniques, *borrowed from human alternative health-care systems, are effective for* **Green Beings** *and related organisms.*

Alternative health-care systems abound for humans and are being accepted into mainstream medical and hospital settings for severely ill patients. Inspired by a human alternative health-care system (the BodyTalk System,™ developed by Dr. John Veltheim) as well as other human energy-healing systems, Dr. Conroy realized that similar principles and techniques could be applied to trees and all plants. After Dr. Conroy's formal education and a lifetime of working with plant health, he was sure that plant health professionals were focusing on disjointed aspects and thus missing something vital about plant health: restoring dynamic balance to the whole system from the inside-out.

Thus, the systems are designed to heal or repair the full range of plant health aspects (botanical, scientific, environmental, physiological, bio-energetic, multicultural, cyclical, multidimensional issues, and more) by borrowing proven "hands-on" human energy-healing techniques such as touching, tapping, intentional concentration, and focused attention.

THE ROLE OF INDIVIDUAL BELIEF SYSTEMS AND RELEVANT SCIENCES

If a person does not believe that a tree or plant is–at some level–alive, then that person may have trouble thinking outside-the-box to understand Tree Whispering, the Green Centrics System, Cooperative BioBalance and Co-Existence Technologies approaches. These are **holistic** *approaches that ask for a temporary suspension of well-known assumptions about how trees and plants should work and an open mind about how people believe the world works.*

When understandings about quantum physics, the human heart and its **biofield**, *plant bio-electromagnetic fields, fractal design, and intentionality are in place, it is possible to make the leap to thinking outside-the-box concerning this new approach to tree, plant, crop, forest, and ecosystem health care.*

QUANTUM PHYSICS

In the early 1900s, a new breed of scientists broke from the Newtonian physics of the previous 400 years. Their experimental results with energy, particles, and light did not fit into the Newtonian principles created during Renaissance times. During the 1900s, quantum physicists explored the nature of matter and of light, determining that everything is energy and all matter is fundamentally connected.

Fritjof Capra, as a quantum physicist and author, drew parallels between the new physics and ancient spiritual principles. In his 1975 classic, The Tao of Physics, *he made three important points:*

1) Everything is energy.

2) All matter is shown to be physically connected at the most fundamental levels, in much the same way that mystics throughout the ages have taught.

3) Linear thought, emphasized by Descartes and Newton during the Renaissance, works for large-scale and practical science, but it does not work at the quantum level. At the level of photons, a new kind of thinking–holistic and systems thinking–is what works. 1

THE SCIENCE OF LIVING SYSTEMS

© Basia Alexander

Since the 1980s, scientists worldwide have studied different aspects of what it means to be a living system. In their search for a fundamental definition, they have explored a full range of systems including biological organisms as well as computer models. Dr. Capra assembled and synthesized all of their work in his landmark book The Web of Life. *He describes three criteria as the new definition of a living system.*

1) "Network Pattern." Trees and plants operate with a complex pattern of organization like a large orchestra. They have countless interacting and interdependent parts and functions that work in feedback loops.

2) "Dissipative Structure." Living systems undergo dynamic change and yet maintain a stable structure. For example, as an Oak tree begins as an acorn and grows into a massive tree, so it has a stable structure while dynamic changes occur constantly.

3) *"**Cognition** as the Process of Life."* All living things show
intelligence or **cognition**. *Not only do sunflowers follow the sun's
progress east to west during the day, but also in the morning, they are
waiting for the sun in the east again. This is not human intelligence,
which is the result of language and culture. It is "cognition" in the
same sense that a single-celled organism in a petri dish will go
toward the food and away from the poison.* **2**

*Trees and plants qualify in all three criteria of living systems. Even
though very different in structure and physiology, trees and other plants
share a similar fundamental cellular biology with humans. All cells
have walls and internal structures, and operate based on energy
exchanges and patterns. Aggregates of cells–called "systems"–must
interact in coordination with other systems for the benefit of the whole.
This is the same in all living organisms. According to Dr. Lipton in his
book* The Biology of Belief, *every cell–whether animal or plant–is
itself intelligent. The membrane of cells must "decide" what to allow in
and what to keep out.***3**

INTELLIGENCE WITHIN NATURE

Jeremy Narby's inquiry into knowledge, a book called Intelligence in
Nature, *builds a strong case not only for the mechanism of cognition as
conceived by the scientists about whom Capra reports, but also for the
reality of intelligent decision-making by species other than humans. For
Narby, the bottom line on plants, specifically, is that plants do not
"have" brains as much as they "are" brains. According to the
authorities Narby interviews, an entire plant organism uses chemical
signaling in a way that parallels neuron activity in animals.*

*Narby focuses his examination of intelligence on both animals and
plants through both conventional and unconventional means. In many
chapters, he reports on pleasant conversations with world-renowned
scientists. In others, he describes personal experiences of immersion
into shamanistic rituals and journeys. His quest is more for insight than
for the one and only "right" answer.***4**

*The Society of Plant Signaling and Behavior welcomes interdisciplinary
approaches to ferret out the physical basis of adaptive behavior and
signaling processes in plants. They call themselves a community of
scientists interested in sensory plant biology and communicative
ecology in plants. Several of the members' papers are quoted in the
body of this book and are referenced in the Citations.***5**

HUMAN ENERGY FIELDS, ALSO CALLED *"BIOFIELDS"*

In the 1990s, sensitive new equipment and new human experiments revealed that the heart has as much neural tissue as the brain-in-the-head. More than that, the heart has a measurable bio-electromagnetic field which it generates. This discovery led scientists to declare that the heart is a brain, too. As such, it is like radio technology: both a transmitter of information and a receiver. Coherence between the heart-brain and the head-brain leads to enormous health benefits for people.

The Institute of HeartMath leads both research and education initiatives in order to establish heart-based living and global coherence of consciousness by inspiring people to connect with the intelligence and guidance of their own hearts. Since 1991, The Institute of HeartMath has conducted basic research into psychophysiology, neurocardiology, and biophysics. They are frequently in collaboration with universities, research centers, and health-care-system partners. This research has advanced understanding of heart-brain interactions and heart-rhythm coherence. Their research interests also include the electrophysiology of intuition and exploring how all life is globally interconnected at a deep, fundamental level via electromagnetic fields and biofields.

The HeartMath Institute has discovered that the human heart is more than a pump. The heart is another brain and communicates with the brain in the head in four different ways:
1) neurologically: It's got circuitry that interprets body conditions.
2) biochemically: It produces a hormone nicknamed "the balance hormone."
3) biophysically: It produces pressure waves in the arteries that travel faster than the flow of blood.
4) energetically: The heart emits a bio-electromagnetic field that is stronger than the brain's field and can be detected several feet away from the body.

In addition to the extensive neural communication network linking the heart with the brain and body, the heart also communicates information to the brain and throughout the body via electromagnetic field interactions. The heart generates the body's most powerful and most extensive rhythmic electromagnetic field.

© Basia Alexander

Compared to the electromagnetic field produced by the brain, the electrical component of the heart's field is about 60 times greater in amplitude and permeates every cell in the body. The magnetic component is approximately 5,000 times stronger than the brain's magnetic field and can be detected several feet away from the body with sensitive magnetometers. **6, 7, 8, 9**

Initial research performed by the HeartMath Institute in 1998 made promising inroads into scientific proof of a mechanism that could explain how energy medicine, such as the laying on of hands, might work. The research suggests that an exchange of electromagnetic energy produced by the heart occurs when people touch or are in close proximity. It showed that one person's electrocardiogram (ECG) signal registered in another person's electroencephalogram (EEG) when there was hand-holding and also when the two people simply sat within 18 inches of each other. **10**

In the 1972 classic, The Fields of Life, Our Links with the Universe, *Harold Saxton Burr reported on his forty years of research at Yale University School of Medicine. He and his colleagues confirmed that all living things have electrodynamic fields–called "L" fields–which can be measured. His research showed that human "L" fields vary with a person's physical and mental condition.* **11**

In her 2002 paper, Dr. Beverly Rubik suggests that the biofield is a complex, extremely weak electromagnetic field of an organism. It is hypothesized to involve electromagnetic bio-information for regulating homeodynamics. She declares the biofield to be "a useful construct consistent with bioelectromagnetics and the physics of nonlinear, dynamical, nonequilibrium living systems. It offers a unifying hypothesis to explain the interaction of objects or fields with the organism, and is especially useful toward understanding the scientific basis of energy medicine, including acupuncture, biofield therapies, bioelectromagnetic therapies, and homeopathy. The rapid signal propagation of electromagnetic fields comprising the biofield as well as its holistic properties may account for the rapid, holistic effects of certain alternative and complementary medical interventions." **12**

PLANT BIOENERGY FIELDS, ALSO CALLED "GROWTH ENERGY"

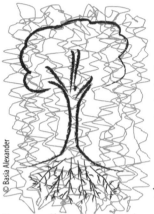

When it came out in the 1960s, The Secret Life of Plants *was a best-seller. It was full of historic and anecdotal information about plants as living organisms and about the people who worked with and studied them. Most notable was lie detector expert Cleve Baxter, well known for hooking up his lie detection equipment to a houseplant in his office. He threatened the plant with fire. The results were amazing: The plant's energy fields were detectable. He extended his work to other living organisms.*[13, 14]

Every cell in a tree or plant produces bio-electromagnetic energy (Growth Energy) because of countless interacting and interdependent inner processes that operate in complex feedback loops. Feedback loops are indications of a living system in operation. Stephen Buhner's book, The Secret Teachings of Plants, *offers a wealth of information and accounts about the heart as an organ of perception and plants as generators of bio-electromagnetic fields. His bibliography is full of other references on this and other topics.*[15]

OVERLAPPING ENERGY FIELDS

To recap: Human Beings generate measurable bio-electromagnetic fields—also known as bioenergy fields— primarily from their hearts. Trees and plants, as whole organisms, have smart cells and countless inner functions operating in complex feedback loops. Like human Beings, trees and plants also generate bioenergy fields.

Just as the waves that bring signals to a cell phone can't be seen, waves that interact between people or between a person and a plant can't be seen, but they do exist. Information is exchanged between the bioenergy fields of living systems.

When coherent energy patterns overlap as interference patterns, a third pattern is produced. This third pattern is proven to contain new information.[16]

SELF-MAKING

The three criteria defining living systems discussed earlier in the Science of Living Systems section, can be expressed in another way as proposed by Gail Fleischaker: A living system must be self-bounding, self-generating, and self-perpetuating.

Together, these concepts suggest that a living system or living Being, such as a plant, forest, or an ecosystem, not only defines itself but also continuously recreates itself by interacting within itself in feedback loops.[17, 18]

FRACTAL DESIGN

All of Nature's Beings use self-bounding, self-generating, and self-perpetuating intelligent design in their organizing patterns.

For example, fractal patterns are self-similar, self-repeating organizing patterns seen throughout Nature.[19]

Note the simple branching design that repeats at different sizes and levels of complexity in the Soybean leaf.

In the Sunflower's center, note the fractal Fibonacci sequence inside the petals: 1, 1, 2, 3, 5, 8, 13, 21, 34, 55, 89, 144, etc. [20]

HUMAN INTENTION IN USE

In her book, The Intention Experiment, *Lynne McTaggart reports on studies performed in the last 100 years, and mostly in the last twenty years, involving the use of targeted human thought, intention, and focused attention to impact matter, including living systems.*

Studies relevant to plants include:

• *Fritz-Albert Popp has proven that light emanates from organisms. He has proven that photons are generated by the DNA of all organisms.*

• *Konstantin Korotkov's bioenergy fields research shows that there is a two-way flow of information between living Beings. It is thought that this research confirms Cleve Backster's lie detector work.[21, 22]*

Recent work photographing water as it freezes into snowflakes, by Japanese scientist Dr. Masaru Emoto, reveals amazingly beautiful crystals. As might be expected, water taken from pure sources produces well shaped, beautiful crystals, while water from polluted sources produces misshapen, ugly forms upon freezing. Pictures can be seen in The Hidden Messages in Water *and other of his books.*

What was not expected in Dr. Emoto's work was the effect that attention, prayer, the written word, music, meditation, and focused intention had on water. All of those activities had a dramatic effect in changing the appearance from the original crystal photo to the resulting crystal photo. For instance, "thank you" written on a container of water changed the resulting appearance of the ice crystal. If free-floating water can be influenced by intention or music or words, what effect might happen to the water in human bodies or in trees and plants?[23]

ENERGY MEDICINE

David Feinstein, PhD, and Donna Eden address six properties of energy medicine for humans. These six properties draw attention to the strengths of approaches that could serve to augment conventional human health-care models. These include the ways energy medicine (1) addresses biological processes at their energetic foundations; (2) regulates biological processes with precision, speed, and flexibility; (3) fosters healing and prevents illness with practical interventions that can be used easily, economically, and noninvasively; (4) includes methods that can be utilized at home or on a self-help basis, thereby fostering patient empowerment and a stronger patient-practitioner relationship; 5) adopts nonlinear concepts consistent with the following: the healing impact of prayer, the role of intention in healing, and compatibility with quantum resonance;

6) *strengthens the integration of body, mind, and Spirit, leading not only to a focus on holistic healing, but also to greater well-being, peace, and passion for life.24*

Some Alternative and Complementary Human Health-Care Approaches:

Therapuetic Touch™	*Reiki*	*BodyTalk System*™
Touch for Health™	*Yoga*	*HeartMath*®
Chiropractic	*Various massage*	*Homeopathy*
Acupressure	*EMDR*™	*Matrix Energetics*®
Acupuncture	*EFT*™	*Feldenkrais Method*®

Changes are generated in these approaches through:

Breathing	*Tapping*	*Movement*
Imagining	*Focused attention*	*Application of energy*
Visualizing	*Intentional*	*flows*
Touching	*concentration*	

*Tree Whispering, Green Centrics, Cooperative BioBalance and Co-Existence Technologies make use of similar concepts and techniques. These approaches impact **Life Force** by adjusting alignment, removing blockages, reconnecting functionality, and redirecting the patterns of energy flow.*

ILLUSTRATIONS DEPICT STAGES OF INTERACTIONS RELEVANT IN COOPERATIVE BIOBALANCE

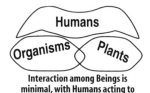

Interaction among Beings is minimal, with Humans acting to dominate and control.

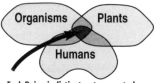

Each Being is distinct, yet connected. The overlap in the center shows the sum of all parts.

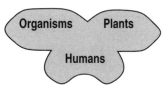

Wholes interrelating with wholes is greater than the sum of all parts. It's transformational, like a caterpiller becoming a butterfly.

Glossary: What Is Meant by Bold Words

Bioenergy and Biofield: inherent energy arising from within and surrounding any living Being. May be the essence of a living Being. Sometimes referred to as "vibration."

Bodymind: the inseparable combination of physical, mental, emotional, and spiritual bodies of a living Being, specifically a human. This is a modern, wholistic view of human Being. The idea of inseparability is gaining acceptance, and is in contradiction to views put forth by René Descartes and other Renaissance era philosophers and scientists. See the next entry.

Cartesian: refers to René Descartes (1596–1650), French philosopher and writer. He is famous for the statement, "I think, therefore I am." Descartes forwarded a highly influential form of body-mind dualism. He suggested that through scientific methodology, the natural world's Beings could be studied as things—separate from the human self and divisible by reductionist methods. He felt that a mechanical–or clocklike–approach to studying objects should be able to lead humanity to a firm and unchanging knowledge of itself and the natural world. This line of thinking impacted nearly 400 years of thought in Western civilization, but has been proven unsound by the last century's advances in quantum physics showing that there are no objects—all energy in the universe is now considered entangled—and modern studies of whole, living systems showing their interrelatedness.

Co-creative or co-creation: cooperation in a creative effort, usually an equal and mutually beneficial alliance between two or more intelligent Beings to attain a shared purpose.
In a co-creative endeavor between a human and the consciousness of Nature, the human would provide the definition of what is wanted, and would ask Nature's innate intelligence and wisdom about how to achieve the goal. Such inquiries result in Nature's consciousness providing indications of how to accomplish the goal efficiently, wisely, and sustainably.

Cognition: perception, the process of knowing.

Communicate or commune: to give and receive mutually; to make known; the overlapping energy fields and exchanging of information; being joined; the expression of thoughts and feelings; is not limited to any particular methodology.
Communication between living Beings occurs when information is shared or exchanged, or when sensory or emotional perception is acknowledged.

Compromised: unable to function, vulnerable to danger, impairment, weakened.

Decline: deterioration or pulling in and down of Growth Energy; prequel to death.

Dynamic balance: the ever-moving center of stability of a living system. Static equilibrium or perfect symmetry is considered impossible in a living Being. Here, the word dynamic indicates the vitality and changing conditions which occur in living Beings constantly. Dynamic balance exists within sustainable limits. Imbalance or instability shows up as disproportionate or unsustainable fluctuations.

Feedback loop: the path, process, and signal by which the output of a system is returned to the input. A living system is defined as a system that is composed of complex, cycling interactions that interrelate and regulate its own balance. Related to the entry above: dynamic balance.

Energy medicine: complementary and alternative therapies, usually involving either "veritable" electromagnetism or "putative" approaches such as Yoga, Reiki, Therapeutic Touch, Qi Gong, or acupuncture. Such therapies are gaining wide accepance and are often a supplement to conventional medicine in hospitals for cancer and heart patients.

Green Being: any member of the Plant Kingdom

Growth Energy: the aggregate of a Green Being's physiology and its Life Force.

Healthy-looking: A tree or plant that appears–visually and superficially–to be healthy, but may not have healthy inner functionality.

Holistic: of the whole; an entire system or complete Being; total, comprehensive, integrated; may also imply a spiritual wholeness.

Internal functionality: the aggregate of a living Being's parts and systems as mutually interactive and supportive operations. It's the universe of all interactions within a living Being.

Intelligence: capacity for knowing, ability to perceive and comprehend meaning, ability to manipulate one's environment, the design and resultant manifestation of innate wisdom. Sometimes considered the consciousness of a living Being.

Intention: an act of purposeful and beneficial focus or the result of that focus, usually involving meaning or significance; the directed use of attention for creating a concept or vision; sometimes an aim that guides action or a process of healing; commitment; volition.

Life Force: a living Being's source of vitality, spirit, energy, strength; may be a Divine source.

Mother Nature or **Mother Earth:** the totality of all ecosystems and elements; the force of consciousness, which is the aggregate of all form and greater than the aggregate. Sometimes referred to as "Gaia."

Nature: all form, including the elements, natural structures such as mountains, the biological world including all plant, insect, fungal, microscopic, and mammalian life as well as human kind. Not limited to physical manifestations; may be multidimensional.

Nature Consciousness: a phrase used to indicate something ineffable, spiritual, or Divine. Readers may choose to use a different word or phrase of their liking. This glossary will not attempt to define "consciousness" but will point to various attributes intended by the phrase "Nature Consciousness."

Nature Consciousness contains the intelligence or cognition shown to exist within living Beings, addressed in Chapter 3. The phrase represents the real but invisible energies embodied in all form. It is considered to operate in multidimensional spaces, in overlapping network patterns and in self-repeating fractal scales. The phrase is also used in this book to address the Spirit within all Life. A model of Nature Consciousness is proposed through which people can communicate, interact, and make co-creative requests of the vast, inherent intelligence responsible for creating and maintaining the form of living Beings.

Paradigm and Paradigm shift: a set of basic assumptions; the philosophical framework of a scientific disciple or cultural patterns of thought and belief that are widely held at a given time. An example is the flat-earth thinking that defined travel during the Middle Ages but is considered archaic now.

A paradigm shift is considered to be the transformation of one framework/model for human thinking and acting toward another framework/model. A paradigm shift usually occurs when the old pattern becomes unworkable, unsustainable, or is proven inaccurate–such as flat-earth thinking.

Usually considered to be a cultural phenomenon, a paradigm shift must occur in each individual's life through changes in beliefs or behavior. Conditions that can facilitate acceptance of a new set of ideas include organizations providing legitimacy, leaders and media make proclamations, governments giving credence, educators teaching, conferences that convene to discuss the new ideas, and population groups gathering to embrace the new model.

The case is currently being made that there are multiple paradigm shifts occurring globally in human consciousness.

For more information, please consult the reading list at www.TreeWhispering.com.

Citations and More to Learn

Basia says: Welcome to the Citations. Not only will you find details here that will allow you to pursue further reading, but also I offer comments, suggestions, and even give a few thumbnail reviews.

CHAPTER 2, YOUR TRAIL GUIDES, P.9

1. www.GenesisFarm.org

CHAPTERS 3, 5, 6, AND 8
DETAILS ABOUT TREE WHISPERING® WORKSHOP GRADUATES QUOTED. ALPHABETIZED BY FIRST NAME.

Adaela McLaughlin, Haverhill, Massachusetts, professional gardener and landscaper, Peaceful Valley Gardens Organic Gardening and Lawn Care, www.PeacefulValleyGardens.com.

Alexandra Soteriou, MA, Passaic County, New Jersey, energy healer and business owner, World Paper, Inc., a tree-free paper company, www.WorldPaperUsa.com.

Alana DuBois, Robbinsville, New Jersey, massage therapist, Reiki and Integrated Energy Therapy™ master instructor.

Ann St.Germaine, Eatontown, New Jersey, educator, writer, and photographer, www.STGnature.com, annstgermaine@gmail.com.

Carol Hulley, Kings Park, New York, gardener.

Carol Ohmart-Behan, Endicott, New York, author and guide of spiritual journeys to Glastonbury, England, www.GoldenSpiralJourney.com.

Carraig "Rocky" Romeo, Princeton, New Jersey, businessman and Druid.

Cheryl Smith, PhD, University of New Hampshire, extension professor and plant health specialist (plant pathologist), http://extension.unh.edu/Agric/AGPDTS/PlantH.htm and www.facebook.com/UNHPDL.

Chuck Winship, Town of Springwater, New York, maple syrup farmer, Sugarbush Hollow, LLC, www.SugarHouseSyrup.com.

Danielle Rose, Northern New Jersey, author of a spiritual novel for young adults, *MindKey*, newspaper columnist, www.DanielleRoseWriter.com.

David Slade, Guilford, Connecticut, arborist and owner of Family Tree Care, LLC, www.Family-Tree-Care.com.

Debbra Gill, New York, New York, energy medicine healer, holistic nutritionist and wellness director for the Art Ranch for Kids, www.TheArtRanch.net, debbragill@aol.com.

Dorrie Rosen, RLA, New York, New York, plant information specialist, New York Botanical Garden.

Dwight Brooks, Katonah, New York, arborist, horticulturalist, organic land-care teacher, www.Dwight-Brooks.com.

Georgette Hritz, Scotch Plains, New Jersey, postal worker, homeowner and longtime Tree Whispering student.

Gerry Verrillo, Guilford, Connecticut, arborist, www.ChristensenLandscape.com.

Ilona Anne Hress, L.C.S.W., C.M.T., Rev., Madison, New Jersey, spiritual healer, www.GrowingConsciousness.com.

Jeff Dawson, Napa, California, horticulturalist, curator of gardens, Round Pond Winery.

Joan Lenart, North Haven, Connecticut, gardener and homeowner.

Jude Villa, Martha's Vineyard, Massachussetts, professional landscaper and designer.

Judy Perry, Maine, artist and landowner, www.JudyPerryStudio.com.

Leslie Ashman, Reston, Virginia, project manager and Gaia Consciousness advocate, www.ChironBlue.com.

Leo G. Kelly, West Haven, Connecticut, arborist and master gardener.

Linda S. Ludwig, USA, divine healer and business owner, The Life Force Institute, Ltd., http://TLFI.wordpress.com/.

Liz Wassell, New Paltz, New York, copy editor, Reiki practitioner, animal and Nature communicator, www.HVCReiki.org, LizWassell@gmail.com.

Lori Myrick, East Windsor, Connecticut, I.E.T. (Integrated Energy Therapy™) master and animal Reiki practitioner. lmyrick555@att.net.

Madeline "Groweesha" Thompson, Boonton, New Jersey, licensed professional counselor and drug addiction specialist, owner of Growing with the Seasons: A Center for Inspiration, www.GrowingWithTheSeasons.com.

Maria Petrova, New York City, New York, professional graphic designer and energy medicine healer, www.MariaPetrova.com and www.MariaPetrova.com/Bodytalk.

Marise Hamm, Sag Harbor, New York, feng shui consultant, www.LivingEnergyDesigns.com.

Mary McNerney, Lincoln, Massachusetts, attorney, marymcn@earthlink.net.

Melanie Buzek, Cornville, Arizona, physical therapist, advanced certified BodyTalk instructor and practitioner, www.MelanieBuzek.com.

Mike Nadeau, Sherman, Connecticut, holistic land-care practitioner, www.PlantscapesOrganics.com and www.MichaelNadeau.org.

Paul O'Kula, Center Moriches, New York, arborist, O'Kula Tree Care, www.OkulaTreeCare.com.

Robin Rose Bennett, Hewitt, New Jersey, visionary herbalist, renowned teacher, and author of *Healing Magic—A Green Witch Guidebook to Conscious Living* and *Green Treasures—Herbal Medicines from Mother Earth*, www.RobinRoseBennett.com.

Sally Malanga, West Orange, New Jersey, tree protector and founder of EccoBella Natural and Organic Beauty products, www.EccoBella.com.

Sylvia D'Andrea, Fair Lawn, New Jersey, graphic designer and homeowner, Meadow Art & Design.

Tchukki Andersen, Billerica, Massachusetts, arborist.

CHAPTER 3, MESSAGES FROM TREES, P. 21

1. http://en.wikipedia.org/wiki/Diffraction_pattern

2. http://en.wikipedia.org/wiki/Definition_of_life

3. Peter H. Raven, Ray F. Evert, and Susan E. Eichhorn, *Biology of Plants, Sixth Edition* (New York: W. H. Freeman & Co., 1999), pp. 150–51.

4. Steve Curwood (Interviewer) and Mark Moffett (Interviewee) 1994, "Life at 150 Feet" (Interview transcript). Retrieved from Living on Earth website: http://www.loe.org/shows/shows.htm?programID=94-P13-00019

5. http://en.wikipedia.org/wiki/Rheum_nobile

6. http://en.wikipedia.org/wiki/Heliotropism

7. http://en.wikipedia.org/wiki/Plant_defense_against_herbivory

8. Linda Walling, "The Myriad Plant Responses to Herbivores," *Journal of Plant Growth Regulation* 19 (2000): 195–216. http://www.cepceb.ucr.edu/resources/biblio.htm#phloem

9. J. Engelberth, H. T. Alborn, E. A. Schmelz, and J. H. Tumlinson, "Airborne Signals Prime Plants Against Insect Herbivore Attack," in *Proceedings of the National Academy of Sciences of the USA* 101:6 (2004): 178–85. www.ncbi.nlm.nih.gov/pmc/articles/PMC341853/

10. Stephen Harrod Buhner, *The Secret Teaching of Plants; The Intelligence of the Heart in the Direct Perception of Nature* (Rochester, VT: Bear & Company, 2004), p. 45.

11. Fritjof Capra, *The Web of Life* (New York: Anchor Books, 1996), pp. 159–76 and 266–70.

12. David R. Hershey, "Plants Are Indeed Intelligent," *American Biology Teacher* (accepted as guest editorial), 2002. http://www.fortunecity.com/greenfield/clearstreets/84/intell.htm

13. Susan Milius, "No Brainer Behavior," *Science News* 175:13 (2009): 16.

14. Richard Karban, "Plant Communication: Sagebrush Engage in Self-recognition and Warn of Danger," *physorg.com*, 2009. http://www.physorg.com/news164652485.html

15. František Baluška, "Recent surprising similarities between plant cells and neurons," *Plant Signaling and Behavior* 5:2 (2010): 87–89.

16. František Baluška, Stefano Mancuso, Dieter Volkmann, and Peter W. Barlow, "The 'Root-Brain' Hypothesis of Charles and Francis Darwin Revival After More Than 125 Years," *Plant Signaling and Behavior* 4:12 (2009): 1121–27.

17. Günther Witzany, "Plant Communication from Biosemiotic Perspective. Differences in Abiotic and Biotic Signal Perception Determine Content Arrangement of Response Behavior. Context Determines Meaning of Meta-, Inter-, and Intraorganismic Plant Signaling," *Plant Signal Behavior* 1:4 (2006): 169–78.

18. Mark Greener, "It's Life, But Just As We Know It. A Consensus definition of Life Remains Elusive" *European Molecular Biology Organization* 9:11 (2008): 1067–69.

19. Society for Plant Signaling and Behavior, mission statement on website, http://www.plantbehavior.org/about.html

20. http://www.merriam-webster.com/dictionary/intelligence.

21. Dorothy Maclean, *Call of the Trees* (Everett, WA: Lorian Press, 2006), p. 42.

22. http://www.findhorn.org/

23. The Findhorn Community: Peter Caddy, Eileen Caddy, and Dorothy Maclean, *The Findhorn Garden*, (London, England: Harper Colophon Books, Harper & Row Publishers,1975) pp. 2–19, 54–99.

24. http://en.wikipedia.org/wiki/Deva_(Hinduism)

25. http://www.siriuscommunity.org

Chapter 4, Be a Better Receiver, p. 51

1. Rollin McCraty, Raymond Trevor Bradley, and Dana Tomasino, "The Resonant Heart," *Shift: At the Frontiers of Consciousness*, December 2004–February 2005, p. 15. www.HeartMath.org/research/research-library/research-library.html#energetics-research *Basia says:* This article explains how the heart works in a few simple and easy-to-understand pages.

2. Doc Childre and Howard Martin, *The HeartMath Solution, The Institute of HeartMath's Revolutionary Program for Engaging the Power of the Heart's Intelligence* (New York, NY: Harper Collins, 1999), pp. 28–52. *Basia says:* This book is great for your own health, too, so I recommend reading the whole thing.

3. Rollin McCraty, Raymond Trevor Bradley, and Dana Tomasino, "The Resonant Heart," *Shift: At the Frontiers of Consciousness*, 5 (2004–05): pp.15–19. www.heartmath.org/research/research-library/research-library.html#energetics-research.

4. Rollin McCraty, Mike Atkinson, and Dana Tomasino, *Science of the Heart, Exploring the Role of the Heart in Human Performance,* Publication 01–001 (2001): 20. www.heartmath.org/research/research-library/research-library.html#energetics-research.

5. Rollin McCraty, Mike Atkinson, Dana Tomasion, and William Tiller, "The Electricity of Touch: Detection and Measurement of Cardiac Energy Exchange Between People," K. H. Pribram, ed., *Brain and Values: Is a Biological Science of Values Possible?* (Mahwah, NJ: Lawrence Erlbaum Associates, Publishers, 1998): 359–379. Proceedings of the Fifth Appalachian Conference on Behavioral Neurodynamics.

6. Bruce Lipton, PhD, *The Biology of Belief: Unleashing the Power of Consciousness, Matter and Miracles* (Santa Rosa, CA: Mountain of Love–Elite Books, 2005), pp. 75–94. *Basia says:* Dr. Lipton is a first-class speaker; he is very entertaining when he tells his stories and explains his reasoning. The reference on p. 117 of his book will lead to to James Oschman's book called *Energy Medicine*.

7. Fritjof Capra, PhD, *The Web of Life* (New York, NY: Random House, 1997), pp.157–221. *Basia says:* There's a great chart depicting the three principles of the new definition of "living system" on p. 161, but you really have to read the whole book to understand how they are interrelated. I deeply appreciate the input and guidance that Dr. Capra gave me about the sciences "relevant" to Tree Whispering during a break at his Omega Institute workshop.

8. Beverly Rubik, PhD, "The Biofield Hypothesis: Its Biophysical Basis and Role in Medicine," *The Journal of Alternative and Complementary Medicine,* 8:6 (2002): 703–17. Published by Mary Ann Liebert, Inc., New Rochelle, NY. The article can be found at www.liebertpub.com/products/product.aspx?pid=26. The website is www.liebertonline.com. *Basia says:* A colleague of Dr. Rubik's is Dr. Gary E. Schwartz, author of *The Energy Healing Experiments– Science Reveals Our Natural Power to Heal*. I strongly recommend this book for a deeper understanding of bioenergy.

9. Beverly Rubik, PhD, "The Biofield Hypothesis: Its Biophysical Basis and Role in Medicine," *The Journal of Alternative and Complementary Medicine* 8:6 (2002): 704. Published by Mary Ann Liebert, Inc., New Rochelle, NY. The article can be found at www.liebertpub.com/products/product.aspx?pid=26. The website is www.liebertonline.com.

10. http://en.wikipedia.org/wiki/Kirlian_photography

11. http://commons.wikimedia.org/wiki/File:Kirlian_aura_leaf.gif

12. Stephen Harrod Buhner, *The Secret Teaching of Plants; The Intelligence of the Heart in the Direct Perception of Nature*, (Rochester, VT: Bear & Company, 2004), pp. 87–88. *Basia says:* This whole book is about the deep experience of communication with Nature. Initially, I found it a bit hard to read but then I came to appreciate that it opened the doors to many of the other books now on the *www.TreeWhispering.com* reading list.

13. Stephen Harrod Buhner, *The Secret Teaching of Plants; The Intelligence of the Heart in the Direct Perception of Nature,* (Rochester, VT: Bear & Company, 2004), pp. 89–115.

14. http://en.wikipedia.org/wiki/Interference_(wave_propagation) and http://en.wikipedia.org/wiki/File:Two_sources_interference.gif

15. http://science.hq.nasa.gov/kids/imagers/ems/uv.html

16. www.naturfotograf.com/UV_flowers_list.html#top

17. www.mindsetmoment.com/Mindsetlist.html. *Basia says:* My alma mater, Beloit College, is now famous for the Mindset List™ that professors Tom McBride and Ron Nief compile yearly.

Chapter 7, The Five Heralds–Healing The Tree Whisperer's Way, p. 119

1. Peter Tompkins and Christopher Bird, *The Secret Life of Plants,* (New York, NY: Harper and Row, 1973), pp. 4–45. *Basia says:* Plants' reactions to being threatened by burning matches—as registered on the lie detectors in Cleve Backster's school for polygraph experts—has become the stuff of legends. You may want to read about similar experiments in the book that Cleve Backster wrote himself, *Primary Perception: Biocommunication with Plants, Living Foods, and Human Cells* (Anza, CA: White Rose Millennium Press, 2003).

Chapter 8, What You Can Do, p. 137

1. Doc Childre and Howard Martin, *The HeartMath Solution, The Institute of HeartMath's Revolutionary Program for Engaging the Power of the Heart's Intelligence* (New York, NY: Harper Collins, 1999), pp. 28–52.

2. www.wikipedia.org/wiki/Transpiration. *A fully grown tree may lose several hundred gallons of water through its leaves on a hot, dry day. About 90% of the water that enters a plant's roots is used for this process. Transpiration ratio is the ratio of the mass of water transpired to the mass of dry matter produced; the transpiration ratio of crops tends to fall between 200 and 1000 (i.e., crop plants transpire 200 to 1000 kg of water for every kg of dry matter produced).*

3. http://thesaurus.com/browse/courage

4. www.glcoherence.org/about-us/about.html

CHAPTER 9, THE TREE WHISPERER'S INSIGHTS, P. 183

1. Edmund Bourne, *Global Shift–How a New Worldview is Transforming Humanity* (Oakland, CA: New Harbinger Publications, Inc., 2008), pp. 104–16. ***Basia says:*** In succinct chapters, Dr. Bourne paints the picture of global changes that have been occurring since the 1940s and even before. In thinking about my life, I related to the trends that he outlines. Perhaps you will, too.

2. J. Engelberth, H. T. Alborn, E. A. Schmelz, and J. H. Tumlinson, "Airborne Signals Prime Plants Against Insect Herbivore Attack," in *Proceedings of the National Academy of Sciences of the USA* 101:6 (2004): 178–85. www.ncbi.nlm.nih.gov/pmc/articles/PMC341853/

3. Richard Karban, "Plant Communication: Sagebrush Engage in Self-recognition and Warn of Danger," *physorg.com,* 2009. www.physorg.com/news164652485.html

4. http://en.wikipedia.org/wiki/Joyce_Kilmer

CHAPTER 10, AN IDEA WHOSE TIME HAS COME, P. 219

1. http://marinebio.org/Oceans/Conservation/Moyle/

2. http://en.wikipedia.org/wiki/Neolithic_Revolution
http://en.wikipedia.org/wiki/Paleolithic
http://en.wikipedia.org/wiki/History_of_the_world
http://en.wikipedia.org/wiki/Axial_age

3. http://en.wikipedia.org/wiki/Reductionism
http://en.wikipedia.org/wiki/Mechanism_(philosophy)
http://en.wikipedia.org/wiki/Renaissance
http://en.wikipedia.org/wiki/Enlightenment_Era

4. HRH The Prince of Wales with Tony Juniper and Ian Skelly, *Harmony, A New Way of Looking at Our World* (New York, NY: HarperCollins Publishers, 2010), pp. 145–183. ***Basia adds:*** This book is a thorough and elegant review of the history of how humanity has done damage to the earth and what new actions people may take to restore harmony to their own Spirits as well as to benefit the environment. I highly recommend it.

5. www.amonymifoundation.org/Home_Page.html. Page 25 of the following pdf:
http://www.amonymifoundation.org/uploads/NA_Approval_Form_Scan.pdf

6. Buckminster Fuller's website is www.bfi.org. *Basia adds:* Bucky Fuller was way ahead of his time. Go to the Buckminster Fuller Institute website to learn about the innovative work still being done from his inspiration.

7. Werner Erhard, "Nothing Is So Powerful as an Idea Whose Time Has Come: The Hunger Project," *Special Edition of The Graduate Review*, January 1978. www.erhardseminarstraining.com (click on Graduate Review) *Basia adds:* I was serendipitously introduced to the Hunger Project by one of its founders, Werner Erhard, on a flight from London to New York in 1977, before the public announcement. It was created as a strategic organization, designed to mobilize a global constituency committed to the end of hunger.

8. The Hunger Project, *Ending Hunger: An Idea Whose Time Has Come* (Santa Barbara, CA: Greenwood Publishing Group; Praeger, 1985). www.thp.org

9. Edmund Bourne, *Global Shift–How a New Worldview is Transforming Humanity* (Oakland, CA: New Harbinger Publications, Inc., 2008). pp. 53–66.

10. Paul Hawken, *Blessed Unrest–How the Largest Movement in the World Came Into Being and Why No One Saw It Coming* (New York, NY: Viking Press, 2007).

CHAPTER 11, FUTURISTIC VISION IN PRACTICE NOW, P. 231

1. The Omega Institute, www.eomega.org

2. Charles E. Little, *The Dying of the Trees* (New York, NY: Penguin Books, 1995). *Basia says:* In one depressing but true chapter after another, Mr. Little tells the stories of trees, forests, and swaths of the planet devastated by the effects of pollution and other human-related insults. This book was written in the mid 1990s. The state of tree health hasn't generally improved since that time.

CITATIONS FROM THE APPENDIX, P. 263

1. Fritjof Capra, PhD, *The Tao of Physics: An Exploration of the Parallels Between Modern Physics and Eastern Mysticism* (Boston, MA: Shambhala Publications, Inc., 1975). www.shambhala.com.

2. Fritjof Capra, PhD, *The Web of Life* (New York, NY: Random House, 1997). www.anchorbooks.com.

3. Bruce Lipton, PhD, *The Biology of Belief: Unleashing the Power of Consciousness, Matter and Miracles* (Santa Rosa, CA: Mountain of Love–Elite Books, 2005) pp. 75–94.

4. Jeremy Naraby, PhD, *Intelligence in Nature, An Inquiry into Knowledge* (New York, NY: Penguin Group, 2005).

5. The Society for Plant Signaling and Behavior, www.PlantBehavior.org

6. Institute of HeartMath, heartmath.org/about-us/about-us-home/mission-vision.html heartmath.org/about-us/our-focus/ihm-programs-services.html heartmath.org/research/research-home/research-center-home.html

7. Rollin McCraty, Raymond Trevor Bradley, and Dana Tomasino, "The Resonant Heart" *Shift: At the Frontiers of Consciousness*, 5 (2004–05): 15–19. www.heartmath.org/research/research-library

8. Rollin McCraty, Mike Atkinson, and Dana Tomasino, *Science of the Heart, Exploring the Role of the Heart in Human Performance* Publication 01–001 (2001): 20. www.heartmath.org/research/research-library/research-library.html#energetics-research.

9. Doc Childre and Howard Martin, *The HeartMath Solution, The Institute of HeartMath's Revolutionary Program for Engaging the Power of the Heart's Intelligence* (New York, NY: Harper Collins, 1999), pp. 28–52.

10. Rollin McCraty, Mike Atkinson, Dana Tomasino, and William Tiller, "The Electricity of Touch: Detection and Measurement of Cardiac Energy Exchange Between People," K. H. Pribram, ed., *Brain and Values: Is a Biological Science of Values Possible* (Mahwah, NJ: Lawrence Erlbaum Associates, Publishers, 1998), pp. 359–379. This is from the Proceedings of the Fifth Appalachian Conference on Behavioral Neurodynamics.

11. Harold Saxton Burr, MD, *The Fields of Life, Our Links with the Universe* (New York, New York: Ballantine Books, Inc., 1972).

12. Beverly Rubik, PhD, "The Biofield Hypothesis: Its Biophysical Basis and Role in Medicine," *The Journal of Alternative and Complementary Medicine* 8:6 (2002): 703–17. Published by Mary Ann Liebert, Inc., New Rochelle, NY. The article can be found at www.liebertpub.com/products/product.aspx?pid=26. The website is www.liebertonline.com.

13. Peter Tompkins and Christopher Bird, *The Secret Life of Plants* (New York, NY: Harper and Row, 1973), pp. 4–45.

14. Cleve Backster, *Primary Perception, Biocommunication with Plants, Living Foods, and Human Cells* (White Rose Millennium, 2003).

15. Stephen Harrod Buhner, *The Secret Teaching of Plants; The Intelligence of the Heart in the Direct Perception of Nature* (Rochester, VT: Bear & Company, 2004).

16. wikipedia.org/wiki/File:Two_sources_interference.gif

wikipedia.org/wiki/Diffraction_pattern

wikipedia.org/wiki/Interference_(wave_propagation)

17. Fritjof Capra, PhD, *The Web of Life* (New York, NY: Random House, 1997), p. 208. www.anchorbooks.com.

18. Gail R. Fleischaker, "Origins of Life: An Operational Definition," *Origins of Life and Evolution of the BioSphere* 20 (1990) 127–37.

19. wikipedia.org/wiki/Fractal

20. www.relativitybook.com/CoolStuff/erkfractals.html (scroll down to Golden Ratio & Fibonacci Fractals)

21. Lynne McTaggart, *The Field–The Quest for the Secret Force of the Universe, Updated Edition* (New York, NY: HarperCollins Publishers, 2008).

22. Lynne McTaggart, *The Intention Experiment, Using Your Thoughts to Change Your Life and the World* (New York, New York: Simon & Schuster, Inc., 2007).

23. Masaru Emoto, *The Hidden Messages in Water* (Hillsboro, Oregon: Beyond Words Publishing, Inc., 2004) www.hado.net.

24. D. Feinstein and D. Eden, "Six pillars of energy medicine: Clinical strengths of a complementary paradigm," *Alternative Therapies* 14:1 (2008): 44–54.

CITATION FOR IMAGE ON THE FACING PAGE

The interconnecting network pattern seen at the back of the Deputy Badge on the facing page was inspired by the network analysis work of Valdis Krebs. www.thenetworkthinkers.com and www.orgnet.com. **Basia says:** Mr. Krebs has timely and insightful things to say about how people are socially networked, and also how companies compete, political parties interact and product popularity can be traced. His views on what I would call cooperation and partnership within information are, to me, on the leading edge and make it easier to understanding the soup we live in every day.

Basia says: Thank you for reading the Citations. I hope they were entertaining.

You will find a reading list at *www.TreeWhispering.com*. I do my best to keep it updated with the books and other resources that I believe to be relevant to Dr. Jim's and my work.

Participate

BE DESIGNATED AS A DEPUTY

Now that you have read this book, you can become a Deputy in the Peace Pipe Global Network Pattern. You will be invited to participate as Dr. Jim directs local and global tree-healing sessions. You can offer healing to the Plant Kingdom in coherence with other Deputies around the world. The sum of the work will be greater than the parts. You'll also receive updated techniques and information so you can help your own trees and plants. Go to www.TreeWhispering.com to find out how to qualify so you can get your Deputy Badge.

SEND YOUR STORY

As a result of reading this book, if you have an interesting experience or get a message from a tree or plant, please submit your story to Messages@TreeWhispering.com. Dr. Jim and Basia would like to hear it and could consider it for inclusion in future books.

TAKE A WORKSHOP

Enroll in Tree Whispering® classes for a deeper experience of connection with trees, plants, and other Beings of Nature. Learn the Holisic Chores™–practical activities done in partnership with trees and plants. Receive all of the Healing Whispers™–experiential bioenergy healing techniques done in cooperation with trees and plants.

To go a step further, the full Tree Whispering Workshop provides both a profound experience with Green Beings as well as a system of healing techniques. Advanced classes in Green Centrics™ and trainings for people to lead introductions are planned. Gain insight into your own health in the class Trees Are Your Healers.

Discover an idea whose time has come in the new field of study called Cooperative BioBalance™–Partnering with Nature. It is the peace treaty among people, all plants, insects, diseases, and related organisms. Practice new guardianship by touching, asking, healing, saving, and loving the Beings of Nature.

FORWARD AN INITIATIVE

The Institute for Cooperative BioBalance offers initiatives in which people may participate. Contact Participate@CooperativeBioBalance.org.

INNOVATIONS, PRODUCTS, AND SPECIAL OFFERS

Check TreeWhispering.com for relevant innovations, supportive products, and special offers as they become available. These include audio downloads of the "Try This" exercises, the companion Tree Whispering: Trust the Path notebook, and other supplementary materials and opportunities.

Contact and About the Authors

Dr. Jim Conroy, The Tree Whisperer®
Whisperer@TheTreeWhisperer.com

Ms. Basia Alexander, The Chief Listener
Listener@TreeWhispering.com

P.O. Box 90, Morris Plains, NJ 07950 USA

Together, Dr. Conroy and Ms. Alexander offer classes and workshops in Tree Whispering.® Through these educational experiences, people gain paradigm-shifting principles and easy, simple practices for restoring inner health to trees and plants, while feeling good in body, mind, and Spirit.

TreeWhispering.com and CooperativeBioBalance.org.

Dr. Jim Conroy, The Tree Whisperer,® earned his PhD in Plant Pathology from Purdue University, Indiana. After 25 years as a plant and tree health senior executive in top 50 agricultural chemical companies, he did a 180° turn-around. He started to come from the plant's point of view. Now, he is an authority on Nature-based communication and a global expert who holistically heals stressed trees, plants, crops, forests, and ecosystems.

His breakthrough to develop integrated ecosystem healing and balancing, called Cooperative BioBalance,™ came through his research and profound spiritual connection with the Plant Kingdom. In 2002, Dr. Jim developed the Green Centrics™ System, a holistic, bioenergy healing, hands-on, no-product, green-friendly, and sustainable solution to restoring tree and plant health from the inside-out. He since created and developed Co-Existence Technologies.™ As a practitioner, he works on estates, golf courses, forests, botanical gardens, municipalities, and people's properties to heal stressed or declining trees by restoring functionality to internal parts and systems.

He is also a NOFA certified organic land-care specialist, educator, on the faculty at Omega Institute and The Nature Lyceum, keynote speaker, healer, rose grower, founder and president of Plant Health Alternatives, LLC, and co-founder of the Institute for Cooperative BioBalance.

TheTreeWhisperer.com, StrengthenForests.com, and CooperativeBioBalance.org.

Ms. Basia Alexander, The Chief Listener, innovator and leader in the new field of Conscious Co-Creativity and an expert Nature communicator, Basia develops leading-edge, synergistic concepts and produces transformative and inspirational curriculum. She has also produced manuscripts on topics including spiritual expansion, personal organizing, health, and creativity. She founded ReVitalizations™—a health and creativity coaching and training business and co-founded Trees for Tomorrow—a local environmental action group in Wayne, New Jersey. As Training Director for an Apple Computer dealership and as an Adjunct Professor at Essex College, New Jersey, Basia wrote and delivered trainings in advanced desktop publishing. She created a Track II Bachelor of Arts in Communications at Beloit College, Wisconsin.

After gaining certification as a BodyTalk System™ practitioner, her love of plants led her to form a partnership in Plant Health Alternatives, LLC, with Dr. Jim. Basia writes all Tree Whispering® manuals and teaches, side-by-side, with him. As co-founder of the Institute for Cooperative BioBalance, Basia directs its educational and philanthropic initiatives.

TreeWhispering.com, PartnerWithNature.org, and CooperativeBioBalance.org.